The Future of Governing

STUDIES IN GOVERNMENT
AND PUBLIC POLICY

The Future of Governing
Second Edition, Revised

B. Guy Peters

 University Press of Kansas

© 1996, 2001 by the University Press of Kansas

Published by the University Press of Kansas (Lawrence, Kansas 66045), which was organized by the Kansas Board of Regents and is operated and funded by Emporia State University, Fort Hays State University, Kansas State University, Pittsburg State University, the
University of Kansas, and Wichita State University.

Library of Congress Cataloging-in-Publication Data

Peters, B. Guy.
    The future of governing / B. Guy Peters. — 2nd ed., rev.
        p. cm. — (Studies in government and public policy)
    Includes bibliographical references and index.
    ISBN 978-0-7006-1129-4 (cloth : alk. paper)
    ISBN 978-0-7006-1130-0 (pbk. : alk. paper)
    1. Public administration. 2. Comparative government. I. Title. II. Series.
    JF1351.P393 2001
    351 — dc21
                            2001026314

British Library Cataloguing in Publication Data is available.

Printed in the United States of America

10 9 8 7 6 5 4

The paper used in this publication meets the minimum requirements of the American
National Standard for Permanence of Paper for Printed Library Materials Z39.48-1984.

Contents

Preface to Second Edition

Since the first edition of this book was published, governing has continued to change. Some of that change has simply been the persistence of patterns that were discussed in the first edition. The ideas of the market and participation and deregulation continue to be implemented. These ideas are being refined and some of the rougher edges have been taken off the earlier reforms, especially those based on the market model; yet they continue to have an important impact on the way in which most countries are governed. Other changes in governing have resulted from direct reactions to the problems created by those initial reforms. Governing is far from an exact science, and even the best-designed reforms may produce negative as well as positive consequences. Therefore, one attempt at change often produces another, and then another.

While these reforms are occurring in the affluent, industrialized democracies, the less developed countries of the world are now being induced to adopt many of the same types. Some of the pressure for reform comes from those governments themselves, but much of it comes from international donor organizations that want to impose their conception of "good governance" on those governments. Some of the same ideas about reform that have been popular in the industrialized democracies have been transmitted to the developing and transitional countries, even though those less affluent countries are often incapable of implementing those programs effectively. Thus, the use of the reforms in a wide range of countries raises yet more questions about the adequacy of the theory available to guide changes in the public sector.

Perhaps the most interesting question arises from the study of recent administrative reforms: why do governments continue to reform even in the face of minimal success and the need to invest significant amounts of political capital in the process? This behavior represents the triumph of hope over experience and says something about the perceived needs to get the administrative system "right" in an age in which the public is skeptical about the ability of the public sector to perform and to provide good services at an acceptable tax price. Although governments may never really be able to get the administrative system right once and for all, they do continue to try to make it better.

As was true for the first edition, a number of people have contributed to the completion of this book. Over the past year I have had the opportunity to work with Geert Bouckaert and Derry Ormond in the actual reform of a government; and they, and our colleagues in Finland, have helped me to understand the process of change more clearly than before.My work with Jon Pierre on governance has also enhanced my understanding of reform within a broader context. This book and many others have been enriched by the ideas of the late Vincent Wright, and I am grateful for the opportunity I had to spend time with him in Oxford. Once again Fred Woodward had to be extremely patient but has remained supportive throughout the process. The errors and omissions are, of course, my own.

Preface to First Edition

Change in the public sector is the rule rather than the exception. The quest for the perfect way of structuring and managing government has gone on as long as there has been a government, always to be met with disappointment. The problem has been in part that there is no single definition of what constitutes perfect administration. Further, each solution tends to create its own new set of problems, which in turn will create a new set of reforms. Although this cycle of reform is good for those of us interested in the process of change, it is less beneficial to those involved in the process. Frequent changes tend to create cynicism about reform efforts, both inside and outside the public sector. Yet such efforts can be a politician's best friend, given that reform is at times the only possible reaction to intractable policy problems.

Although change has been a common experience in the public sector, the reform activity during the 1980s and 1990s has been extraordinary. This is true not only of the number of reform initiatives but also of the fundamental nature of the changes being considered. In some cases, e.g., New Zealand, it is not excessively hyperbolic to say that a revolution has occurred in the public sector. The traditional Westminster model of government in that country has been replaced by ideas drawn from public-choice economics and private management. Even countries that appear on other criteria to be performing more than adequately have found it necessary to invest a great deal of time and effort in reforming their public sectors.

Perhaps because of the ubiquity and fundamental nature of change in these decades, the administrative reforms being implemented are far from intellectually consistent. Although they sometimes parade under broad umbrella terms such as "reinvention," a number of different strands of thinking about change are being advocated. Further, those patterns of thinking are often inherently incompatible even though they are being implemented as components of the same reform program. In such a case it is crucial to understand the ideas that undergird reforms. This is as true as ever intellectually, but it also is true for more practical reasons. If a number of the reforms now being implemented are indeed incompatible, then we cannot expect them to be successful, and these probable failures can only exacerbate the already pervasive conception that government is incapable of doing anything right.

Although the ideas contained in these reform efforts may be incompatible, it is even more important that contemporary reforms are driven by ideas. Each of the four models of change to be discussed in this book has a set of ideas beneath the more practical reform proposals being implemented. Some of these models, e.g., the market, have a substantially clearer intellectual basis than do the others, but all do have some identifiable theoretical foundations. This characteristic distinguishes this current round of reform from some of the "tireless tinkering" that has tended to characterize administrative reform. Most discussion of the reforms has taken place in the context of individual countries or groups of countries, but it is also important to look at the common ideas that have guided and motivated the transformations.

Although I am interested primarily in the ideas undergirding reform, I am also concerned with how they have been manifested in different national settings. Context is extremely important for understanding politics and administration. The various political and administrative traditions of the developed democracies have provided a set of lenses through which to interpret contemporary ideas for making government perform better. These various lenses sometimes produce confusion, with the same concept being interpreted to mean very different things in the various national settings. Despite that possible confusion, the differences are useful indications of the differences among administrative systems and therefore can serve as the basis for interesting comparative analysis.

This comparison could extend across almost the entire world, and certainly across the entire developed world. I will provide examples from a number of countries, including some in the developing world, but I will focus attention on examples from the English-speaking democracies. This emphasis is in part a function of ease of access to information, but there is also more than a little intellectual justification for it. These countries have been innovators in a number of ways and collectively also have reformed more extensively than have most other countries. And some of the Anglo-American countries were in need of more extensive reforms than were many other developed democracies.

Although there is only one name on the title page, there have been a number of people who have had a significant influence on the development of this book. Perhaps the individual to whom I owe the greatest debt of gratitude is Donald Savoie. Through Donald's good offices I have been able to develop a continuing relationship with the Canadian civil service and a large number of capable and dedicated civil servants. We have worked together as senior fellows of the Canadian Centre for Management Development (CCMD) for several years, and that collaboration has been crucial in developing my own thinking about government and public administration. Several other individuals at CCMD have been extremely supportive of my research on public administration and have contributed to it. In particular, Ralph Heintzman and Maurice Demers have encouraged and helped fund the research and provided their own valuable insights into the practice of public administration.

A number of other colleagues have helped shape the ideas in this book, sometimes without being aware of how much contribution they were making. Vincent Wright provided me with a visiting position at the Centre for European Studies, Nuffield College, Oxford. The opportunity to have several months of virtually uninterrupted time to think and write was crucial to finishing the book. Numerous stimulating, if sometimes rushed, conversations with Vincent also contributed to my thinking about contemporary administrative change. Jon Pierre and his colleagues at Forvaltningshogskolan at the University of Gothenberg provided a similar, if alas shorter, opportunity to do more of the same. Patricia Ingraham asked me to write a paper that became the foundation of this book. She and her colleagues at the Maxwell School, Syracuse University, also provided a number of interesting insights on the reform process at conferences in Washington, DC, and in lectures in Beijing, China. Several colleagues in Norway, including Tom Christensen and Morten Egeberg, have provided interesting and important feedback on some of the ideas contained here. Here in Pittsburgh several colleagues have helped me think through some of the ideas, and others assisted (in their own way) by making it impossible for me to rush through the manuscript.

1

Changing States, Governance, and the Public Service

Governance is a scarce commodity. Governments have created a vast array of institutions designed to exercise collective control and influence over the societies and economies for which they have been given responsibility. Those efforts at building institutions and "steering" capacity (Pierre and Peters 2000) have certainly provided comparative politics with an interesting array of data, but it is much less clear that they have moved governments any closer to solving the problems of regulating the behavior of people and organizations. If anything, these efforts at governance now may be less successful than were similar efforts in the past. Government also has lost some policy autonomy to external actors such as international organizations and amorphous international markets.[1] At the same time that external forces impinge on governing, there has been an apparent sharp increase in popular resistance to being governed (Norris 1998; Putnam and Pharr 2000). Moreover, large organizations in the private sector are proving themselves more capable of avoiding attempts by government to regulate their behavior.[2] Political leaders in the world today must ask whether what they do in their national capitals really does very much to shape the lives of their citizens.

Fortunately, governments, government leaders, and their civil servants continue attempting to find better ways of governing. I say fortunately not just because these efforts keep us students of the public sector in business but also because there is a great capacity to do good for citizens, individually and collectively, through effective public action. It is now fashionable to malign government, and the people working in it, and to point out gleefully all their failures, real and imagined. Such skepticism and cynicism about government is cheap; it requires much greater commitment and courage to continue attempting to solve problems that almost by definition exceed the capacity of any individual or private actor to solve. If the problems had been easy or profitable, they probably would have remained in the private sector, and government would never have been made responsible for them. Despite the popular mythology to the contrary, it is rare that governments are imperialistic and go looking for new problems to solve; they are more likely to be handed the poisoned chalice of an insuperable problem.[3]

It remains crucial for governments, and the individuals who constitute them, to continue their search for innovative mechanisms for making government work better and to serve society better. This search will continue, even in the face of problems that are "ill structured" (Simon 1973), or "intractable" (Schön and Rein 1994), or "wicked" (Dunn 1988), and often in the service of a mass public that does not either recognize or appreciate the effort involved. That mass public is also ever more reluctant to provide increased funding for the public sector, and public managers often must do more with less. Contemporary public servants are neither martyrs nor saints; they are simply individuals charged with making collective decisions and enforcing previous decisions on behalf of the public interest.

The leaders of government are also charged with reforming and improving the internal performance of their organizations. Many of the efforts at reform that I will discuss have been internally generated, an indication that the public sector is not resisting change, as many of its critics assume, but in some cases is actually leading the charge for change (Tellier 1990; Peters and Savoie 1994; Derlien 1995; see chapter 7). Of course, there are at least as many reforms that have been imposed from the outside, some of which have indeed been resisted vigorously by the "entrenched" civil service. There is no monopoly on virtue or on vice in the world of administrative reform.

My purpose in this book is to examine the efforts that are being made to make government work better. Numerous efforts of this sort have been occurring all over the world for at least the last decade and a half. In most industrialized democracies these reforms have originated internally (see Pollitt and Bouckaert 2000), but in many of the less developed countries they have been imposed by external-aid agencies as conditions of receiving assistance (United National Development Programme 1988). Even countries that appear to be extremely successful from the outside, e.g., Japan, have engaged in large-scale administrative reforms (Krauss and Muramatsu 1995), in part as a means of keeping pace with other countries.

The discussion will focus largely on the Anglo-American democracies, in part because these have been the most active and innovative reformers. I will, however, also use examples from other countries when they can illuminate the analytic point being made. My purpose is not so much to describe the numerous efforts at administrative reform—that has been done extremely well in a number of other places (Savoie 1994; Zifcak 1994; *International Political Science Review* 1993). Rather, the intent is to examine the ideas that motivate reform and that provide a diagnosis of the problems in the public sector as well as the basis for prescriptions to remedy the problems. Given that purpose, and the ubiquity of reform, the focus on a smaller number of cases is not particularly damaging.

Among the industrialized democracies, the discussion will focus on the

Anglo-American democracies but will also give special attention to the problems of reform in developing and transitional countries (see chapter 8). Much of the administrative reform encountered in those systems is not the product of endogenous force but is the result of the concepts and programs of outside actors, especially international donors. This imposition of reforms, combined with the particular administrative and political problems of many of these countries, means that the managerial and political consequences of reform are rather different from those of the more industrialized and democratized countries.

Understanding administrative reform requires understanding the traditional model of governance that is the backdrop against which attempts at reform must be viewed. Rather than being a set of intellectual principles, this traditional model tended to evolve from practice and rarely has been articulated as a distinct model. Despite its lack of a single, coherent intellectual foundation, the traditional model was once thought to be the way in which the public sector should be organized, and indeed it worked rather well for decades.[4] During the height of optimism about government's capacity to solve social problems, e.g., the 1950s through the early 1970s, this basic model appeared to require little fundamental debate. The task then was to refine the model, to make it more "rational" with techniques such as program-budgeting (Novick 1965) and cost-benefit analysis (Mishan 1988), and then merely to let the governing system continue to produce effective policies and socioeconomic improvements.

Certainly some conservative politicians and thinkers did raise questions about the virtues of those (by then) traditional governance ideas and especially on the increasing role of the public sector (Friedman 1962; Hayek 1968; Sawer 1982). For most people in and out of government, however, the parameters of acceptable public action then were broad and well established. There was a pervasive belief that government could regulate the economy through taxing and spending and that it had sufficient economic resources to ameliorate social problems such as poverty, sickness, and poor education. The 1950s and 1960s were the period of the "mixed-economy welfare-state" and of "treble affluence" (Rose and Peters 1978) as well as of the promise of an ever brighter future through public action.

Those two decades were also the period of consensus politics (Kavanagh and Morris 1994) in most countries of Western Europe and North America, and both scholars and practical politicians proclaimed the "end of ideology" and the creation of a "post-industrial society" (Gustaffson 1979).[5] Even a conservative such as Richard Nixon said, "We are all Keynesians now" and attempted to create new social programs (Spulbar 1989) rather than roll them back, as subsequent Republican presidents and Congresses attempted to do.[6] Similarly, Christian Democrats in Germany preached the virtues of the "social market economy" as a desirable alternative to unbridled capitalism (Peacock and Willgerodt 1989). Clearly something has changed in the economy and in the popular mind since that time, and with that change has come a change in the definition of what constitutes good government and acceptable public administration. Before we look at what has changed, however, I will present a somewhat more complete idea of the traditional model and something of its strengths and weaknesses.

TRADITIONAL PUBLIC ADMINISTRATION: THE OLD-TIME RELIGION

Dwight Waldo (1968) once wrote that public administration has had so many identity crises that in comparison the life of the average adolescent appeared idyllic. Professor Waldo was discussing public administration as an academic discipline, but its contemporary practice displays much of the same uncertainty. Questions of practice that now appear extremely uncertain include such basic issues as the structure of government, management of those structures, and the proper role of public administration in governance (Harmon 1995). Many old certainties about government and the public service are now either totally altered or are subject to severe questioning.

The old model of public administration may not be singular (Richards 1992), but at least five old chestnuts have guided our thinking about the public service and its role in governance (Peters and Wright 1996). These five ideas clearly are simply no longer as canonical as they once were in the public sector.[7] What is sometimes forgotten in the discussion of alternative approaches to public management is that these principles evolved over periods of time and generally represent responses to a number of problems that existed in public administration at earlier times. Indeed, there is a real chance that some of the problems for which the old chestnuts were designed may reappear once they are replaced with more "modern" conceptions about how to run government (for consequences of initial attempts at reform, see chapter 6).

Reforms solve problems existing at one time, often in the process creating a new set of problems that may generate subsequent reforms (Kaufman 1978; Aucoin 1990; Peters 1995). This admonition of caution about administrative reform does not mean that the old ways of running government were necessarily better. What the appeal to prudence does argue is that these approaches to public management did solve certain problems, albeit creating some additional problems of their own. Overturning those older modes of administering certainly has solved some problems but in the process perhaps revived older difficulties and perhaps even created new ones. If the potential costs of discarding the existing system of public administration are not recognized, then change may appear entirely too attractive.

An Apolitical Civil Service

The first of these five principles is the assumption of an apolitical civil service and associated with that the politics-administration dichotomy and the concept of "neutral competence" (Kaufman 1956) within the civil service. The basic idea is that civil servants should not have known political allegiances of their own and that they should be able to serve any "master," meaning any government of the day. Civil servants may have views about particular policies and are almost expected to as members of an organization responsible for making and implementing policies (Aberbach, Putnam, and Rockman 1981). What they are not expected to have are partisan views that might lead them to be disloyal to a government of one party complexion or another.

The principle of an apolitical civil service has been largely an Anglo-Saxon preoccupation, when compared to administration in other industrialized democracies (Silberman 1993). However, even in countries with a more overtly politicized civil service, such as Germany and France (Derlien 1991; Bodiguel and Rouban 1991), the concept of competence comes at least as high as political allegiance when selecting civil servants. Similarly, the civil services of the Scandinavian countries tend to be less overtly politicized than that of Germany, but in these countries political allegiances are often known or assumed (Ståhlberg 1987). What is true in all these civil service systems is that objective qualifications are the first hurdle for recruitment, followed then by any political questions.

Although the concern with depoliticization of the civil service has been very much an Anglo-American concern, it is also a rather recent administrative value. In the United States, for example, the spoils system dominated recruitment until the mid-1880s, and even then the number of merit appointments under the Pendleton Act of 1883 was rather small (Skowronek 1982; Ingraham 1995a). By 1904 only half of total federal employment was under the merit system, and most of that was in lower-level clerical positions (Johnson and Libecap 1994, 30–33). In the United Kingdom the merit system was initiated only slightly earlier than in the United States, although it spread throughout the administrative system more quickly (Parris 1969). The historical record in other Anglo-American democracies is not significantly different, with patronage appointments either being replaced by merit gradually under British rule from the end of the nineteenth century, or with former colonies institutionalizing merit systems quickly after gaining independent status (Braibanti 1966; Koehn 1990).[8]

Associated with the concern for maintaining an apolitical personnel system was the argument that politics and administration were, and more important should be, separate enterprises. In the United States this position was stated first by Woodrow Wilson (1887) and restated more forcefully by Goodnow (1900). In the United Kingdom the argument was made about the same time, first implicitly in the Northcote-Trevelyan Report (1853) on the civil service and then later in the Haldane Report (Cmnd. 9320, 1918) on the structure of government. In both countries the argument was that the job of the civil service was to implement the decisions made by its political masters and to do so without questioning the sagacity of those decisions.[9] Other Anglo-American political systems have had similar apolitical civil services and are now encountering some of the same problems of increased politicization (Gregory 2001).

Despite the ideological advocacy of an apolitical civil service, it is increasingly clear that civil servants do have significant, if not necessarily dominant, policy roles in most contemporary governments (Peters 1992; Kato 1994; Peters and Pierre 2001). It is also clear to most analysts that governance is better, on average, because they do (Terry 1995). The policy role of civil servants is most obvious at the implementation stage, where the role of implementors in determining real policies occurred as early as the 1930s (Gulick 1933; Almond and Lasswell 1934). In addition to the policy that emerges from "street-level bureaucrats" dealing with individual cases (Lipsky 1980; Adler and Asquith 1981; Vinzant and Crothers 1998), the public bureaucracy has a more systematic role in making public policy through implementation. Yet the recognition of both the empirical reality of the role of the bureaucracy in governance and that some benefits arise from that involvement has not prevented the continuing ideological advocacy of separating politics and administration.

The manifest policymaking role of the public bureaucracy arises most clearly in the promulgation of "secondary legislation," or "regulations" in the language of American government (Baldwin 1995; Page 2001). Very few legislatures in the world are capable of writing laws that specify the necessary details for complex policy areas and thus depend on their bureaucracies to fill in that legal and technical content. For example, in the United States, although Congress passes only a few hundred bills annually, something approaching five thousand final rules are passed each year.[10] This accumulation over the years has produced, for example, over ten thousand pages of rules in the *Code of Federal Regulations* just for agriculture policy (Kerwin 1994, 18–19). In other industrialized democracies the volume of secondary legislation is no less; even in the European Union there are at least ten times as many secondary rules written as there are pieces of primary legislation adopted (Blumann and Soligne 1989).

The civil service also has a significant, if now threatened, role as policy adviser at the formulation stage. Though ministers may be elected to make policy decisions, they often lack the capacity to do so effectively (Blondel 1988). Even in countries where civil servants are generalists by education and career patterns, through experience they can gain greater command of the details of policy than can ministers who are only in office for a short time (Peters 1992). Although in policy formulation and advice the role for the civil service is important in the developed countries, it is perhaps even more crucial for developing and transitional governments, where the need for expertise and the demands for a "committed bureaucracy" are that much greater (Peters 1995a; Goetz 1999).

The institutional design problem then becomes how to structure government in ways that recognize the reality, and even the desirability, of the significant policy role for civil servants while simultaneously preserving the requirements of democratic accountability. This is a difficult balance for designers of government institutions to achieve, especially given the historical legacy of thinking about the neutrality of the civil service and the current reality of public demands for enhanced accountability (Day and Klein 1987; Cooper 1995; Aucoin and Heintzman 2000). Furthermore, political leaders have become ever more aware of the policy role of civil servants and in response often have attempted to minimize it (Campbell 1993; Peters and Pierre 2000). Reducing the role of the civil service has been done in part for ideological reasons (they were perceived as too far right or left of their masters) or simply for reasons of preserving institutional differences.

The struggle over competence and authority to make public policy therefore is now more obvious to individuals working within government, as well as to citizens, than in the past. The politicization of the functions of the civil service, if not its members themselves, may make the delicate balance of policy competencies between the permanent civil service and its political masters even more difficult to maintain. Long years of one-party domination, e.g., the Thatcher and Major years in the United Kingdom, mean that civil servants often become identified with the policies of a particular party, rightly or wrongly. Further, the prevailing assumption, if not always the reality, is that civil servants must accept the party line of the incumbent government or face termination or at least face being excluded from important decisions.

Hierarchy and Rules

The second significant change in government relevant to this discussion is the decline in assumptions of hierarchical and rule-bound management within the public service as well as the authority of civil servants to implement and enforce regulations outside it. The neat Weberian model of management (Wright and Peters 1995) does not apply within public organizations as it once did, and in its place we encounter a variety of alternative sources of organizational power and authority. As one example, the market is an increasingly significant standard against which to compare the structure and performance of government organizations (Lan and Rosenbloom 1992; Hood 1990; Boston 1991). Moreover, within organizations market mechanisms for managing personnel have replaced, or at least supplement, traditional hierarchy. Though it can be argued that the inherent differences between the public and private sectors are crucial to understanding governance (Savoie 1995a; Self 1993; Perry and Rainey 1988), even governments on the political left have implemented market-based reforms.[11]

For transitional and developing regimes, the demands for greater economic efficiency in the public sector must be balanced against the needs to create some of the predictability, universality, and probity associated with Weberian bureaucracy. The changes being introduced in industrialized countries assume that the employees implementing market-based reforms will have at least some of the public values that have informed the civil service. Without those values, market-oriented reforms run the risk of justifying corruption and becoming a publicly sponsored version of the excesses of capitalism. Those excesses to some extent have occurred already in the former Soviet Union and may well emerge in other transitional regimes. These aberration, unfortunately, have not been entirely absent from the industrialized democracies where market-oriented reforms have been implemented.[12]

There are other challenges to hierarchy in addition to those coming from the market. Another alternative to the market model, as well as to traditional models of bureaucracy, is the "dialectical" or participatory organization. This model has been discussed by scholars and reformers for a number of years, but government organizations are now being placed under increasing real pressure to accommodate the interests of lower-level employees, as well as those of their clients, into their decision-making processes (Barzelay 1992). This change in management is at once a manipulative mechanism for increasing efficiency and a genuine moral commitment to participation (Thomas 1993). Whether the participation is authentic or not, it is difficult for an organization to deny involvement and access to its employees and even to its clients.

Contemporary public organizations also must negotiate societal compliance with their decisions and negotiate compliance with contracts for service delivery, instead of implementing public programs directly through law and other authoritative means. The spread of network conceptualizations in the social sciences has been paralleled by a proliferation of network practices in governance (Scharpf 1991; Kenis and Schneider 1991). No longer can governments impose their wills through legal instruments and, if necessary, coercion; they must now work to achieve something approaching consensus among a large group of self-interested parties who have some influence over the policy. Governing in most industrialized democracies has become a process of bargaining and mediating rather than of applying rules (Kooiman 1993).

Further, civil servants increasingly are expected to make their own decisions about what constitutes the public interest, and they at times are compelled to make determinations diametrically opposed to the stated policies and desires of their nominal political masters.[13] If civil servants and other appointed officials are indeed to become entrepreneurial, then they must become less dominated by the dictates of their "masters." If practiced, this would alter fundamentally ideas of accountability and ideas of management in the public sector, especially in the Westminster democracies (Wilson 1994c). All of these changes make the role of civil service managers even more difficult than it had been and also make the role of civil servants within governments even more ambiguous. Further, the general absence of a formalized normative structure in government may make preserving accountability more difficult (*Public Money and Management,* 1995).

For developing and transitional regimes these changes are even more problematic than for the industrialized countries. Bureaucracies in European and North American countries are searching for ways to become more entrepreneurial and less constrained by red tape, but governments in many developing and transitional regimes confront different challenges. The problem of many governments in these countries is first to create the Weberian and rule-directed bureaucracies that are now being supplanted in the industrialized regimes. Going back to the earlier characterization of bureaucracies in transitional regimes by Fred Riggs (1964) as "prismatic," one of the challenges of public management in contexts of low universality of rules is to ensure equality and uniformity of the rules.

Permanence and Stability

The third change in the assumptions about governance and the public bureaucracy concerns the permanence and stability of the organizations within government (Kaufman 1976). Further, employment as a public servant is usually conceptualized as being a lifetime commitment, a "social contract," with civil servants trading a certain amount of income for secure employment (Hood and Peters 1994). Joining a public organization is sometimes conceptualized as joining a Japanese corporation once was—lifetime employment. The permanence of public organizations is frequently overestimated (Peters and Hogwood 1988), but it has been an important partial truth about government. Increasingly, this pattern of permanent organization is being attacked. The growing recognition of the dysfunctions of permanence, as well as the recognition that many significant social and economic problems currently exist within the interstices of existing public organizations, has led to some discussion of alternative forms of government organization.

The character of the alternative organizational structures remains somewhat inchoate at present, but the discussion has begun. In particular, ideas about task forces, "czars," interdepartmental committees, and similar structures have generated options for thinking about more flexible governance.[14] Another possibility that has been advanced is the "virtual organization" as a means of linking a range of individuals, and with them institutional interests, employed across a range of government organizations. Given the spread of information technology, the necessity of having people sit in the same place in order to have many characteristics of an organization has diminished. Therefore, forming alternatives to traditional organizations has become practical.

For individual public employees, the possibilities would also be diverse, with contracting and consultancy arrangements, temporary employment at peak times (tax and recreational employees, for example), and an increasing number of positions that are clearly not intended to be tenurable. Even in the senior civil service the idea of a distinctive career structure is being questioned and abandoned. This is true even in countries such as the United Kingdom, where the civil service has been very much a group apart from other employment streams. The Treasury—long the homeland of the mandarin—has embarked on a process of reducing its own staff and of thinking about how best to involve outside talent in its own work (HMSO 1993; HMSO 1994a).

The traditional sense of permanence in public organizations is being questioned from several perspectives. One is simply as a means of "deprivileging" the civil service at a time in which almost all organizations and employees are being confronted with downsizing and other threats to their existence. Another view is that permanence and stability tend to ossify policy lines and to make coordination of policies even more difficult. If temporary organizational structures are more common, this could have two benefits. First, it would enable more organizational experimentation in solving problems (Campbell 1982) without the fear that a future dinosaur was being created (Kaufman 1976). Further, it could permit the creation of organizations with primarily coordinative tasks that could address a particular problem of interaction among programs and organizations and then disappear. The conventional wisdom would argue that government organizations would not disappear, but neither has there been much real attempt to create such organizations explicitly.[15]

Governments of developing countries seem even more impacted by the permanence of public organizations and employment. Government is a major employer in all these countries, often serving as employer of last (or first) resort to maintain full employment. These governments absorbed in particular large percentages of the relatively small professional and educated segments of the society. It is difficult for any government to dismiss existing workers, but they also may perceive the need to hire additional, politically loyal, personnel. One instance in which it may make sense to dismiss existing employees on political grounds is when those employees have been compromised by their participation in a regime with serious human rights abuses (Peters 1995), but even then a government may wonder where the adequately trained replacements will come from. In any case, the tendency for public employment to be conceptualized as permanent presents real problems for these governments.

An Institutionalized Civil Service

The fourth fundamental assumption undergirding traditional public administration is that there should be an institutionalized civil service that is governed as a corporate body. This concept is a somewhat recent development in some industrialized democracies, with patronage or personal service to the crown or both being the older model for managing the state. For the intellectual father of contemporary bureaucracies, Max Weber (1958; see also Mommsen 1989), the development of authority and bureaucracy—beginning with charismatic and traditional authority using patrimonial organizations and ending with rational-legal authority employing bureaucratic organizations—represented the development of the modern state (especially in Germany). Although some analysts consider it central to political modernity, the concept of a distinctive and professional civil service has also been brought into question in a number of countries seeking to establish a more committed and activist civil service.

In addition to the impermanent government organizations being created, the personnel commitments of government have become less permanent. Government organizations increasingly expand and contract to meet variable demands for work, e.g., in tax offices or recreation programs. Though this style of personnel management may save governments money, it produces several empirical and normative questions for public managers and policy makers. Temporary employment for a significant portion of the public labor force may produce even more difficulties for citizens than the presumed indifference of permanent employees. Citizens will have to cope with public employees who may lack the commitment to service and other public values that, in most instances, characterized the career civil service. At a more practical level, temporary employees may lack the training and information necessary to do their jobs properly.

Even if the civil service system itself has not been challenged, the manner in which it traditionally has been managed is being questioned. For example, one of the common principles of personnel management in the public sector has been a uniform set of grades for personnel across the civil service, based on their qualifications, the difficulty of the tasks with which they are charged, or both, with relatively equal pay within each grade. Further, advancement was to be based on merit, demonstrated either by performance on the job or by a series of examinations. It is now less clear that merit is to be measured within the context of the public service and the public sector, again with forces and priorities of the market being used to "test" the worth of individuals as well as policies.

Internal Regulation

Yet another chestnut is that the civil service should be acquiescent and respond almost without question to policy directives issued by its nominal political masters. This demand goes beyond mere political neutrality. Many of the problems associated with government, and especially with public bureaucracy, are a function of controls imposed by political leaders seeking greater control and accountability (Kaufman 1977; Walters 1992b). Government organizations are generally among the most stringently regulated organizations in any society (Wilson 1989), especially in Anglo-American democracies. Therefore, if the skills and entrepreneurship of public employees could be engaged more freely, then government is likely to be able to perform more efficiently and effectively (Osborne and Gaebler 1992).

Still, it is less clear that deregulation is the most appropriate response to the needs of developing and transitional regimes. Certainly many of these governments have been characterized by extremely high levels of internal regulation (Beyme 1993) that have stifled creativity and produced problems in dealing with citizens. Further, in many instances, international organizations and private-sector lenders are pressing for loosening restraints on government action. Yet deregulation may not be the most appropriate response for the governments of transitional countries. The need in these regimes generally is for greater predictability and accountability rather than for the greater entrepreneurship demanded in more developed regimes.

Equality

The final characteristic of the traditional model of governance and public administration is that there should be as much equality of outcomes as possible. The traditional system of personnel management stressed equal pay and conditions of employment for similarly qualified employees across the civil service. Further, there are also strong norms in the traditional bureaucratic model that the decisions made by the public service with respect to their clients should also be as similar as possible throughout the organizations. In a traditional conception, clients with the same objective characteristics should receive exactly the same benefits, no matter where or from whom they receive them. In this Weberian conception of bureaucracy the civil servant applies the rules *sine irae et studio* (without anger or bias) to produce equitable outcomes for all clients (Thompson 1975).

Like almost everything else in the old system, this conception of equality is also being questioned through several related types of reform. First, market-oriented reforms have tended to decentralize and disaggregate government departments and to provide an enhanced amount of autonomy to managers. The assumption is that they will still be obliged to follow the laws of the programs they administer, but there does appear to be much greater room for discretion. That discretion is especially important if it is seen as possibly saving money for government. In this view the creation of differential levels and patterns of service generates a quasi market of sorts so that citizens can exercise some choice over what they will receive (and perhaps what they will pay for) from government.[16]

The attacks on equality of services also arise from an entirely different quarter: the participatory ethic in relationship to public services and public employment. The concept here is to "empower" lower-echelon workers in organizations and enable them to make more autonomous decisions about services. The argument is that the rigidity of bureaucratic structures designed to ensure greater equality of services for clients restricts the freedom of employees both to "self-actualize" on the job and also prevents them from making more creative and humane decisions about their clients. If these shackles are removed, then public employees will be happier and will also deliver better services to their clients. Particularly for social services, programs that were intended to be humane and helpful have become bureaucratized (in the pejorative sense of that term) and frequently harm (if only in subtle ways) in addition to helping their clients (Smart 1991). Further, some of the models of administrative reform argue for the empowerment of clients to make more of their own decisions, an approach that may be diametrically opposed to the empowerment of the workers administering benefits for those clients (see chapter 3).

In addition to raising questions about how happy both public employees and their clients are, the issue of equality points to important issues of accountability and the law. Do clients want the outcomes of their demands for service to be contingent on getting the "right" worker? Do other taxpayers want public employees to have so much latitude in delivering the services that are paid for with tax money? Is it legal (or ethical) for people with the same characteristics and the same rights to be treated differently by government, or are these other public values equally or more important than the values of empowerment? Unfortunately, these issues do not appear to be addressed adequately in the contemporary debates about change in the public sector.

Summary

Rather than looking back to vestiges of past thinking about governance, in this book I will be prospective and examine several alternative paths for the development of the public service. I will examine and develop several alternative models of the state that are emerging in practice and then look at their implications for the civil service. Except for the market model these alternatives have not been articulated in a comprehensive form; they have appeared more clearly in government documents than in the academic literature. I therefore will have to extract them almost as ideal types from academic and practical discussions of governing.

Further, there is some similarity of analyses and prescriptions across the alternatives, although the meanings attached to the prescriptions may be quite different in each model. Most reforms have the effect, however, of "hollowing" out the state and making it, and particularly the career public service, a less significant actor in society (Rhodes 1994; Milward forthcoming). Interestingly, however, one of the approaches to changing government may have the (probably unintended) consequence of enhancing both its powers and the powers of the civil service within it. Although focusing on alternatives, I argue that one possible model is a vigorous restatement of the status quo ante. For many civil servants, and for some politicians, the "oldtime religion" may still be the best way to run a government, even if they must face massive skepticism from the public.

WHAT HAPPENED?

This traditional system of administration persisted for decades and was, on the whole, extremely successful. It fought several world wars, produced and administered a massive expansion of social programs, instituted large-scale economic management for the public sector, and did a host of other remarkable things. This system, however, has now gone from "hubris to helplessness" (Downs and Larkey 1986). What happened to cause such a large-scale rethinking of governance as has been occurring during the 1980s and 1990s? There is no single answer, but there has been a confluence of events that has caused a fundamental rethinking of governance and some attempt to move administration far away from its roots. Although this can be seen most dramatically in the Anglo-American democracies, the changes extend into virtually all industrialized democracies, including some such as Japan that are usually thought to be highly successful (Krauss and Muramatsu 1995).

One (too) facile reply to all these changes is that there were such significant shifts in the economy that governments were forced to respond. Presumably, this meant that as economic growth slowed, became less certain, or both, government could no longer realistically count on the fiscal dividend of growth to fund increasing costs. Certainly any significant new programs were unlikely to be adopted. Further, if the costs of delivering existing service commitments could be reduced by making administration more efficient, then by all means that should be done. The desire to be economically competitive in an emerging global economy (Savoie 1995), it has been argued, began to outstrip most other concerns on the agenda of government so that any reductions in tax costs, regulation, and perceived public-sector inefficiencies were welcomed.

This economic explanation for the advance of the governmental and administrative reforms is a bit too facile. Certainly there were economic problems, but in the recent past these might have been addressed by *expanding* the role of the public sector rather than by reducing it. Clearly Richard Nixon's confession of his Keynesianism would appear to argue that. Further, the economic problems were not as great as at some other times during the postwar period that produced much less overt response from reformers, especially those within the public sector itself. There is a need to specify other influences that may help explain why these questions about the performance of the economy produced such massive responses.

One of the possible contributory factors is demographic change. The populations of almost all industrialized democracies are rapidly becoming older. This means that the level of entitlement expenditure for programs such as old age pensions, medical care, and the like is doubtlessly going to expand and will have to be paid for by a declining number of working-age people. Reviews of these commitments, such as the that of Kerry/Danforth Commission in the United States (Bipartisan Commission 1994), have pointed to the rapid escalation of entitlement expenditures that will occur over the next several decades under existing law. Reforming public-sector management is unlikely to be able to do anything about these problems per se, but it may be able to reduce at least some of the total costs of government and create some greater capacity for future spending on entitlements. Further, making government appear better managed may be important symbolically if it needs to go to the people for additional taxes.

The concern about entitlement spending belongs largely to the political elite; relatively few people in the mass public are aware of entitlement obligations, other than their own future benefits. The concern over governance, however, has not been just an elite phenomenon and indeed has become a force approaching a populist uprising in some countries.[17] That populist reaction against government has a number of dimensions. On the political right there has been a reaction against taxation, public spending, and the degree of regulation being imposed on business. Even many working- and lower-middle-class citizens who may be net beneficiaries of the public sector now oppose government spending, and especially taxation (Petersen 1992; Sears and Citrin 1985). This reaction to the public sector has been the more common one, with demands that government simply shrink. The dominant assumption is that government cannot do anything well so should do as little as possible.

There has also been a populism of the left, although it has been less visible and less successful than that coming from the political right. This alternative version of populism has attacked the large, bureaucratic structures that have been developed to deliver a range of social and economic services. These bureaucracies are claimed to be insensitive, inefficient, and often hostile to the very clients they were intended to serve (Smart 1991). Further, it is argued that government as a whole has become increasingly divorced from the people it serves and is dominated by the affluent, the educated, and the powerful. In the extreme version of the argument, government is conceptualized as "regulating the poor" rather than actually serving them through social programs (Piven and Cloward 1993; Squires 1990). Part of the lack of success of this version of populism is that it attempts to strengthen the positions of the poor and other groups with relatively little political clout.

The cultural change manifested in populism has not been felt uniformly throughout the Western world. Even some of the more successful welfare states in the past, e.g., Sweden and Denmark, have undertaken administrative reforms that are derivative from the market model (Andersen 1994; Lundell 1994). Other countries such as Norway, however, have attempted to maintain the old values and even to increase the democratic and collective elements of policy and administration. Although the wealth of Norway helps to explain some of the persistence of these values, the collective values being implemented also reflect the importance of those older values and of mass political participation within the culture.

Indeed, the economies and societies that governments are meant to control and regulate have become less governable (Mayntz 1993; Kooiman 1993). This decline in the capacity of government to regulate society effectively results from several interrelated causes (Cohen and Rogers 1994). First, there is increasing social and political heterogeneity among populations. The role of the welfare state in rectifying market-based inequalities has been reduced, and income inequalities have been increasing in most industrialized societies. Further, the ethnic and racial heterogeneity of these societies has also been increasing through immigration, with a related increase in social tensions.

The second cause for increasing difficulties in governance appears to be that the issues confronting contemporary governments have shifted from being bargainable to being less bargainable. Certainly economic issues are important in the political debates in all societies and indeed have been returning to a more central position in many. The general problems of sustainable economic growth, distribution, and employment are more important in the 1990s than they appear to have been at any time since the end of World War II. That having been said, however, these economic issues are supplemented by a set of issues such as race, gender, participation, and equality, problems that are more difficult to solve through the mechanisms of conflict resolution created in postwar politics. The "post-materialist values" (Inglehart 1990) that undergird these conflicts tend to be more absolute rather than marginal, so that divisible goods such as money are often inadequate to the task of addressing them.

A closely related third point is the decline of stable organizations as the focus for government interventions as well as for the source of inputs into governing. One of the most effective means of addressing economic policy issues during the postwar years was "corporatism," existing in its various guises throughout Europe and to some extent in North America (Schmitter 1989; Pross 1992). Even when government was attempting to cope with numerous economic demands and economic policy, a constellation of stable and reasonably well-structured interest groups existed with which government could bargain. Yet even in the most successful of these regimes, there has been some decline in the proportion of the workforce represented by unions,[18] and in the commitment of members to their unions, so that the bargaining partners of government are now less reliable. Further, corporatist structures began to erode when, in the 1970s and 1980s, they were no longer able to distribute economic growth and new benefits but began to have to think about distributing cuts in programs.

As soon as the public sector begins to have to make policy about these post-materialist issues, the constellation of interest groups becomes less stable and less able to deliver its members' consent to any deal. Members of "attitude groups" do not need to retain their affiliation, as do members of unions or employers organizations, so if they disagree with the policies approved by their leadership there is little or no cost to their leaving and forming other organizations. Thus, the possibilities of making binding deals are much less than in traditional economic policy negotiations, and governments may have a harder time framing the issues adequately, much less implementing effective policies.

VISIONS OF THE STATE AND GOVERNANCE

Few governments have remained untouched by the wave of reform that has swept through the public sector over the past several decades. The magnitude of reform undertaken in most political systems may have been unprecedented, at least during peacetime, but reform also may have tended to be extremely piecemeal and unsystematic (Peters and Savoie 1994). The absence of clear visions and integrated strategies may partly explain why the results of the reforms have tended to disappoint so many of their advocates (Caiden 1990; Ingraham 1995b). Apparently, what often has happened is that governments have selected "off the shelf" reforms derived from one set of assumptions (implicit or explicit) at the same time that they selected others based on quite different, or even directly contradictory, premises. The political and administrative leaders made these selections, expecting all the changes to work well together. It is therefore little wonder perhaps that in practice the sets of reforms have not worked together in a large number of instances and that also at times the interactions have proven to be negative.

What I will do in this book, therefore, is to explicate several more integrated visions of possible futures for the state and its bureaucracy. The nature of each vision will in turn influence the manner in which governance, considered more broadly, would be practiced if such an administrative regime were to be implemented in toto. These reform agendas must not be considered in isolation from other political and cultural movements in society. For example, the emphasis on market models of reforming government represents but one strand of thinking about the need to inculcate market ideas into a whole range of social institutions, such as universities. Likewise, the drive for making administration more participatory is but a part of a general ethos (largely contradictory to the market model) stressing greater opportunities for participation in these same institutions.

If the implications of these alternative visions are more fully explored and understood, and contrasted with the traditional conceptualizations of governance, then there is some possibility of producing more effective planned change in government. There is certainly no guarantee of success even with more coherent programs, and the possibility that even the best-planned administrative changes will be diverted and subverted is inevitably present (March and Olsen 1983).

The practical significance of this exercise, however, will be secondary. My purpose is primarily to enhance the understanding of what has been happening with governance and to clarify the future implications of the alternative conceptions. Gaining a clear insight into contemporary reforms is not easy. Speaking of the changes occurring in British government, Sue Richards (1992, 15) argues that it is a confusing picture of changing patterns of behavior, of informal and emergent rules, and of shifting power plays. We need greater clarity so that public managers and other practitioners of public service may be assisted in their understanding and so that a wider public may have better access to these changes.

It appears almost certain that the status quo ante is no longer a preferred option in the public sector, in Britain or anywhere, so we must understand what patterns are emerging. Academic and practitioner analysts must explore the assumptions of those models, along with the particular proposals derived from those assumptions. Without that analysis and interpretation, it will be difficult to comprehend the emerging form of the state in society—both industrialized and transitional—and to think about the fundamental problems of governing in the next century.

My concern in this book with alternative visions should not be read to mean that any of these schemes is superior to the traditional model of the civil service in governance. I tend to think that is not the case, although certainly the traditional model is far from perfect and could be made to function better. I also tend to believe that continuing reform in government is probable or even inevitable under the current political climate, and if that reform is to occur it is more likely to be effective if the changes are systematic and integrated. Readers should also remain cognizant of the internal contradictions inherent within some of these approaches to governance. It may be that like Simon's now classic discussion (1947) of the "proverbs of administration" there are also "proverbs of reform" that are equally contradictory (Kaufman 1978; Peters 1995). Thinking about the complexities of the public service, even when guided by a relatively strong set of theoretical assumptions, tends toward constructing situational rather than systematic remedies. This emphasis on situational rather than systematic analysis can be seen most clearly with cycles of reform, with centralization efforts following decentralization, followed by yet another round of decentralization.

That having been said, however, we do need to think about the context within which any particular vision of governance is to be implemented. For transitional regimes in Central and Eastern Europe it may be that a Weberian system of highly constrained administration is perhaps the most suitable tool for restoring some legitimacy to government (Hesse 1993; Derlien and Szablowski 1993). The values inherent in that system may need to be institutionalized first, then to be followed by the more marketized systems of administration later. The politicization and extreme arbitrariness of the old system may have to be purged from people's minds before a more decentralized administrative system can be legitimate.

Nevertheless, some Third World regimes that have been dominated by a bureaucracy (perhaps in the pejorative sense of the word) may find the alternative models to be discussed just as applicable and desirable as do the industrialized countries (Grindle and Thomas 1991). One difficulty in the reform process has been that advocates have assumed that one size fits all and that any government could be improved by the institutionalization of their preferred new pattern of government. Indeed, some of the problems with reforms, such as "reinvention" (Osborne and Gaebler 1992) in the United States, arise from their being based on assumptions about government derived from the experiences of small local governments that may not be appropriate for central governments.

As I develop these four alternatives to the traditional system of governance, the implications and prescriptions of each "vision" for several aspects of governing will be examined. The first and most basic is the *diagnosis* of the problem. Reform efforts imply a desire to change something, and each of the four alternatives contains a fairly clear idea about what is producing problems in the public sector. Thus, the models attempt to take the (often) vague sense of uneasiness and malaise that citizens feel about their governments and translate it into a specific cause-and-effect relationship. As with any attempt to impose such a construction on complex social and political institutions, this exercise often produces some oversimplification. The identification of a cause, however, also produces the clarity that may be needed to engage in the complex and difficult battles to reform government.

The other four dimensions of analysis are more specific conceptualizations of problems and particularly of alternatives to the status quo. The second dimension is *structure:* how should the public sector be organized? Governments have tended to be organized in a hierarchical manner, the principal format being large departments headed by a cabinet minister. This pattern remains the default option in most governments, but there is also a variety of alternative structures being introduced, more or less successfully, in almost all political systems. Thus, the structure of government is no longer the given that it once was, and there is a need for scholars and practitioners to think about the options available to them and the relationships of structural decisions to the several emerging models of governance. Though some students of organizations tend to see structure as a relatively insignificant aspect of making an organization effective, I will argue that it needs to be coordinated with other aspects of governance if the public sector is to be effective.

The third dimension of the models is *management:* how should the members of the public sector be recruited, motivated, and managed, and how should the financial resources of the public sector be controlled? There has been a clearly articulated model for personnel management that has dominated thinking in the public sector. Although the thinking about structure has tended to question the conventional wisdom while largely retaining it, in personnel management the dominant pattern has been to eliminate the old ways of doing things. These changes tend to replicate personnel management in the private sector and also tend to weaken the long-term commitment of government to its employees. Working for the public sector is less different from working for the private sector now than it has been in the past, and we should consider the implications of those changes.

Similarly, there has been a dominant managerial ethos about the control of resources through budgeting and purchasing rules. These rules have tended toward the ex ante control of decisions by powerful central agencies. In this view management was largely a central function, with other actors following the direction of the central masters. There might have been some latitude for personal decisions for organizational heads, but the principal managerial tasks were conforming to rules rather than exercising discretion. As I will point out, the emerging models of governing tend to shift thinking about management toward greater autonomy and discretion for lower-echelon officials.

Fourth, there is always some conception of the policy and the *policy process:* what should the role of the career public service be in the policy process, and more generally how should government seek to influence the private sector? These questions involve a variety of difficult issues about the procedures through which government should make its decisions as well as the content of those decisions. Too often, those two issues are conflated, with the assumption that certain actors (civil servants) will produce certain types of policies (interventionist). Therefore, more market-based instruments (vouchers, for example) that keep the bureaucrats out are preferable. Further, we need to examine the impacts of internal rules and regulations, e.g., civil service laws, in the policy process as the means that legislatures and judiciaries use to ensure that policies are made appropriately, if not always quickly.

Finally, these four emerging visions of governance each contains some conception of the *public interest* and an overall conceptualization of what constitutes "good government." These conceptions are often implicit in the models, but they are certainly apparent after a little reflection. They all have answers for the question, "How should government govern, and what should it do?" This view of the public interest is perhaps the most important component of the entire exercise, given that the fundamental question that anyone in government should be asking is whether the programs of reform adopted and the outcomes of the policy process are likely to benefit the public more than the system that is being abolished. As I will point out, all the reformers do believe that their changes will be for the best, although they often operate with very different conceptions of the public interest.

By way of preview, readers should examine these four models and the four dimensions of evaluation (see Table 1.1). Looking carefully at these dimensions of change will enable us to understand the strengths, weaknesses, implications, and interactions of these four models, as well as of the specific reforms that are derived from them. That careful examination will also enable us to understand why several of the contemporary packages of change have been disappointing to their advocates and have confirmed the suspicions of their critics. Changing the public sector, or any other significant aggregation of large organizations, is not an easy task. I hope that with a more thorough and dispassionate examination the difficulties, and the possibilities, will become clearer.

REFORM CONTINUES

To this point I have talked about the dismantling of a traditional form of governing and of administering programs in the public sector. The problem with successful reform is that this quickly becomes the new orthodoxy and in turn becomes subject to challenges and changes. This has certainly been the case for the reforms of government that were implemented during the 1980s and 1990s. Although these provided a series of possible solutions to the problems of governing, they also generated their own problems, and thus there have been reactions to changes that advocates had seen as the solutions to governing.

What has happened in the public sector after the four types of reforms were implemented is discussed in chapters 6 and 7. I am arguing that there have been four principal reactions to the first rounds of reform. The first has been to emphasize performance and quality in government in contrast to the concern with econ-

Table 1.1. Major Features of the Four Models

	Market Government	Participative Government	Flexible Government	Deregulated Government
Principal diagnosis	Monopoly	Hierarchy	Permanence	Internal regulation
Structure	Decentralization	Flatter organizations	"Virtual organizations"	No particular recommendation
Management	Pay for performance; other private-sector techniques	TQM; teams	Managing temporary personnel	Greater managerial freedom
Policymaking	Internal markets; market incentives	Consultation; negotiation	Experimentation	Entrepreneurial government
Public interest	Low cost	Involvement; consultation	Low cost; coordination	Creativity; activism

omy and efficiency, which were emphasized in the first round of changes. Governments are now using performance and quality standards as the means for assessing management and policy, with economic efficiency being one of a number of standards that are being applied to managers and their programs.

Besides the emphasis on performance, the more recent set of reforms has been stressing the need for coordination. The initial rounds of reform tended to disaggregate the public sector, both structurally and procedurally. Reforms such as Next Steps in the United Kingdom, and the creation of a number of autonomous and quasi-autonomous organizations in many countries, have made the familiar problem of coordination in the public sector even more difficult to achieve. Similarly, ideas of empowerment have tended to cause many managers to assume that they should be concerned with their own programs to the exclusion of any responsibilities they may have for the public sector as an entity.

The third dimension of reactions to initial reforms has been to reregulate the public sector. The initial reforms did a rather thorough job, at least in some countries, of removing the rules and regulations that had shaped public management and that had to some extent produced problems for efficient management. It has appeared to many observers that these reforms went too far and reduced some of the capacity of central agencies and political leaders to ensure equality and probity in government. There is one important difference between the old approach and the regulations being implemented in the more recent round of changes — they tend to be ex post facto, with central organizations now assessing what organizations have done and then imposing controls when they believe that they or their managers have behaved inappropriately.

Closely related to the attempts to reregulate government are general concerns about accountability. As well as removing a number of organizations from direct ministerial responsibility, advocates of the first round of reforms tended to assume that managers and even lower-echelon employees could make more of their own decisions and that means to hold them accountable were unnecessary. At least the mechanisms of parliamentary accountability did not seem as appropriate as they once did after those associated with New Public Management had been established. Therefore, new means of accountability have had to be found to replace what has been lost, and these often focus on both performance management and reregulation.

This second round of reforms lacks the strong intellectual roots that characterized much of the reform implemented during the first round of change. The one exception to that generalization is the quality movement in government, which, as I will demonstrate, does have a good deal of academic development and an extensive literature. The other three brands of reform, however, are in many ways restatements of some traditional ideas in public administration, albeit modified to some degree to meet the demands of a changed public sector. Still, these reforms are more complementary than were those in the first round of change. The changes in the second round point, in one way or another, toward restoring some of the older values associated with governing and the restatement of those old virtues.

We also must ask whether the reforms, and the style of governing associated with them, are appropriate as universal standards or whether they are bound in culture and in particular socioeconomic systems. The ideas associated with management reform have now been spread to many developing countries, usually in connection with the programs of one or another donor organizations. Though they may have produced some notable results in the industrialized democracies, these programs appear unsuited in many ways to the administrative and cultural conditions of developing societies. In particular, public administration in developing and transitional countries often lacks the institutionalized value systems that make deregulated and more autonomous governing feasible—feasible, that is, assuming that any government must maintain its accountability and integrity, as well as being efficient. With these concerns in mind, I shall examine the spread of ideas about public management reform and their effects on government in a range of countries outside the industrialized democracies (see chapter 8).

In summary, governing continues to present challenges to the individuals who choose to make its pursuit their career. They have been proving themselves to be creative and persistent in meeting those challenges, but they have not yet found the philosophers' stone that will produce good government in the large, complex, and often recalcitrant systems within which they function. The evidence presented here, however, is that they continue to try; and they do respond to failures, and even to successes, as they continue to design new instruments for governing. As we examine their efforts we should always remember that the tasks of governing are almost inherently more difficult than the tasks of managing in the private sector, given the multiple goals, the constraints on action, and the demands for accountability that characterize the public sector. We can only hope that the pursuit of better ways to manage the public's business will continue.

2

Market Models for Reforming Government

If there is a single alternative to the traditional model of public administration favored by contemporary politicians, academics, and probably also the public, it must be the market model. Instances in which this model has been applied, or claims have been made that it has been applied, are perhaps too numerous to list here.[1] The fundamental point is that the dominant Zeitgeist of reform in government has been to use the market and to accept the assumption that private-sector methods are almost inherently superior for managing activities (regardless of what they are) than are those of the traditional public sector. Whether administrative change is being considered in the most affluent country of Western Europe or the poorest country of Africa,[2] the operative assumption appears to be that the best, or even only, way to obtain better results from public-sector organizations is to adopt some sort of a market-based mechanism to replace the traditional bureaucracy.

In this view of the world, the principal problem with traditional bureaucracies has been that they do not provide sufficient incentive for individuals working within them to perform their jobs as efficiently as they might. Given this dearth of motivation, individuals will usually attempt to maximize other qualities in their job. One such quality might be "on-the-job leisure" (Peacock 1983), with the result that the familiar image of the slothful, indolent bureaucrat is created. Then there is the argument that bureaucrats frequently maximize the size of their agency budgets as a means of enhancing their own personal power and income (Niskanen 1971; McGuire 1981). This view raises the specter of the activist, megalomaniac bureaucrat—certainly the antithesis of sloth—and assumes further that administrators can gain personally from a larger budget.

Further, bureaucrats and their organizations are sometimes conceptualized as overzealous, not about personal rewards but about the exercise of public policy, especially those that are alleged to damage industry and impose "internalities" on the society as a whole (Wolfe 1988; Booker and North 1994). Once

created and granted a mandate to regulate a certain area of policy, an organization may become difficult to control. Bureaucratic drift (Shepsle 1992) may
occur, in which the organization tends to move further and further from original
legislative intentions and more toward its own definition of good policy. This
regulatory activity is usually conducted with good intentions, but for the regulated industries such activism is generally unwelcome.

Here, then, is a set of complaints concerning traditional public administration, ills which the market model is assumed to be able to cure. The problem is,
however, that these diagnoses are rather different, and indeed contradictory, perceptions of the failings of the old model of administration, and this single type of
reform is expected to be capable of correcting all of them. That characterization
of internal contradiction is perhaps somewhat unfair, given that the market
"model" itself is to some degree significantly differentiated and comprises several components. Still, this observation does point out that there is a strong element of ideology in almost all efforts to improve the public sector, and one must
be extremely thorough when evaluating any claims being advanced. Claims on
behalf of the models are often made by enthusiasts who have not always worked
through all the empirical implications of their ideas. This critique is true for the
market model, but it will be equally true of the other approaches to reforming the
public sector (Moe 1993, 1994). Moreover, the same critique of presenting a pre-
dominantly ideological argument definitely can be made for some advocates of
reaffirming the traditional model of public administration (Goodsell 1995).

After the initial ideological adherence to the market model, and optimism
about its appplicability, the experience of some reformers using it has been less
positive than expected. This is beginning to produce a somewhat more nuanced
understanding of the utility of the market as an exemplar for the public sector. It
is also resulting in some discussion about the need to reintroduce aspects of traditional public administration into the reformed public sector.

THE IDEAS BEHIND THE MARKET MODEL

There really is no single market model, other than the basic belief in the virtues
of competition and an idealized pattern of exchange and incentives (King 1987;
LeGrand 1989). The market model as it has been applied with respect to public
administration has several intellectual roots. Just as there is that internal variation in thinking about government, so too have the programs for change derived
from these strands of thinking been diverse. The task, therefore, is to extract both
from the academic literature and from practice the explicit and implicit ideas
involved in market-based change and then to relate those ideas to the administrative changes being imposed in the real world of government. In some
instances the linkage between ideas and action is clear (or at least meant to be
so). Margaret Thatcher once advised her ministers to read William Niskanen's

work on bureaucracy and then to follow its advice (Hennessy 1989). In other cases, such as the Reagan administration and the Mulroney government, any relationship of actions to ideas was probably accidental (Savoie 1994a).[3] As Peter Self wrote, the ideas of Reagan and his principal advisers appeared "too shallow to be debited to any respectable theorist" (1993, 71).

Although the market model was closely associated with these governments of the political right, it has also been influential among the more leftist governments that have followed them. Tony Blair, Jean Chretien, Bill Clinton, and Gerhard Schroder come from the political parties normally associated with the political left in their countries, but they also have adopted many of the market-based ideas for managing government. This is especially clear for the Labour government in Britain, which has retained and even expanded the market regime begun by Thatcher (Geddes and Martin 2000), somewhat to the dismay of many supporters.

The Efficiency of Markets

The primary intellectual root of the market approach to changing the public sector is the belief in the efficiency of markets as the mechanism for allocating resources within a society. Arising from neoclassical economics, the ideas advanced by the advocates of the market model are that other forms of allocation, i.e., through bureaucracies or law more generally, are distortions of outcomes that would be produced by a free market. Therefore, society would, on average, be better off (at least in economic terms) if the market or analogous competitive institutions were allowed to determine policy decisions. This assumption tends to beg questions about the distribution of those resources among individuals (LeGrand 1991); that is one of the problems that public intervention commonly is designed to remedy. The advocates of the market approach also assume that there are no significant costs of production (pollution as the classic example) that are not included in the price of the product—the familiar externalities problem (Coase 1960)—that would cause social cost and market cost to diverge.

Any number of critiques have been written on the assumptions contained within the neoclassical economic model, and we do not need to explore all the logical and empirical problems here.[4] What we should do, however, is think about what the adoption of this model as the standard for efficient social allocation does for the role of public bureaucracy as that institution has been developed in most industrialized democracies. The quick answer is that the acceptance of the market as a standard tends to require advocates of any deviations from distributions produced by competition to justify those positions. Justifications have been made through the recognition of externalities, the recognition of the social desirability for some redistribution of income (Commission on Social Justice 1994), and the existence of public goods that by definition cannot be allocated efficiently through markets because of their nonexcludability characteristic (Atkinson and Stiglitz 1980). Other analysts, however, believe that market mechanisms can be used to solve externality problems, e.g., pollution.

Even when these deficiencies of the market as a mechanism for social allocation are recognized, that still does not mean that bureaucracies and formalized legal instruments will necessarily be the best, or even better, means of government intervention. The advocates of the market tend to assume that the closer instruments of public intervention come to the market, the better the collective outcomes will be. Therefore, the traditional public sector with its direct mechanisms for intervention will often be characterized as an inefficient "tool" for it to use (Hood 1986; Linder and Peters 1989). In contrast, more market-based mechanisms such as contracts, incentives, and tax expenditures (see Hula 1990; Walsh 1995) emerge as preferable instruments under those assumptions. For example, many policy analysts[5] prefer market-based incentives for pollution abatement rather than the command-and-control mechanisms usually used in that policy area (Schultze 1977; Oates 1995).

Bureaucratic Monopolies

The second intellectual root of market-based reforms is the analysis of the failings of conventional bureaucracies by scholars such as Niskanen (1971), Tullock (1965), Moe (1984, 1989), and a host of other advocates of public-choice analysis (Bendor 1990; Dowding 1991) in political science. These scholars have argued that because of the self-interest of the members of the organizations, especially "bureau chiefs" at the apex, public bureaucracies tend to expand at an unjustifiable rate and to charge their sponsors (read legislatures) too much for the services produced for the public. The permanence of bureaucrats, and especially their monopoly on information, it has been argued (Banks and Weingast 1992), places them at a competitive advantage when dealing with the legislature. The basic root of the failings in the public sector, when visualized from this perspective, is the self-interest of bureaucrats who exploit their control of information for personal gain.[6]

Interestingly, another school of economic analysis argues that bureaucracies *under*supply certain goods and services (Breton 1974), also for reasons of self-interest among the bureau chiefs. The argument here is that bureaucracies have the choice of creating public goods or private goods through their budgets. Given the indivisibility and nonexcludability of public goods, they are not usually perceived as conferring any particular benefits on individual members of society. On the other hand, private goods do benefit particular individuals and thus have a much higher political payoff for the bureaucracy and for their political masters. Therefore, bureaucracies (assuming they have the available latitude) will undersupply public goods and oversupply private goods to their clients. Using similar logic, Anthony Downs once argued (1960) that the public budget would tend to be too small in a democracy, although his logic is that the public does not recognize the value of public goods and therefore does not vote for candidates promising them. Still, his conclusion today appears startling, if not absolutely heretical.

Other scholars (Dunleavy 1985, 1991) have argued for a "bureau-shaping" approach to understanding the maximizing behavior of public bureaucrats.[7] Not all expenditures are equally valuable to the personally ambitious bureaucrats; transfer money that simply passes through the bureau to grant recipients outside, for example, generates work but produces few appropriable benefits for the bureau chief. Therefore, rational bureaucrats will attempt to maximize the "core budget" of the bureau, i.e., that portion of their budget that funds their own staff and operations instead of attempting to expand the total budget. If rational, the bureaucrat would expand the core budget at the expense of other forms of expenditure and perhaps even total expenditures. In this view of behavior in the public sector, bureaucrats will attempt to develop methods of maximizing their nonpecuniary rewards of office, given that their salaries and so forth tend to have been determined by fixed scales. With the shift to performance pay and differential pay policies for public employees (Eisenberg and Ingraham 1993), however, civil servants may rightly become more concerned with their personal salaries.

These perspectives on the public bureaucracy in the economics literature are clearly views in which the individual bureaucrats are personally ambitious, or at least self-indulgent, and attempt to use the monopoly powers possessed by their bureaus to maximize their own personal self-interest (see Egeberg 1995). These officials are able to exercise this power in the budgeting process, in part because they have superior access to information, especially information about the true cost of production of the service, than does their sponsor. If there were effective bureaucratic competition to provide the same service, so the argument goes, the bureaus would have an incentive to drive down their costs of production in order to drive their competitor out of "business." This is the same competitive mechanism presumed to work in the private sector and presumably would result in minimizing the costs of delivering the services.[8] Even if overt competition did not work, if multiple agencies were in competition to provide the service, the sponsor might be able to play one off against another, have them reveal their true costs of production (Downs 1967), and then use that information to control public spending.

The problem with this analysis is that one of the canons of public-sector management (and even in the private sector within a single firm) holds that there should be minimal redundancy of functions (but see Bendor 1985; Landau 1969), thus preventing any effective competition among agencies.[9] This need to minimize redundancy is seen most clearly in the regulatory arena where citizens and corporations complain about multiple and conflicting requirements (Duncan and Hobson 1995; Mastracco and Comparato 1994). Even that regulatory redundancy, however, might be efficient from the perspective of a sponsor seeking to gain information both about the performance of the bureaus and of the regulated organizations.[10]

Even in service provision, however, there are many demands for "one stop shopping" for recipients of social benefits (Jennings and Krane 1994). That integration of services is presumed to provide for greater efficiency for both the client and government. However, it may conflict with an emerging emphasis on providing "customer satisfaction" with government services. People do not want to have to go to several locations to receive their services, but they also want to have their cases considered by a knowledgeable civil servant who can make a decision. Too much emphasis on one-stop shopping and cross-training employees can create as much dissatisfaction as too much (organizational or geographical) division of services. The familiar logic of specialization in providing services is of course quite contrary to the logic of one-stop shopping.

Further, competition does not appear to be an effective solution for the problem of the undersupply of public goods through the bureaucracy. The sponsor would have many of the same incentives as the bureaucracy to attempt to please its own particular clients and to spend less on public goods in order to be able to provide more private goods for those clients. In the case of a mixed bureau providing both public and private goods, budget-shaping of a different sort may permit managers and sponsors to shift resources from public goods to private goods. If anything, the incentives for the sponsor to provide private goods may be higher, given the need for reelection (Fiorina 1989; Miller and Moe 1983) and the generally low electoral appeal of public goods. The strength of these expenditure incentives for the sponsor will vary somewhat, depending on the structure of the legislature. Legislative structures such as that of the United States, with numerous committees responsible for oversight of administrative agencies and with the members of those committees having a pronounced political interest in the activities of the bureau, will be particularly susceptible to the oversupply of private goods and the undersupply of public goods (see Krause 2000). Proportional representation systems that limit the direct connections between individual legislators and particular constituencies (geographical if not always functional) apparently reduce these incentives for bureau-shaping by legislative sponsors.

There seem to be several other difficulties with the assumption that monopoly powers of bureaucratic agencies generate inefficiencies. First, it may be the case that some of the services delivered by government are delivered more efficiently as monopolies rather than through competition. Williamson (1985) specifies some of the conditions for monopoly (whether public or private), including the conventional criterion of natural monopoly. This is almost certainly the case for publicly owned utilities, such as gas and electricity in Europe. Even if privatized, these services tend to retain their monopoly status and must be regulated by government (Wiltshire 1987; Richardson 1994).[11] Moreover, many public services already have substantial competition from the private sector, e.g., private education; private health care, even in government-dominated systems; and the numerous private courier services competing with postal services. Very few public services continue to enjoy a monopoly of provision so that there is already a great deal of effective competition, with little capacity for government agencies to escape those pressures (Peters 1995c, 35). Similarly, government provision or regulation or both may be justified when the social risks involved are too large and too difficult to quantify for reasonable private contracts to be negotiated (Perrow 1984).

Indeed, there is already a good degree of competition over the allocation of resources in government through the conventional budgetary process. Even if an agency is not directly competing with another public agency delivering the same type of service, it is competing with all other agencies for resources at budget time. This competition plays a crucial role in the survival of an agency and is intense. Moreover, the budgetary process is used to elicit a good deal of information from the agencies for the "sponsor" (Savoie 1990; Wildavsky 1992), especially when the sponsor is well structured to exercise such oversight through budgeting (Schick 1990; Kraan 1996). Indeed, sponsors tend to be quite capable in gaining information through the budgetary process and in using it to assess the success of public management and to punish the less effective.

This view of the world of government and its bureaucracy from the market-oriented critics supposes a good deal of autonomy for agencies within the public sector. In this approach, agencies are capable of engaging in a variety of ploys that mask their activities from effective scrutiny by their sponsor. The problem with this analysis is that such a degree of autonomy exists in very few governments, and even in those few cases there are numerous mechanisms designed to restrain it. In essence, the Niskanen model is patterned after structures existing in the United States, with a highly fragmented government and consequent difficulties in exercising effective control (Goodin 1982). Other countries such as Sweden and Norway (Christensen 1994; Petersson and Söderlind 1992) also permit their agencies a great deal of autonomy, albeit within the constraints of a well-articulated legal and budgetary framework that produces adequate coordination without direct control.

Most of the world of government, however, does not permit such great autonomy for its agencies or for the civil servants within them. Either through ministerial structures with stronger internal controls, through the strength of central agencies, or through both (Campbell 1983; Savoie 1995b), agencies are forced to conform more to the wishes of their political and administrative masters. What is particularly interesting, however, is that some of the market-based reforms now being implemented are creating just the type of agency autonomy that is assumed by Niskanen to be one root of much of the difficulty. This change is now being effected in the name of "entrepreneurship" and "efficiency," but the results may not be terribly different from when autonomy was granted to enhance the policymaking powers of the agency—if indeed that was ever a conscious choice to enhance agency autonomy in the United States—or to provide Congress greater control over policy.

In this public-choice view, bureaus also derive some of their power from their influence over the agendas of government (Altfeld and Miller 1984). This power is dependent in part on the relative level of information enjoyed by the bureaucracy. Perhaps the strongest agenda power for an agency is negative, or the capacity to prevent an issue from being considered. This "second face of power" (Bachrach and Baratz 1962) derives from the close contacts of most agencies with their policies as being implemented and their knowledge of problems emerging in an existing program. If this information is suppressed, then the capacity of either the minister in charge or the legislature to intervene to correct the problem becomes limited.

Public bureaucracies also have substantial control over one aspect of the policy agenda, the issuing of secondary legislation, or "regulations" in American political parlance. When legislatures pass any major piece of legislation, they tend to leave a great deal of the elaboration of the specific meaning to the bureaucracy. Legislatures cannot specify all the particulars that may arise in these instruments and so delegate substantial authority to their bureaucracies (Schoenbrod 1993). The agencies then have the ability to pick and choose among the options and thereby to shape policy.

Given the amount of legislation in force in developed democracies, agencies have substantial capacity to decide what they want to do, i.e., to determine their own agenda and to initiate regulatory action. This action can provoke their sponsors to respond, given that bureaucracies sometimes issue regulations not anticipated by the legislature. Some legislatures have sought to control secondary legislation through devices such as the legislative veto (Foreman 1988) or committees that scrutinize secondary legislation (Byrne 1976). In other cases, the executive also attempts to control perceived bureaucratic aggressiveness in legislating through mechanisms for "regulatory review" (McGarrity 1991) or the examination of the costs and benefits of regulations issued and rejection of the more costly ones. That having been said, however, bureaucracies often can set the terms of the conflict between institutions and therefore determine at least part of the agenda of government.

Bureaucracies are also agenda setters in other, less obvious, ways. The public-choice literature on bureaucracy and its role in policy has focused its attention on the capacity of an agency to make proposals about policy that establish the terms of debate in other institutions (Tsebelis 1994; Altfield and Miller 1984). These analysts further explore a set of presumptions about the unit costs of providing public services (Bendor, Taylor, and Van Gaalen 1985) as a part of the agenda-setting process. Although rational-choice analysts discuss this behavior in terms of the ability of agencies to manipulate their sponsor, this power could simply be a function of their command of the details of relevant policy issues. This technical expertise and its associated organizational perceptions enable them to force particular definitions of the policy problems onto the rest of government.

Generic Management

The third intellectual root of the market model is generic management and its ally, the New Public Management (NPM) (Pollitt 1990; Hood 1991; Massey 1993). This corpus of analysis is founded upon the assumption that management is management, no matter where it takes place. In such a view the creation of a separate discipline of public administration and its inculcation with a distinctive ethos would be seen as mistaken.[12] Moreover, this approach argues that the instruments used to organize and motivate personnel are as applicable in the public sector as they are in the private (Linden 1994). It then denies the relevance of most of the traditional model of administration (chapter 1).

In its most aggressive form, this NPM literature argues that much of the infrastructure that has been created around public management was a means of justifying the inefficiencies and the privileges that were inherent in that system. Part of the goal of these managerialist reforms becomes to "deprivilege" the civil service (Hood 1995) and to open up what had been an internal labor market to greater external competition. By using the techniques and motivational devices from the private sector, NPM's advocates argue that good managers can produce (in the optimistic language of the Gore Report in the United States) "better government for less money." Government can be made to work better, they assert, if only the managers are allowed to manage and are not caught up in the rules, regulations, and other constraints on management that have typified the civil service.

The views of the New Public Management become most evident when confronted with issues of accountability and the special obligations of the public sector. Ranson and Stewart (1994, 5) argue that "by overemphasizing the individual to the exclusion of the needs of the public as a whole, consumerism has neglected the inescapable duality of the public domain which defines its unique management task, that is, the requirement of achieving public purpose." Rather than deploring the absence of a sense of the public interest as a guide for policy action—as the public-choice literature often appears to do—the generic management approach to the public sector assumes the lack of meaningful differences between the two sectors. In this view, *if* the incentives are structured properly, private interest and public interest can be made to coincide. Further, in the NPM conception of government, values that tend to dominate the private sector—efficiency most notably—should become more important in the public sector, and the shift toward a managerial perspective will be essential to producing a public sector that will *really* serve the public interest. It may be that this view does not so much lack a conception of the public interest but that it has one so radically different from the traditional concept that it appears to be absent to people accustomed to the older view.

On a relatively high intellectual plane, the recommendations of this variant of managerialist thinking can be based on the ubiquity of principal-agent relationships in public policy (Moe 1984; Shepsle 1989) and the application of trans-action cost analysis (Williamson 1975; Calista 1989; Alexander 1992) in organi-zations, whether public or private. On a lower level of academic development, generic management is often the accepted doctrine of outsiders who want to export their favorite management techniques—strategic planning, MBO, TQM, and so on—to the public sector.[13] At both levels of conceptualization the generic approach has been criticized by insiders (scholars and practitioners alike) who consider management in the public sector a distinctive undertaking rather than simply as running another organization.

Another implicit, and sometimes explicit, consequence of the new manage-rialism is that the role of public servants becomes defined in terms of their man-agerial tasks. These are certainly important and in the past at times have been ignored or at least given only secondary emphasis. The role of senior civil ser-vants has been defined largely as policy advisers to their ministers (Plowden 1994). Now managers must manage, and politicians are attempting to take over principal responsibility for making policy decisions. Taking the policy reins once in office is sometimes more difficult for politicians than they had realized, and advice from the public service remains crucial to making good policy in most areas (Rose 1974; Kato 1994). What the ideological shift to managerialism has done, however, is to reiterate the familiar politics-administration dichotomy (Campbell and Peters 1988) and to make the involvement of civil servants in pol-icy appear even less legitimate than it had been.

We will now explore how these various intellectual arguments about the place of the market in governing work in practice, or more precisely identify the practical "solutions" that have been derived from the ideas. The connections between ideas and practice may be vague at best, yet the reformers tend to believe that what they are doing is derived from a coherent set of concepts and principles. In particular, reformers working from the market perspective tend to believe that what they are doing is emulating so far as possible the workings of private markets within the public sector. In their view of the world, using the market provides a moral claim supporting the reforms in addition to the more practical claim that government will work better. In this and the other cases to be discussed, it is important to remember that the reformers often do believe that they are working in the public interest, even if their critics generally perceive them to be Philistines desecrating the public temple.

STRUCTURE

The market approach assumes that the principal problem with the traditional structure of the public sector is its reliance on large, monopolistic departments that respond ineffectively to signals from the environment. Indeed, most of the critiques argue that the problem is not that these organizations have difficulty in responding to market or other environmental signals but that they do not even want to respond. Rather, these departments are conceptualized more as being self-guiding and concerned more with the personal advancement of participants, and particularly that of their leaders, than with serving either the public at large or their political masters. Self-aggrandizement is a familiar stereotype of public bureaucracies, but public-choice theorists have been able to put some analytic flesh on the ideological and anecdotal bones of that argument, which abounds in most political communities.

The size and complexity of government organizations, combined with their delivery of unpriced goods and services, is seen by students from the public-choice approach to be the root of much perceived government inefficiency and ineffectiveness. In the absence of signals and constraints coming from the market, hierarchy has been used to control organizations. These structural difficulties are accentuated by the emphasis on formal rules and authority as guidelines for action within public organizations (see chapter 5). In the view of the critics, formalized rules insulate decision makers from the need to make choices, tend to preprogram too many decisions, and limit the entrepreneurial possibilities for managers. Rules further exacerbate the tendency of large organizations to respond slowly and cautiously to environmental changes and also may make detecting errors in those changes difficult.

Even if a smaller public organization emerging from reform cannot be subjected to direct competition, proponents claim some advantages inhere just in being smaller and concerned with delivering a single "product." In his analysis of the presumed inefficiencies of the public sector, Niskanen (1994, 106–12) argued that the multiservice bureau would be less efficient and more costly than the sum of the costs if the individual services were delivered by several single-purpose organizations. Therefore, it is argued that splitting large organizations into as many smaller ones as there are "product lines" will reduce costs, even in the absence of effective market signals for the pricing of their products. Further, having single products provided by an organization should also enhance the capacity of the legislative sponsor to monitor its behavior.

These ideas about the structure of government departments is mirrored in much contemporary thinking about the organizations of the private sector (Weir 1992). Business firms in the 1960s and 1970s tended to create huge conglomerates that were engaged seemingly in any and all economic activities, but the tendency in the 1980s and into the 1990s has been to differentiate "product lines" within large firms and to disaggregate some of the conglomerates. Some of this thinking about the structure of the firm revolves around the need to serve the customer better, the customer becoming extremely difficult to identify within large conglomerate organizations. Therefore, even when businesses remain large and diversified, their structures tend toward the "M" form (Lamont, Williams, and Hoffman 1994), with more autonomous subunits acting almost as firms within the firm.

Given these points, the structural prescriptions arising from this diagnosis of the problems in public organizations should be obvious. One central element of the reforms is decentralization of policymaking and implementation. The most fundamental way to break down large government monopolies is to use private or quasi-private organizations to deliver public services. Privatization has been practiced widely in the countries of Western Europe and the Antipodes, where previously there had been significant levels of public ownership (Wright 1994; Feigenbaum, Henig, and Hamnett, 1999). Yet this structural shift toward privatization has frequently produced the need for regulation to control inherent problems of natural monopolies. For many European countries, imposing regulations on economic monopolies was an unfamiliar policy, with the result that at least in the short run substantial inefficiencies in the delivery and pricing of products may have resulted from privatization as a means of structural change in the public sector (Foster 1992).

Decentralization also has been achieved through splitting up large departments into smaller "agencies," or through assigning functions to lower levels of government. This advice is particularly applicable when the goods or services in question are in principle marketable. In extreme versions of this approach, government would create multiple, competitive organizations to supply goods and services, with the expectation that the competitive mechanisms presumed to work in the private sector would also work for the public sector. In the more probable case, government would create a number of smaller organizations, each with a particular service to deliver, these taking the place of the multiple-purpose ministries that have been the tradition in most public sectors.

The advice to divide large departments into smaller segments has been accepted in a number of developed democracies such as the United Kingdom, New Zealand, and the Netherlands (Davies and Willman 1991; Boston 1991) and has been practiced in the Scandinavian countries for decades. For example, beginning in the late 1980s, New Zealand has "corporatized" the former ministries into a large number of autonomous or semiautonomous organizations to supply public services. The policy functions remain in a number of much smaller ministries, with the entire policymaking system continuing to be dominated by the Treasury and the activists who initiated all these changes (Boston 1991, 255; Ministry of Finance 1994).

A similar structural change has been undertaken in the United Kingdom under the rubric Next Steps (Hogwood 1993). This reform represented a major departure from the conventional wisdom in British government, which had favored the large ministerial department linking policy and administration. Beginning with the Ibbs Report (HMSO 1988) almost one hundred executive agencies have been created. Agencies range from very small organizations, such as the Wilton Park Conference Center (thirty employees), to the Benefits Agency, employing approximately seventy thousand people and responsible for delivery of most social service benefits in Britain (Greer 1994, 32–44). These agencies tend to be single-purpose and are more responsible to market forces and other direct means of performance assessment than were the ministerial departments. Their leadership has been drawn from within the civil service as well as from the private sector, and they are meant to be managed more like private sector, or at least quasi-private, organizations instead of like strictly public organizations. For example, the executives tend to be on performance contracts with possibilities for dismissal for poor performance.

New Zealand and the United Kingdom are the most extreme examples of the movement toward the model of decentralized service delivery, other than the Scandinavians, from whom the system was largely copied (Petersson and Söderlind 1992).[14] There are, however, other experiments under way in implementing structures of this type in government. The Netherlands (Kickert 1995) has launched an effort to create a number of agencies. Canada also has begun to experiment with Special Operating Agencies to deliver some services (Canada 1991; Wex 1990; Clark 1991), although the long-standing instrument of the Crown Corporation (Laux and Malot 1988) in Canadian government has some of the same features as agencies. These various structural experiments are now seen as compelling examples of attempts at addressing the familiar problem of how to enhance government efficiency and effectiveness.

Implementing such a system of market-oriented organizations assumes a capacity to monitor effectively and to measure adequately the performance of the decentralized bodies created. Thus, this organizational pattern appears applicable to the "machine" functions (Mintzburg 1979) of government yet probably less applicable to the complex social and developmental tasks that it must also perform (but see Romzek and Dubnick 1994). As I will be pointing out throughout this book, administrative reform needs to be matched carefully to the needs of a society, and to the characteristics of the tasks being reformed, not routinely applied in a simplistic and mechanical fashion. The unwise adoption of market-based reforms, for example, has placed those ideas into some disrepute.

The penchant for breaking up larger organizations and making the resultant ones more entrepreneurial is a case in point for not applying the market model slavishly. It could be argued that the Next Steps initiative and similar structural changes have gone further to create the world that Niskanen was decrying than any other administrative changes before or after. First, the breaking up of the departmental structure, if anything, has tightened the grip of each organization on its policy area. Further, the entrepreneurial element and the loss of civil service rules mean that growth in the budget of the agency (admittedly now often more "earned" revenues along with income from the budget process) is more directly linked to the perquisites of office than ever before.

The market approach to reform has some structural recommendations at the microlevel within organizations as well as for the macrolevel of entire departments. The emphasis on entrepreneurial activity and individual responsibility pushes toward relatively flat organizations, with little of the layering that traditional public organizations tended to consider essential for control and consistency in decisions. Advocates of the approach presume that organizational leadership, as well as the bottom line resulting from the organization's dealings with the external environment, will be more effective than hierarchy in producing appropriate decisions (but see Thompson et al. 1991). This observation points to the importance of integrated and consistent, as opposed to piecemeal, reforms. The structural changes without associated changes in management behavior are unlikely to produce the benefits presumed by the theoretical presuppositions.

Decentralization sometimes also means territorial decentralization and giving local governments more power over policies. Especially in unitary governments there has been a tendency for central governments to dictate policies to subnational ones. Even in federal regimes the financial resources of central governments have sometimes produced a "priority inversion" in which local priorities are squeezed out by central concerns (Levine and Posner 1981). The logic of geographical decentralization is similar to that of creating agencies. First, it reduces hierarchy and places control over organizations somewhat closer to the public. In addition, decentralization reduces the monopoly that single organizations may have had over services so that experimentation, "voting with one's feet," or both can produce different types of controls over organizations.[15]

MANAGEMENT

The managerial implications of the market model should be fairly obvious by this point. If public-sector employees are considered to be much the same as workers in the private sector, then the same managerial techniques should work in government as elsewhere. This assumption also would imply that some cherished traditions of personnel and financial management within government would have to be modified. To generic-management advocates, such changes would be long overdue, assuming that the public sector has been able to maintain its rather arcane system of civil service management for too long already. The generic-management gurus would tend to argue, very much like the public-choice proponents, that the distinct public-sector management system has been used primarily to shield people in government from the real world and to enable them to extract excessive personal benefits.[16]

Among the clearest manifestations of the ideology of introducing private-sector management into the public sector were exercises such as the Grace Commission (United States) and the Nielsen Commission (Canada). These two programs brought a large number of private-sector managers to each of the national capitals and turned them loose to find mismanagement (Peters and Savoie 1994). The results were reports with literally thousands of recommendations for managerial change. Especially in the case of the Grace Commission, many of these recommendations were totally out of touch with the realities of the public sector (Kelman 1985; Peters 1985), in part because the executives who came to Washington apparently did not take the career public servants seriously. The Canadian Report fared somewhat better (Wilson 1988), partly because it had at least some representation from the public service. The simple (or simplistic) assumption that guided these exercises was that public and private management were really the same thing.

Besides the general managerial trends occurring as a result of the implementation of market-based ideas, there are more specific changes in several areas of public management—personnel and finance in particular. I will detail some of those changes and attempt to identify their probable impact on government. I will also point out that these reforms are themselves not exceptionally coherent, and some of the changes appear to be at cross-purposes with some of the other transformations implemented as a part of market reform.

Personnel

The market-oriented reforms are already under way in a number of areas of public personnel management, most obviously in the reward provided public officials for their participation in government (Hood and Peters 1994). One tradition of public personnel systems has been that individuals in the same grade of the civil service are paid the same, with any differentiations based largely on seniority. In this traditional personnel system, merit and ability to perform the tasks were proved prior to entry and constituted the basis for promotion within the public service. There was therefore an assumption that all people in each grade within a uniform system were equally meritorious and therefore should be paid almost exactly the same.

Further, although there was some attempt at least to link movements of public-sector pay to wage movements in the wider economy, the market level of wages was only an indirect indicator of what pay in government should be.[17] In some cases, e.g., Germany, pay for working for the state was governed by the principle that someone in that significant social position should be paid well enough to live accordingly (Derlien 1994). For Anglo-American societies, working for government was expected to provide other tangible and intangible benefits—including some genuine financial perquisites such as early retirement—so that salaries could be less than comparable positions in the market would command. Given that some of those benefits of government employment, such as a virtually permanent job, are being placed in jeopardy by other reforms, pay becomes a more important factor.

This rather rigid payment scheme is being replaced with a merit principle that deems people should be paid more in line with what they could earn in the market and that better performance should be rewarded with better pay, regardless of differences that may emerge among employees. The obvious implication here is that the uniform civil service system that has been developed over a number of years should be replaced. Although there certainly have been some economic motivations among the members of civil service systems, there were also strong commitments to the service as an organization and to public service as an ideal (Peters 1985; see also Schorr 1987). These amorphous, yet real, values and incentives are being replaced with monetary reward as the principal means of recruitment and motivation.

The emphasis on differential rewards for differential performance is especially important at top-management levels of government. For example, one of the earliest schemes for differential rewards was the bonus system for members of the Senior Executive Service (SES) in the United States (Ban and Ingraham 1984). As written into law, SES members would have been eligible for bonuses of up to 20 percent of their annual salaries. The same legislation that established the SES (the Civil Service Reform Act of 1978) also called for extending merit pay, whether through bonuses or differentiating base pay, to middle managers in the federal government. In the end the failure of Congress to fund these bonuses adequately and difficulties in developing the measures to judge meritorious performance have rendered the merit pay system only a hollow echo of its original intent.

Merit pay, or pay for performance, is not being spread across a range of political systems (Eisenberg and Ingraham 1993). It is most common in small, relatively autonomous agencies created as a part of the market approach to governance. In several reward schemes already implemented, managers are hired under contracts that contain specific performance standards. If the agency managers, and their organizations, achieve those standards, the managers are eligible for full pay and perhaps bonuses. If the organization does not reach these goals, then the manager may lose pay or be fired.[18] In this model, managers are individual entrepreneurs responsible for what happens within their agencies and are rewarded accordingly. Lower echelons within these organizations may be rewarded under similar contractual arrangements based on performance standards.

These schemes for differential rewards depend on the capacity of government to measure the performance of employees and their organizations. Any number of studies have demonstrated the severe difficulties encountered when attempting to carry out the seemingly simple managerial task of measuring individual contributions to the performance of large, complex organizations and policy-delivery systems (Boston 1992a; Sjölund 1994a). This is especially true if performance is to be measured at the output or impact level rather than merely at the activity level (Carter, Day, and Klein 1992). This measurement problem means that either performance contracts and effective managerialism will be limited to the relatively few agencies providing marketable and otherwise directly measurable services or that it must depend on inadequate or even specious measures of performance. In either case, the capacity to implement this aspect of the market model appears at least a little suspect. It is even more so when there is a political element in the evaluation of employees.

I should also point out that these managerialist trends are not neutral in their effects on the role assigned to the public service. Measuring performance is substantially easier, even if still difficult, for the managerial and service-delivery functions of the civil service. It is much more difficult to measure for the policy-advice functions. As a result, adoption of managerialist pay schemes tend to contain some implicit bias in the direction of a more managerial and a diminished policy role for civil servants. This may be true both because of changes in the signals coming from evaluators above and decisions by the evaluated that they can maximize their own rewards by playing the managerial game.

Performance-based management and reward techniques run counter to many other ideas motivating reform in the public sector. In particular, one of the increasingly popular means of motivating workers is providing them greater self-determination on their jobs. These participatory ideas are becoming even more important through the "empowerment" approach to reform (see chapter 3). If, however, performance measures are being used to judge individual contributions to organizational goals, then participation and team-building will be difficult to achieve (Behn 1993b). Team concepts and individual foci of management are still difficult to reconcile empirically or normatively. Thus, promoting reform must be done carefully, and all the good (and not so good) ideas that are around cannot be implemented at once.

Financial Management

It is not only personnel management that is being reformed as a part of the drive to introduce generic management, or managerialism, in the public sector. Financial management is also being reconsidered and changed drastically. These reforms have been going on for some time in countries such as Britain (Pliatzky 1989) and Australia (Department of Finance 1987; Campbell and Halligan 1992) and show little sign of abating. These ideas are also being spread to a number of other countries. Financial-management reforms have ranged from simple changes such as better cash management and tighter controls over public loans to some fundamental rethinking of the manner in which the public sector budgets and thinks about the costs of providing public services. As with personnel management, some of the reforms have been well conceived and implemented and others appear almost to have totally missed the point of what government does and how it does it.

One of the several market principles underlying the financial reforms of the public sector is the separation of purchasers and providers and the creation of internal markets (OECD 1993). In traditional public administration such a reform was irrelevant, or perhaps even inconceivable, given that the old model was one of hierarchy and unitary services. In contemporary reforming systems, however, this approach is an important mechanism for ensuring that market principles pervade the public sector. For example, in the National Health Service in Britain the purchasers and providers had been managed as part of one corporate entity. That unified structure has now been replaced with a quasi market in which Area Health Authorities purchase services for their "customers" (citizens) from providers (hospitals, and so on). Likewise, budget-holding general practitioners will begin to negotiate with specialists for their services on behalf of patients. In this management system the separation of the two functions is intended to reduce costs and increase efficiency (Ranade 1995), although there has been substantial public and academic criticism about the real consequences of the changes (Harrison, Small, and Baker 1994; see Robinson and Le Grand 1994).

The government of New Zealand has undertaken a similar separation of purchasers and providers throughout the entire government. Under the Public Finance Act of 1989 the purchaser-provider dichotomy is intended to pervade a good part of the public sector in that country (Pallot 1991). In this system government, through its central agencies, in essence becomes the purchaser of the outputs of the departments actually producing the services (Boston 1993). Those services are meant to be costed fully, including factors such as interest, taxes, and capital depreciation, which frequently have been excluded from the internal "pricing" of goods and services in public-sector budgets. In this approach to public finance, virtually all public-service providers essentially become public corporations, with even more stringent financial controls than usual being applied.

Even the Swedish government, long the model of the welfare state and of skepticism about the market, has begun to think about introducing market reforms into government. For example, very much as in the United Kingdom, a plan for separating purchasers from providers in the health service has been implemented by the counties, and greater choice of physicians for citizens has been introduced (Burkitt and Whyman 1994; Forsberg and Calltorp 1993). Given that the health delivery service tends to be concentrated at the county level and the purchasing through insurance is quasi-public at the national level, the institutional structure for separation was to some degree already established. Similar market-based management schemes are being considered and implemented in a number of other publicly controlled health care systems (Jerome-Forget, White, and Wiener 1995).

The Financial Management Initiative (FMI) in the United Kingdom (Gray and Jenkins 1991) and the Financial Management Improvement Programme (FMIP) in Australia (Keating and Holmes 1990) are two of the principal programs designed to change financial management in central governments. These two reforms have some common elements. The most important of these is the attempt to identify within government the "cost centers" associated with the delivery of services and to allocate total costs of each service more accurately than in the past. For example, the overhead costs of government—central management functions, information technology, and so on—are sometimes difficult to attribute to particular programs so that the programs that consume a great deal of these overhead services tend to be subsidized by those that do not.[19] With the financial management improvements that have been implemented, there has been an attempt to assign true costs more fairly to each program, thus improving the ability to judge the relative efficiency of programs. Following from these efforts the British government has undertaken a number of other attempts at changing the manner in which funds are allocated to programs. For example, "resource accounting and budgeting" is now being implemented as a means of making government even more like the private sector (HMSO 1994b). The idea of these budget reforms is to account for public money, not just in current costs but also in terms of the opportunity costs of the uses of the resources (Mellett and Marriott 1995). This device is designed to reflect more accurately the real impact of the public sector on the economy. Australia meanwhile has reinvigorated the concept of program-budgeting so popular during the 1960s. This return to rationality reflects an attempt to capture better alternative uses of resources within the public sector.[20] This renewed interest in rationality can also be seen in a revived interest in policy analysis and evaluation after something of a hiatus.

Interestingly, these changes, which are largely rationalistic in their motivations, are being implemented in a period of drives to reduce overall public spending more radically. This is perhaps most evident in the United States, with plans such as the proposed balanced budget amendment following already radical changes in the budgetary process, e.g., the Budget Enforcement Act of 1990 (LeLoup and Taylor 1994). In virtually all countries, however, the same desires to reduce public expenditure and to balance public budgets have required cutting exercises that tend to be done across the board or by some other less than fully rational method (Tarschys 1981; 1986). Thus, the simple economy motives of the market advocates at times appear to conflict directly with their own attempts to create greater economic rationality within government.

The growing emphasis on financial management in industrialized democracies has produced an increased emphasis on auditing. This is not old-fashioned financial auditing, however, although certainly the search for "fraud, waste and abuse" continues in all these regimes. Auditing is now directed more toward the three E's of economy, efficiency, and effectiveness, in addition to financial probity. Some government auditors, e.g., the General Accounting Office in the United States (Mosher 1979), have a history of performance-and-effectiveness auditing, and this doctrine has been spreading around the world. Auditors have now been transformed from their green-eyeshade image to being integral parts of the reform and accountability process in many contemporary governments.

Market Testing

The reform of central government departments in the United Kingdom has proceeded to another round, this time focusing more on management than on structural change. The principal component of this most recent round of marketizing government is contracting out (Ascher 1987), or more recently "market testing" (Oughton 1994). The idea of this reform is that virtually all functions performed within government should be subjected to some form of competitive bidding to determine whether the private sector is able to perform the task better, more cheaply, or both. This requirement was imposed on local authorities earlier (1986), with the terminology "compulsory competitive tendering" (Painter 1991). This concept more recently has been extended to the central government as well, through a White Paper, "Competing for Quality" (HMSO 1991). This has been followed by the closely linked idea of "fundamental reviews," which is a test of whether the public sector should be in any way involved in a policy.[21]

The United Kingdom is far from alone in attempting to impose this form of market discipline on its public-sector organizations. Indeed, requirements for competitive bidding for government work have been around for some time in a number of governments. In the United States, OMB Circular A-76 in the mid-1970s required at least 10 percent of all work performed by an agency to be subjected to bidding from outside contractors, with consideration of how much additional work could be performed outside more efficiently. More recently the General Services Administration (GSA), which once had a monopoly on providing services such as office space and automobiles to federal agencies, now must compete with private vendors for over 90 percent of its business (Interview, October 16, 1994; GSA 1993). In Australia and New Zealand, requirements for subjecting government programs to external bidding have been in place for a number of years (Keating and Holmes 1990). In all these cases the government agency can establish the conditions of the bidding, and to some extent it therefore gains an inside track in the competition. However, there have been some good-faith attempts to determine just how money might be saved and whether the usual criticisms about inefficiency within the public sector are correct.[22]

At least in the United Kingdom, this shift has been seen by some critics as undermining the changes undertaken in the earlier structural change of Next Steps (Jordan 1994). First, although Next Steps apparently argues that if the structure is changed, then efficiency will follow, market testing requires that assumption to be proven. Almost before most of the agencies have had any opportunity to settle into a working pattern, they are being forced to develop bidding processes and then prepare their own bids. The employees of the agencies believed they had paid the price for keeping some functions public but now find that they are again required to justify their existence within the public sector. Although some management analysts argue that constant change is functional for organizations, the people who are living through it do not find it so beneficial.

Perhaps more fundamentally, the competitive tendering process and the documents that have established it do not appear to have any real sense of what, if anything, is clearly a public function and therefore not potentially subject to contracting out. One important case is policy advice. Should this function be contracted out, or should it remain an internal governmental activity (Boston 1992a; Australia 1992)? Of course, a certain amount of policy advice has been contracted out in almost all political systems, with consultants, interest groups, political parties, and even academics providing reports and recommendations too voluminous to catalog. Still, governments have retained a dominant in-house capacity to sift through the outside responses and then generate advice to ministers. Should that function be contracted out to the private sector, or is it sufficiently vested with the public interest that it should remain a governmental activity?

It is interesting that the compulsory competitive-tendering concept of the Conservatives has been retained by the Labour government elected in 1997, although in the slightly different guise of "best value" (Boyne et al. 1999). On the one hand, this program places even greater pressures on local governments because it requires thinking about what the best value might be instead of depending entirely on the market to set the price through the contract. On the other hand, the market does not have to be consulted about each possible contract, but relational contracting can be used to develop stable means for providing services (Williamson 1985).

As befits an approach attempting to make government more like the private sector, the market perspective places a great deal of emphasis on "improving" public management. I put the term in quotation marks because there is less than universal agreement that the changes being implemented are indeed positive. For many people committed to the traditional civil service style of running the public sector, these changes have totally misread the nature and purpose of government. The assumptions of generic management, for example, appear to undervalue seriously public administration and its distinctiveness. It seems clear, however, that there can be no return to the (presumably) glorious days of civil service government in the past, so some accommodation between the traditions and the innovations will emerge if government is to move forward.

POLICYMAKING

The third aspect of the marketized vision of the state is its conceptualization of how public policy should be made and, in particular, the appropriate role of the career public service in making it. A fundamental contradiction appears to reside at the heart of the role that the market model assigns to the bureaucracy. On the one hand, it advocates decentralizing bureaucratic functions to multiple, "entrepreneurial" agencies that would be authorized to make autonomous decisions. These decisions presumably would be based on either signals received from the market or simply on the judgment of the organizational leadership. Breaking the (presumably) stultifying bonds of bureaucracy is meant to liberate decision making and to produce greater risk taking and more innovative programs in the public sector.[23] Just as entrepreneurs in the market are expected to be risk takers, so too should public-sector administrators.

On the other hand, the practitioners who advocate this approach expect compliance from these quasi-autonomous organizations with the policy and ideological directives coming from above. One consistent observation concerning the Reagan, Thatcher, and Mulroney governments and other similarly purposive regimes is that they have attempted to impose their own views on the civil service (Savoie 1994a). Bureaucrats were seen as too committed to the growth of their own organizations as well as excessively committed to serving their narrow clientele rather than serving "the public interest." In this view the public administrators and their organizations therefore should be made to follow the directives of their political masters (as the embodiments of the *volonté générale,* or general will) instead of pursuing their own interests.

To many people in government this pressure to conform to prevailing policy doctrines was an attempt to politicize the public service and policymaking. Attempts at politicization of the civil service are by no means new but appear to have become more overt during the past decade (Meyer 1985). Politicization has been seen by defenders of the traditional view of government as the erosion of one of the most important features of merit systems and the civil service. In some ways, however, these demands for conformity are merely a reaffirmation of the traditional view (at least in Anglo-Saxon regimes) that civil servants should be "on tap but not on top" and that political leaders should be responsible for policy. Whether it is part of the traditional conceptualization or not, there is an inconsistency, and civil servants are being faced with a set of perhaps unreconcilable demands and expectations.

Even if that apparent inconsistency could be resolved, there would be additional problems for policymaking arising from the market approach. One of the most important of these is the difficulty in coordination and control that decentralization presents. As one commentator has said, "The ship of state has become a flotilla," and the creation of many small organizations presents significant problems if government is to speak with anything like a single voice. The radical decentralization of policymaking to more autonomous organizations provides relatively little opportunity for either senior bureaucrats or political leaders to coordinate policy effectively (Boston 1992b; Jordan 1994, 96–136).

If one applies some of the economic logic of the advocates of the market approach to examine their own recommendations for reform, one encounters several interesting questions. For example, one of the justifications of the large firm in the private sector is the reduction of transaction costs (Williamson 1975), or the costs imposed by the need to interact with other parties. However, much the same should be true for the large executive department in the public sector. If a number of smaller organizations are operating with substantial autonomy, then there will be (everything else being equal) substantial transaction costs when they must cooperate to deliver a set of services to the same clients (Calista 1989). Indeed, the transaction costs may be borne by clients instead of within government itself, given that the services may not be rendered in an integrated and coordinated fashion. Clients would be forced to go from agency to agency, seeking the full range of services they need.

A similar argument would be that decentralization is to some degree centralizing. That is, if decision-making autonomy is conferred upon a number of independent organizations that previously had been coordinated through a ministry, the need for coordination is not diminished. That being the case, the only remaining locus for this coordination is at the top of government, whether that is through central agencies or through cabinet and the prime minister. Thus, as Wildavsky once argued about program-budgeting (1969), once individual organizations are forced to set priorities, then some superordinate organization will be forced to choose among them.

One critique of the traditional approach to governance has been that de facto the independence of the bureaucracy thwarted consistency across policies and often produced destructive competition among organizations over budgets and policy (Allard 1990; Smith, Marsh, and Richards 1993). The market approach appears to exalt that competition and its potential inconsistency—so long as the actions taken correspond to the ideology of the current political leaders and do not require additional public spending. It is perhaps too much to believe that leadership of autonomous agencies would be content to be managers of these organizations and would not become concerned with the policies being implemented by them (Rhodes 1995). The inconsistency and redundancy produced by applying the market model are bad enough in wealthy societies but may be particularly undesirable when the model is exported to less affluent developing countries, as it so often is by management consultants and international organizations.

At a more conceptual level, there is the problem of the changing role of the citizen. The market model tends to conceptualize the recipients of government programs, and the public more generally, as *consumers* or *customers* (Pierre 1995a; Behn 1993a). This definition is simultaneously empowering and demeaning for the public. When seen as a beneficial change, it is intended to provide citizens with the same expectations of quality services that they have when dealing with a private-sector firm.[24] Although usually conceptualized as components of participatory reforms, changes such as the Citizens' Charter in Britain and PS 2000 in Canada contain many of the elements of consumerism (Lovell 1992). Just as earlier consumer movements attempted to rectify the balance between private-sector organizations and their customers, this movement seeks to redress that balance between public organizations and their clients.

Nonetheless, citizens have been made into little more than consumers, and their role as the holders of rights and legal status vis-à-vis the state appears diminished (Pierre 1995b; Lewis 1994). Government may be concerned with more than buying and selling, and almost certainly should be concerned with more. If governing is reduced to the level of mere economic action, then citizens become less significant figures in political theory than they should be. This shift in conceptualization of the public is important also because it tends to conflict with other movements in contemporary political life. Most significant among the conflicting trends is the tendency of politics to be considered as being about rights (and even obligations) instead of being merely about money.

Although the public's shift to "post-materialist values" discussed by Inglehart (1990; Inglehart and Abramson 1994) may have been overstated, there have been changes in what people expect from government and in the values they want to see maximized through public action. One of these values is participation (see chapter 3), and another is the special claims of groups such as ethnic minorities and women. This value transformation has been under way even longer than the shift toward an acceptance of an enhanced role for market mechanisms in public life. Thus, although there are ideological forces driving toward an economic rationale for policymaking, there are also forces resisting that change and moving toward policies determined by much "softer," humanitarian values. The market and economic values appear to be in ascendance at the moment, but their triumph may be only temporary.

THE PUBLIC INTEREST

The final component of the market vision of governance is how it defines the public interest. Although generally not clearly articulated, this vision definitely does contain such a conceptualization. The first and most central element of the definition is that government should be judged on the basis of how cheaply it delivers public services. Even more fundamentally, the market model asks what things should be public in the first place. Much of the indictment of government in the market model is that it is overly expensive and inefficient. To achieve the goal of lower costs, government may have to undertake its activities in rather unconventional ways, e.g., through creating multiple competing service providers; but in the long run the public—in their role as taxpayers—is better served by government acting in this more businesslike manner.

A second component of the market-based definition of the public interest is that government should respond to signals coming from the market, so that accountability—a fundamental dimension of the public interest in any democratic system (Day and Klein 1987)—is more difficult to identify than in the traditional administrative system. Rather than accountability being defined as progressing upward through ministers to parliament and then to the people, it becomes defined increasingly in market terms. In this model of accountability, instruments such as parliamentary oversight and reviews through the judicial system become less important than the financial bottom line. Indeed, as with the ideas of rules and hierarchy already discussed, these formalized mechanisms are often indicted as the means through which government organizations have avoided meaningful accountability.

This emerging conception of accountability would use output measures to replace the process measures used in the traditional model. As with several other aspects of the market model of governing, this version of accountability appears to beg a number of questions. The most important of these is the measurement issue. Can we measure the performance of public organizations, even in their marketized format, sufficiently well to be able to use nonprocedural devices for defining accountability effectively (Glynn, Gray, and Jenkins 1992)? Even if analysts could make those measurements effectively, could they attribute differences (whether across time or across organizations) to the management of those organizations? What level of performance is "good enough"? The "new evaluative state" (Henkel 1991) runs the risk of attempting to fire its analytic cannons before they are fully loaded.

The third component of the market vision of the public interest is that citizens should be conceptualized as consumers as well as taxpayers (Lewis 1994). Therefore, besides providing guidance to policymaking, the market vision can also serve the public interest by allowing citizens to exercise freer choice in a market for public services. This autonomy is instituted in place of forcing citizens to consume a package of services determined by the legislature, the bureaucracy, or both. This enhanced choice for consumers can be created either by breaking up the monopolies that traditionally have provided most public services or through improving the wherewithal of citizens to exercise freer choices among service options.

The options for citizens exercising autonomous consumer choices can be expanded through several means. One is to permit private firms to enter into competition with services that traditionally have been public monopolies. This has already happened in the case of postal services, for example, where private courier services have taken over a large share of the most profitable end of the market. Private providers have also been able to compete in most countries in the field of education for a number of years. What is happening is that some services that were thought to be the peculiar concerns of government, e.g., managing prisons (Black 1993; Goodman and Loveman 1991) or providing personal social services (Llewellyn 1994), are now considered appropriate targets for private-sector providers.

Choice can also be created by providing vouchers for services such as education and perhaps housing (Chubb and Moe 1990; Adley, Patch, and Tweedy 1990). If the argument is correct that one of the principal reasons for the perceived failings of education in many countries—especially Anglo-American countries—is the monopoly held by the state over education, then the creation of competition through vouchers may be a useful mechanism for both improving education and leveraging private resources for it.[25] It is not entirely clear, however, what limits there are to voucher plans for social and educational programs. The Conservative government in Britain, for example, has considered a plan to convert virtually all primary and secondary education in the country to fee-paying systems supplemented by vouchers. Nor is it clear what role public education should play in a democratic society, especially in the United States, which has relied on public education as a major component of the system for enculturating immigrants.

The choices available to the public may further be increased by simply expanding the information offered to citizens about the service options already open to them. One feature of bureaucracies, especially those that also have a professional component, is that they tend to deny autonomous choices to clients. This is done in the perceived best interest of the client, who is assumed to be incapable of making informed choices about complex legal or technical matters, or both, e.g., in medicine. Both the market and the participatory models of reform argue for greater openness and more real choice for the public. No matter how individual choice is to be enhanced, the idea of creating a genuine market for the goods and services that have been provided through monopolies (whether bureaucratic or professional) is a central element in the prescription of the market approach.

SUMMARY

The market vision has become the most popular alternative conceptualization of the state and government. This view conceptualizes traditional public bureaucracies more as instruments of personal aggrandizement by civil servants than as instruments for unselfish service delivery to the public. It also conceptualizes public-sector agencies as facing the same managerial and service-delivery tasks as do organizations in the private sector and, therefore, as being amenable to the same techniques for managing them. An acceptance of the models of traditional public administration is seen to be little more than a means of protecting bureaucrats against control and accountability. Market-oriented analysts also assume that if the rule-based authority structure usually associated with public bureaucracy is removed, or at least de-emphasized, then there can be a flowering of the creative and administrative talent of individuals working in the public sector.

Although usually associated with the political right, some devotees of the market approach believe that its successful implementation would result in a more effective and efficient public sector, whether in delivering defense or social services. Indeed, one of the strongest test cases for this approach has been the experiment in New Zealand by the Labor Party (Walsh 1991). Moreover, several elements of a market approach have been introduced into Scandinavia by governments of the political left (Olsen 1991). There appears to be a Zeitgeist that pervades contemporary thinking about government and that has pushed many governments in the direction of reducing public-sector controls on the private sector and toward using more market-based instruments within the public sector.

Although the market perspective is extremely popular with politicians and also with many people in the mass public, one must still inquire how well it both describes the failings of the old system and offers possible avenues of positive change. I have pointed to some of the weaknesses of this approach while discussing its specific features. This doubt about the market is not simply a knee-jerk reaction to change in government but is an attempt to understand better just what possibilities there are for improving its performance. It is meant to be a recognition that the old system was not entirely bad and indeed did some things rather well.

Not only did the old system of administration do some things extremely well, but most proposals for movement away from it will be far from costless. All these reform proposals have substantive as well as transitional costs for government. They will certainly be borne by employees within public bureaucracies, and they may also be felt by the clients of programs. Some programs may be eliminated entirely while others may be reduced and their delivery "streamlined" in ways that many clients may find undesirable. Therefore, when deciding to make the move to new forms of government, those costs and the losses of positive features of the older administrative system must be understood, just as the potential benefits of the reformed system are understood.

Further, the market model—despite its emphasis on exercising choice through vouchers—tends to provide little real choice for citizens about whether to search out new levels or varieties of service provision. In this view of the "policy marketplace," the dynamic element appears to be lacking, and impersonal forces, rather than human agency, seem to make the policy selections. Further, the choices offered in the "policy market" are often about implementation rather than about whether there will be a program or not. That more basic type of choice appears to be in the province of the participatory model of change, which we will examine next.

3

The Participatory State

The second alternative approach to reforming governance—participation—is almost the ideological antithesis of the market approach. The political ideologies that most of its advocates use to justify their concept reject the market and search for more political, democratic, and collective mechanisms for sending signals to government. Their assumption is that governing should be about finding out what the public wants and finding ways of delivering those services.

Participation is one of the dominant political themes of the 1990s. Bill Clinton and Al Gore gained substantial political advantages by having town hall meetings and riding across the country in a cavalcade of buses. Tony Blair more than any previous British prime minister has opened mechanisms for political participation, even if these opportunities have no direct consequences for policy other than to legitimate them. Consultation and citizen involvement in policymaking have become central components of Canadian government, including the budgetary process (Lindquist 1994), and the government seeks even more ways to open policymaking to the public (Kliksberg 2000). These examples from the Anglo-American democracies are impressive but are actually rather insignificant when compared to the opportunities for participation in the Scandinavian countries. This is clearly an age in which government finds it difficult to legitimate its actions without active public involvement.

Despite the ideological differences in the participatory and market approaches, in some instances the analysis and recommendations derived from the two appear remarkably similar. What is perhaps most common in their views is that conventional bureaucracies are an impediment to good government and that if nothing else is changed there must be new means for delivering public services. These common strands in thinking, however, have been the source of substantial confusion in the administrative reform literature as well as in practice. One of my principal purposes in writing this book is to identify more clearly the

differences among the four approaches to change in the public sector and to identify where and when they are and are not compatible.

While monopoly appears to be the principal villain for the market model,
hierarchy is the evil most directly addressed by the participatory model. The
assumption is that the hierarchical, top-down style of management in traditional
bureaucracies restricts the involvement of employees in their own jobs. This
absence of real involvement alienates public-sector employees and reduces their
commitment to the organization. Advocates of the market and the economics of
organization also argue against hierarchy, preferring a set of contracts that can
structure behavior within the organization (Miller 1992). They further argue that
hierarchy imposes enforcement costs on government that voluntary contracting
would not. Hierarchy within a single organization appears more acceptable to that
group of scholars, however, than does monopoly within a set of organizations.

I am calling this approach the "participatory state," but it has been discussed
using a number of different names (see Kernaghan 1992).[1] An alternative characterization might be the "empowerment state" in which segments of organizations and societies (presumably) excluded under more hierarchical systems are
permitted greater organizational involvement (Kernaghan 1992; Clarke and
Stewart 1992; Peters and Pierre 2000). Very much like the market and the deregulatory approaches, the participatory approach considers the hierarchical, rule-
based organizations usually encountered in the public sector as severe
impediments to effective management and governance. However, this approach
does not concentrate attention on the upper echelons of managerial leadership in
public organizations who are conceptualized as the protoentrepreneurs within
government as does the market approach. Rather, it pays much closer attention
to the lower-echelon employees as well as to the clients of the organizations.

The fundamental assumptions informing this approach to governing are that
a great deal of energy and talent lies fallow and underutilized at the lower echelons of hierarchies and that the workers and clients closest to the actual production of goods and services in the public sector have the greatest insight and
information about the programs. It is assumed further that if those ideas and tal-
ents were harnessed adequately, then government would perform better. The general prescription for making government function better, therefore, is to foster
greater individual and collective participation by segments of government organizations that commonly have been excluded from decision making.

For some advocates of this approach, increased participation should be
structured to include the mass public in addition to, or even instead of, individuals directly benefiting from a policy. The argument is that bureaucratization has
produced segmentation of the public sector, with only consumers and producers
within the particular policy area having influence over policy or implementation
(Muller 1985; Tonn and Feldman 1995). Further, the bureaucratization and segmentation of policies limit the capacity to coordinate programs and to produce
coherent policy regimens that span multiple policy areas. Thus, there is little

attention given to the overarching concerns of the public in their roles as citizens and taxpayers and to their desires to have an effective and democratic government.[2] Further, this argument points out that participation may not be an undivided benefit but that it has virtues contingent upon how it is structured, even in a democratic regime.

Somewhat predictably, advocates of the participatory approach tend to be associated with the political left (Bachrach and Botwinick 1992). However, some theorists from the political right, concerned with issues such as empowerment, community, and self-management by clients as instruments for enhancing efficiency, also advocate versions of it.[3] Further, in the domain of mass politics, the manifestations of this approach often appear from the political right, with its rejection of bureaucracy in favor of various populist approaches to governing. Except for true elitists, participation is a value that can be embraced by the entire ideological spectrum within a political democracy. This broad acceptance of the concept leaves only the problem of sorting out just what is meant by participation within those different political camps.

THE IDEAS OF THE PARTICIPATORY STATE

The intellectual roots of the participatory approach are diverse, indeed substantially more so than those of the market approach. The manner in which participation has been conceptualized varies from pragmatic attempts to motivate public employees through enhanced involvement in their jobs to more complex, philosophical statements concerning the true meaning of democracy in a mass society (Pateman 1970; Pennock and Chapman 1975). These various conceptions of participation are bound together by their common concerns with minimizing hierarchy and technocracy (Fischer 1990; Meynaud 1969) in governing. I will discuss four interpretations of participation that are relevant to our concern with the management of public organizations and their role in the governing process. These four ideas about participation are not entirely managerial, however, and are also concerned with broader questions about the relationship between state and society and the opportunities for involving the mass public in decision making.

The idea of enhancing participation in government organizations is hardly new. In fact, it has been one of the recurring themes in administrative reform as well as in more general reform efforts for the public sector. A number of countries already had made significant advances in improving participation in their administrations prior to the contemporary round of reforms. For example, there have been any number of attempts to enhance the involvement of workers within their organizations and to make the climate in public organizations more participatory. The Scandinavian countries and Germany developed principles of workplace democracy and codetermination some years ago (Hancock, Logue, and

Schiller 1991; but see Werth 1973), in both the public and private sectors. Even extremely modest participatory programs, such as flexible working hours, apparently have had substantial positive impact on morale and productivity. These ideas are not new, but the extremes to which several of its contemporary advocates appear willing to extend it are indeed new.

Participatory Management

At its simplest level, participation in this analysis means involvement of employees in the organizational decisions that affect their working lives and a substitution of collective decision making for some aspects of hierarchy. A large body of literature argues that involvement and participation are the most effective means for motivating individual employees, even if those practices do have the potential to become manipulative (USGAO 1995a). This literature argues that most employees desire greater scope to exercise their own initiative and to make independent decisions on the job and would be willing to invest more time and energy in the organization if they were granted a greater level of personal involvement (Perry 1994; Garvey 1993). Employee involvement and job expansion have been dominant themes in management in both the public and private sectors for a number of years. Identification, analysis, and advocacy of this style of management goes back at least to the famous Hawthorne study (Roethlisberger and Dickson 1941) and has been carried forward by a long line of management scholars including Argyris (1964), Likert (1961), and Follett (1940). These scholars have advocated "organizational humanism" as the best way to promote both efficiency and morality in organizations.[4]

In American public administration one of the milestones of thinking about participation in public organizations was the Minnowbrook Conference and *Toward a New Public Administration* (Marini 1971; see also Frederickson 1997). This book reflected the beliefs of a cadre of younger scholars of public administration whose ideas have been shaping transformations of both theory and practice. The initial work was followed by a number of other works advocating and/or analyzing greater opportunities for participation in public organizations (Simmons 1972; Frederickson 1980). More recently, Robert Golembiewski (1995) has argued that one of the major contemporary challenges for public administration is managing diversity, or simply the differences that exist among employees and clients of public organizations. He sees traditional administrative structures as impediments to meeting that challenge.

These analyses correspond to what Stillman (1991) refers to as the "stateless tradition" of bureaucracy, especially within the context of the United States and the American aversion to bureaucracy. Stillman argues that this American approach to governing searches for means of delivering public services in ways that are not destructive of human values for either employees or clients. This more open approach is in contrast to traditional hierarchical bureaucracy, which is claimed to be destructive of those values. That view of hierarchy, of course, may itself reflect the negative, "stateless" Anglo-American view of bureaucracy as contrasted to a more positive conception of both government and bureaucracy commonly held in much of continental Europe. That is, in some political traditions bureaucracy, by ensuring equality of treatment for citizens, is considered necessary for democracy rather than antithetical to it (Derlien 1999).

Although many of the ideas about job expansion and organizational participation are quite old, they have been rediscovered and dressed up in the new language of "empowerment." The idea is simply that if the workers within an organization, and especially a white-collar organization, are empowered, then a number of positive outcomes will result (Sagie and Koslowsky 2000). In addition to the humane aspects of permitting people greater control over their own lives, this change in management style, it is argued, will also produce substantial benefits for the organization (Romzek 1990). As the older analyses of organizational participation asserted, workers will be more productive if they are more involved in the organization and more empowered to make decisions on their own. More empowered workers also should be willing to work harder, share more ideas with management, and treat their clients more humanely since they are themselves being treated better.

One of the more commonly cited contemporary manifestations of the empowerment concept is Total Quality Management (TQM). As with many of the managerial practices in the market approach, TQM has been borrowed from the private sector, indirectly from Japanese management to be precise (Deming 1988). TQM is very much a participatory program, however, rather than a market-based idea.[5] The basic idea is to inculcate in employees the concept that the quality of their product is their major consideration. To produce a quality product requires (in this view) several things. One is the commitment of all members of the organization to quality. Further, the members of the organization should work together as a team, not be linked only through hierarchical authority and the division of labor. The absence of hierarchy implies that ideas of all members of the team are valuable so long as they can contribute to quality and organizational productivity. The organization therefore should create mechanisms through which participation and communication in all directions, not just downward, are encouraged.

There is some question about whether TQM is really suitable for the public sector, although this doubt has not prevented numerous attempts at implementing it. For example, during the first Bush administration a Federal Quality Institute (FQI) was established in Washington.[6] Its mission was to spread the idea of TQM and "quality" throughout the federal government (Brockman 1992; Burstein 1995). Following that, the National Performance Review (NPR—the Gore Report) placed a great deal of emphasis on similar issues, albeit couched in rather different terms (Kettl and DiIulio 1995; Ingraham 1995). Because of the existence of NPR, as well as the obvious political reasons, the Federal Quality Institute was terminated early in the Clinton administration.[7]

The quality movement has been even more influential at the state and local levels of government in the United States than at the federal level (Durant and Wilson 1993). These levels have been at the heart of the reinvention and quality movements, and they began implementing ideas of this sort well before the federal government began to do so. Their use of the quality program also has been assisted in part by having responsibility for services that have outputs and impacts that are somewhat easier to quantify than are those of the federal government.

Skeptics question whether TQM is really suitable for the public sector (Swiss 1993; Walters 1992c). In the first place, there may not always be the latitude for involvement and job-shaping in the public sector that is found in the private sector. The duties and obligations of public employees are shaped by law, so that they simply cannot decide that doing something different, or doing the same thing in a different manner, is a good idea (Gilbert 1993). Certainly for some routine activities that latitude may be available, but for actual delivery of services it most often is not. Second, definitions of quality may also be more contestable in the public sector, lacking any clear bottom line to assess whether a program has been a success or not. Measurement of quality and success is a general problem for all service producers (Bowen and Schneider 1988), but the problems are exacerbated in the public sector (Bouckaert 1995).

The argument can be made that quality in the delivery of public-sector services depends to some extent on cooperation in production rather than on government employees simply delivering the service (Walsh 1991). This may be true to some extent for most service industries, but it is particularly true for the public sector. If social service programs are to be effective, for example, the beneficiaries must ultimately want to change some of their behaviors—either economic or social—and no amount of social service delivery will be successful without that value change. This perspective on quality goes very much in the direction of the emerging communitarian emphasis on coproduction of services. In this view, the only really effective and efficient service programs are those that demand participation rather than passivity from the clients.

Empowerment has been an appealing idea for politicians and for civil servants. Indeed, one of the reform documents most clearly stating the case for empowerment—PS2000 in Canada—is largely the work of the civil service itself (Tellier 1990) rather than an idea forced down their collective throats. This is a marked contrast to many of the market reforms that have been implemented (Peters and Savoie 1994a). For the public service the concept of empowerment provides a means of fighting back against the several decades of imposed market reforms. It further reinforces the sense of collective identity within the public service that has been threatened by more individualistic methods of evaluation and reward. In this style of managing, members of the public service can work together instead of perceiving themselves to be in competition.

Street-Level Bureaucracy

Another strand of literature on participation and empowerment argues that the lower echelons of public organizations are central to their effective functioning and as a simple empirical reality the role of "street-level bureaucrats" needs to be recognized (Lipsky 1980; Prottas 1979; for France, see Dupuy and Thoenig 1985). While the empowerment literature exalts the potentiality of the lower echelons of organizations for improving performance, the literature on street-level bureaucrats attempts more to recognize and describe the powers that these employees already possess. It then attempts to identify the consequences that this bureaucratic power has for individuals who come to public organizations seeking benefits from government. One common finding is that workers often identify with their clients in their wish to debureaucratize agencies, and they also want to provide clients services to which they might not formally be entitled (Goodsell 1981b). The debureaucratization in turn provides clients an important locus of participation within the administrative system.

Just as the participative management literature has deep intellectual roots, so too does street-level bureaucracy, which goes back to some of the earliest empirical studies of public administration (Almond and Lasswell 1934; Blau 1960). After that initial research, there was a great deal of interest in involving clients in decisions that affect them, especially in programs such as urban renewal and Model Cities (Rogers and Mulford 1982). Though the evidence is strong that these well-intentioned efforts at democratization of programs were largely unsuccessful and even counterproductive (Moynihan 1969; Millett 1977), the values of participation and programmatic democracy continued to be espoused. Indeed for some clients, e.g., middle-class parents and their children's education, participation is considered absolutely essential to successful service delivery.

When thinking about the outcomes of governing for individuals, one might first consider whether they receive the benefits they sought or not. There may be other consequences as well, which may be of greater significance to the bureaucratic system itself than they are to the clients. The face-to-face contacts between public employees and the public help to define the relationship between state and society (Katz and Danet 1973; Goodsell 1981a). For most citizens, government is a relatively amorphous entity. They may see pictures of leading politicians on the television and may respond to certain national symbols, but government is something that happens somewhere else and involves somebody else.

Nevertheless, the public has a number of encounters with representatives of government, most of whom are street-level bureaucrats. These range from relatively mundane encounters with postal workers, schoolteachers, park rangers, and the like to more serious and potentially threatening ones. Citizens in financial distress must interact with social workers who have a decided impact on their immediate economic well-being. We as citizens also must from time to time interact with policemen, whether as victims, speeders, witnesses, or whatever. Even the most honest of citizens may have their tax returns audited and be required to justify their interpretations of the forms and their rights under them. In short, citizens do see government face-to-face and often develop their impressions of it from those encounters (Katz and Danet 1973).

The good news is that most of these encounters are positive, at least for the industrialized democracies.[8] Most of the empirical studies available report that citizens are satisfied with the way they are treated by their public servants. This is true even for encounters in some of the more threatening circumstances, e.g., in tax offices.[9] There are, of course, exceptions that frequently make the newspapers, but the average encounter between the bureaucracy and its public is a positive one—on average as good as with private-sector employees. Now for the bad news. These positive encounters with public employees do not appear to add up to a positive impression of government in general. Paradoxically, it appears that a remote and inefficient administrative structure is composed of pleasant and efficient individuals (Bodiguel and Rouban 1991). There seems to be yet another Zeitgeist that makes public bureaucracy a popular object of abuse even though its individual members appear to the public to be perfectly decent people.[10]

The other discussions of participation and empowerment tend to be normative and ameliorative. The discussion of street-level bureaucracy as an approach to participation has somewhat less of that reformist zeal itself, but the implications for change are clear. If government is to be effective, then a good deal of attention needs to be paid to the work of these "bureaucrats." They are already participating in reality, but it is not very well structured or even understood (OECD 1987). Further, their participation is often conceptualized almost as illegitimate, as if their appropriating authority is not rightfully theirs. The problem may be that the responsibility is indeed theirs, but it has not been designed in a way that "empowers" them; it only makes them appear, and feel, that they are operating on their own without any support from above, or even from the clients below.

Another way to link participation and street-level bureaucracy is to think of participation as a means of overcoming the problem of "contravention." As Dexter (1990) has argued, the politics within an organization is at least as important, and contentious, as those among organizations, and members of an organization must be able to work together effectively in order to achieve collective goals.[11] A basic problem in any organization, public or private, is to ensure that all its members will do approximately the same thing when faced with similar "stimuli" from the environment. That is, all regulators should find the same objective conditions in a factory as in or out of compliance with the environmental laws, and all social workers should give clients with the same objective criteria the same decisions concerning their eligibility for benefits. Adequate participation within an agency cannot guarantee that, but it can help.

Internal political struggles of public organizations may to some extent be exacerbated by participation and empowerment, largely because these democratic ideals are so important in contemporary politics that we are attempting to empower everyone. Street-level bureaucrats are a primary target for empowerment, as are their clients. Further, part of the managerialist movement in public administration is to empower managers. The problem is that you cannot empower everyone at once without creating conflicts among groups, all of whom believe that they rightly possess the power to make decisions (Peters and Pierre 2000). Thus, in the end, some of the attempts at empowerment may actually be alienating, by creating the sense of power without actually transferring that power.

Discursive Democracy

The participatory model of governing is concerned also with managing the participation of citizens and the relationship between state and society. In its simplest form, participatory government is plebescitarian, with the public being asked to decide all manner of policy issues by a direct vote. State and local governments in the United States have something of this character (Cronin 1989), as does Swiss government (Kobach 1993), and there has been an increasing use of referenda for policy issues in other European countries (*Economist* 1995; Butler and Ranney 1994; Budge 1996). Although broadly inclusive, referenda tend not to permit the public to make more than a yes or no choice about a decision that has been set for them by political elites.

At a somewhat higher conceptual level, and with a more intensive conception of public participation, perhaps various strands of literature on "discursive democracy" (Dryzek 1990), "associative democracy" (Hirst 1994), "strong democracy" (Barber 1984), and other similar concepts call for reforming government fundamentally. These ideas have a much broader conception of popular participation and democracy than conventional representative democracy. These scholarly works argue for enhanced participation by clients, workers, and especially the public at large in the identification and clarification of problems within government as a whole, as well as by those dominating particular public organizations (Handler 1986).

The fundamental concept behind this version of participation is that the "experts" in a bureaucracy do not have all the information or perhaps even the right type for making policy (Majone 1989). Therefore, isolating important decisions from public involvement will generate policy errors. As Jan Kooiman (1993, 4) has put it, "No single actor, public or private, has all knowledge and information required to solve complex dynamic and diversified problems; no actor has sufficient overview to make the application of needed instruments effective." For example, although pharmaceutical regulation in the United States is far from perfect (Roberts 1995), the openness of the system to information and argument from a variety of interested parties appears to help minimize errors.[12] In contrast, the relatively secretive system of drug licensing found in the United Kingdom (*Observer,* May 7; see also Harrigan 1994) and in several other European countries does not permit that error correction.

Further, the deliberative models contain an implication at least that representative democratic institutions are far from perfect in transmitting the wishes of the public into policy. This is hardly a new thought (Rose 1974), but what distinguishes this perspective from others is the assumption that more direct democracy can be made to work, even in complex modern societies. In this view, therefore, there is a need to involve a wider range of citizens in the shaping of issues, in the formulation of responses, and perhaps also in the implementation of programs once they are adopted; this style of governing has come to be known as *Bürgernähe,* or closeness to citizens, in Germany. Government should be forced to become more open to a range of views, it is argued, not just to those of the policy experts and bureaucrats managing the program.

This manner of thinking about democracy and governing is often associated with continental social theorists such as Jürgen Habermas (1984) and Niklas Luhmann (1990). Habermas, for example, has developed the concepts of the "ideal speech community" and "communicative rationality" to describe the conditions under which participation would be most effective. In such an idealized setting there would be no hierarchy of individuals or of ideas. Rather, in this equal and open forum all ideas are equally valuable and should be voiced in order to ascertain the true range of opinion within the community. Clearly, decision making in this model of management or governing would not be easy or quick. The democratic virtues of participation, as well as the chance of developing innovative ideas about how to solve policy problems, are seen as justifying the extra expenditure of time and energy (White 1988, 70–71).

In many ways this vision of democratic governance is not dissimilar to the somewhat older ideas of participative management already examined. The major difference appears to be in the scope of the discussion that would be permitted under each model. In the participative management or empowerment mode of thinking, the discussion would be primarily about how to administer a program that was already accepted as policy.[13] Further, the discussion would be primarily among the members of the public organization charged with delivering that service. For the advocates of discursive democracy, however, the subject matter of the discussion and the types of participants involved would be much broader. The discussion would focus on what should be done as well as about how it should be done. Not only would public employees be involved but also members of the community at large, including perhaps some citizens with quite different ideas about what constituted good policy.

Critics of this conception of governing can readily point to the practical problems that it would generate. The public wants to be involved in making decisions, but it also wants government to be able to act swiftly and decisively. Would not participation simply be another form of red tape that would slow down a system that is already perceived as being too slow? Further, does the public at large really have much useful information to add to a discussion about the details of complex policy issues such as genetic engineering or nuclear power?

It sometimes appears that the experts have sufficient problems reaching any consensus on issues among themselves without involving a whole host of amateurs whose ideas may only waste time. There are also a number of legal constraints on the capacity of government to do simply what it and other participants in the policy process want, and when and how they want to do it, so participation may be the beginning of the process rather than the end.

As well as permitting more participation, the deliberative model might require government itself to become more transparent. Transparency has been one type of reform implemented during the 1980s and 1990s in a number of countries (IMF 1998). The basic idea is that the public sector should let the public know more about its operations and the decisions it makes. This information, in turn, provides the basis for involvement in decision making by the public. In some cases, transparency covers just decisions made about the individual, but in other instances the information available covers policy issues more broadly, thus providing the basis for effective public participation.

Governments are further constrained by the practical point that often the only way that they are able to make difficult decisions is to limit participation instead of fostering it. For example, in order to be able to close military bases that were no longer necessary at the end of the cold war, the American government found it necessary to create a base-closing commission and to limit the capacity of politicians and other potential participants to influence their decisions (Koven 1992b). Likewise, both New York City and more recently Washington, DC, have had to establish financial "boards of control" to limit the growth of deficits created through more participatory, democratic government. Even that strategy has not been fully successful in producing fiscal restraint, but there is more chance of achieving the goals if participation is minimized.

If we move away from the ideal version of the model and examine some empirical examples, we can see that many industrialized democracies are attempting to construct patterns of policymaking that approximate the requirements for dialogue and discourse (Handler 1986). They have been doing this without necessarily building in all the practical constraints that would so severely restrain the capacity to reach decisions in a timely fashion. For example, "issue network" and "policy community" frameworks for understanding policymaking have become popular over the past decade (Rhodes and Marsh 1992; Jordan 1990). Although it is unclear whether these structures have existed all along and social scientists have just discovered them or whether they truly have been developing, their increased prominence in the discussion of policy does provide a more participatory cast.

The basic theme of these ideas about communities and networks is that surrounding each policy area is a host of interest groups, professional associations, scientists, activists, and so forth, all of whom have something they want to say about the policy. The trick for government then is to structure discussions in a way that allows maximum input but still permits making decisions in a timely fashion (Barker and Peters 1993). The balance that is struck may be a function of cultural factors, with the Scandinavian countries, for example, generally willing to tolerate longer delays in order to gain maximum participation (Meier 1969; Laegreid and Roness 1997) and the Anglo-American countries much less concerned with full participation and more about making a decision. Even in the less consultative regimes, however, political pressures are now forcing much more complete public consultation before a policy can be made legitimately.[14]

Moreover, government must make related decisions about how broadly to cast its net in seeking and accepting input from groups and individuals when making policy. At the extreme, corporatist systems might constrain participation to a very few selected interest groups, thus obviating the real meaning of public participation in the eyes of many discursive theorists (Schmitter 1974; Micheletti 1990). Other methods, such as public hearings, town hall meetings, and "teledemocracy" permit broader participation but present real difficulties in reaching policy decisions (Pierce 1992; Etzioni 1993). The task for government again is to balance the need for timely decisions with the need for participation and to develop some criteria for the probable germaneness of inputs from prospective participants.

In considering public administration as the focus of much of the reform activity in government, it is interesting to note that in some ways the decisions made by these (presumably closed) organizations are in some ways more open to public participation than the decisions made by representative, nominally democratic institutions. For example, in the United States, the Administrative Procedure Act of 1946 mandates that each regulation (secondary legislation) issued by the bureaucracy be subjected to one or another mechanism for public input into the decision. The simplest is "notice and comment," in which the public has so many days to respond to a published notice about a proposed regulation (Kerwin 1994; Page 2001). Other types of regulations and licensing decisions will require open public hearings before the decision can be made. These mechanisms are far from perfect and depend on a very attentive public (usually only interest groups respond to notices), but the system is indeed more open than might be expected.

There are movements in place to make the regulatory process in the United States even more open and consultative. The principal device in this quest is "negotiated rule making." As the name implies, this method of making regulations would permit the actors affected to negotiate among themselves and with the agency the nature of the rules that would become law (Harter 1982; Pritzker and Dalton 1990). This method is intended both to enhance the democratic nature of the process and to improve the quality of the rules adopted. That is, the assumption is that the information brought to the table by the affected interests will improve the technical quality of the decisions. Further, given that all or most affected parties would be participating in the negotiations, the probability of the regulatory agency being captured by the interests might be less than under other systems of regulatory decision making.

The access of the public to rule making in the United States is far from perfect, given that relatively few average citizens have the desire to read the *Federal Register* on a regular basis, but it is still better than in many other countries. Other even more open systems of participation for rule making exist in the Scandinavian countries. In these cases public agencies are required to circulate a request for opinions (*remiss*) about proposed legislation (primary or secondary) prior to its being issued. This system tends to involve primarily affected interest groups, but given the large number of groups sent the *remiss* and the organizational intensity of Scandinavian societies, most segments of society will be contacted before rules are made.

Even simple changes in political life can be used to enhance participation and the influence of citizens over policies. For example, I spoke of decentralization in local governments as a part of the agenda of market reformers. Yet this structural change can also enhance public participation. For one thing, local governments by their very size make participation more likely and more meaningful. Further, they tend to have more mechanisms permitting direct citizen involvement than do national or regional governments. The famous New England town meeting in the United States (Elder 1992) and the annual meetings in some Swiss cantons are perhaps the extreme cases (Frenkel 1994), but all manner of procedures such as open meetings of governing bodies, public zoning hearings, and citizens' advisory bodies enhance participation at the local level in ways that would probably be impractical for national governments. Even in countries with limited transparency at the national level, e.g., the United Kingdom, local governments appear more open than national government.

Communitarianism

The development of the set of political ideas usually labeled as "communitarian" is also important for understanding the emergence of participatory models of government (Etzioni 1993; Spragens 1990). Its basic thrust is that the individualism implied in the market, as well as in some of the preceding participatory ideas, is misdirected. Rather than thinking about individual gain and individual power in formal political structures, the citizen should think first about the impact of policy on the community, however defined, and about how the community can be more directly involved in the production of the services. Communitarianism, therefore, denies the central importance of bureaucracies in the delivery of public services and instead looks for means of "coproduction" and personal involvement as the way to make government perform better (Koven 1992). Bureaucracies may still be necessary for some public services, but the people themselves can play a larger role in helping themselves (see Racine 1995).

Communitarianism is sometimes discussed as a means to revive the salad days of the political left and as a way to replace the market-driven ideas of the 1980s with a more "humane" vision of governing for the 1990s and beyond

(Mulhall and Swift 1992). This may be true, but only partially, and there are some communitarian strands of thinking on the political right as well. At the level of mass political activity, the "conservative populism" manifested in Swedish elections in 1991 (Taggart 1995), in Canadian elections in 1993 (Lemco 1995), and in the American congressional elections of 1994 can be seen as a form of communitarian revolt against big government and its bureaucracy. Unlike most earlier populist movements (Kazin 1995), this manifestation conceptualizes big government as one of the enemies (Boyte and Riessman 1986), if not the major enemy, of the people. In the past, populists had conceptualized the public sector as a solution to the economic and social problems created by big business.

At the more elite level, some conservative thinkers visualize communitarianism's reviving volunteerism as an alternative to social and educational services provided by government (Willetts 1994). Their view is that the expansion of the mixed-economy–welfare state has stifled all forms of individual and collective initiative so that alternative forms of provision—including the family—that once flourished are now moribund. If community action and involvement can be given a moral claim on people's time and energies, then there will be less need for government as well as better and more caring public services (see Jenkins 1995). This version of communitarianism, like that on the political left, appears somewhat utopian, but it is also very appealing to large numbers of people.

Whether attached to and promoted by the political left or right, communitarianism would emphasize the growth of the "third sector," meaning nonprofit organizations other than those in the public sector, as a solution for many problems of contemporary society (Gidron, Kramer, and Salamon 1992). The way to reform government, therefore, is to use its power to foster the creation of more groups in this third sector. Interestingly, the actions of the market reformers in creating more autonomous "agencies," especially the now famous "quangos" existing between the public and private sectors, may be a step in the right direction from the point of view of communitarians.[15] The structures needed for some of their reforms are therefore already established. All that is now required is to inculcate those structures with those desirable communitarian values and greater public involvement, and the problems of governing society will be solved.

In this light it is interesting to note how little attention students of public administration have paid to the third sector and its relationship to government. This is less true in the United States (Kearns 1996) than in Europe (but see Pierre 1997), given the power of the volunteer sector in areas such as social services, but even in the United States it appears that these organizations often have been perceived as the competition rather than as potential allies in solving problems (see Anheier and Seibel 1990). In some ways public/private partnerships with business have been more successful than relationships of government and nonprofits (Kernaghan 1994; Pierre 1997). Economic realities as well as ideological changes appear to be encouraging a shift in the relationships between the sectors.

The participative approach to reforming the public sector is not short on ideas. Yet they are rarely as clear as the ideas that have animated the market approach, and they address the problem of governing from several levels of abstraction. That having been said, however, there is a rich lode of conceptualizations that can and have been applied when thinking about how to make government perform better. "Better" here means something quite different from what it means to the advocates of the market approach. However, some of the strands of thinking, e.g., consumerism in the market approach and empowerment of clients, are not totally opposed to one another. Indeed, both approaches see large institutions as a source of the perceived problems of the public in coping with government and propose to remedy them by breaking down the institutions.

We will next examine at how the participative approach deals with the issues of structure, management, policymaking, and the public interest. Given that there are at least four versions of this one (presumed) approach for change in government, there may be some internal contradictions in terms of specific reform ideas and recommendations for change. These recommendations, however, will be held together by their common search for a way to involve more people—lower echelon workers, clients, and the public at large—in the governing process and to break some of the bonds of conventional bureaucracy.

Besides these internal contradictions, there will be some contradictions to the market approach. This is to be expected, given the different ideological and philosophical roots of the approaches. Nevertheless, these contradictions do make a difference because specific reforms based on each group of ideas are being implemented simultaneously within the same governments. The failure to understand the logical basis of reforms and to make them compatible with what else is being tried in a government is a prescription for failure, and perhaps even worse. That is, implementing incompatible reforms can lead to negative synergy as easily as it can to positive synergy, or more easily, and with that to an actual reduction in the effectiveness of government.

STRUCTURE

The structural implications of the participatory approach to reform are somewhat less clear than those of the public-choice approach using the market as the exemplar. Participation as a guide to reform appears to focus more on process than on the structures within which the processes take place. At one level, formal organization may be irrelevant if there are other opportunities for the workers and clients to participate in decisions. There are, however, structural reforms that may make their participation easier, and therefore this approach is not entirely silent on the design of public organizations. In considering both participation and decision making we need to note the extent to which enhanced participation by one group—whether lower-echelon employees or clients—may reduce the capacity of the other to participate effectively. The advocates of participation talk about this virtue as if there were a limitless supply of opportunities, but it may in fact be a limited commodity in something approaching a zero-sum game.

The most obvious implication of participation for structure is that, much like the public-choice approach, public organizations would become much "flatter" and have fewer tiers between the top and bottom. If the lower echelons are perceived as having a great deal of insight and expertise to offer in decision making and are highly motivated to provide good services, then hierarchical levels of control are merely impediments to good performance in an organization. Further, if this shift in the locus of decision making is going to take place anyway, then eliminating the middle-management tier is a good way to save money. This flattening of organizations clearly has been happening in the private sector, under the rubrics of "delayering" and "downsizing," and the pressures on the public sector to save money through the same techniques are at least as intense.

The alternative implication, however, is that if clients and lower-echelon employees are to be permitted substantial involvement in making decisions, there may be a need for *greater* control from above to ensure that public laws and financial restraints are adhered to faithfully. The latter may be especially true if values of public service and accountability are not well institutionalized in transitional political systems. The street-level bureaucracy literature points to the extent to which employees may become advocates for their clients rather than administering the law *sine irae et studio*. Therefore, empowerment may produce a countervailing need to look over the shoulders of employees instead of assuming that all is going well.[16]

These possible implications point to yet another of the contradictions in the mind of the public and experts about government. On the one hand, people want government to be decisive, efficient, and less burdened by red tape. On the other, people want to ensure that public employees are adequately controlled so that they do not waste money, violate laws, or assist the wrong people. It is difficult to have it both ways, and therefore there is a constant battle between these two forces in the design of public organizations and the processes that control them.

Another structural implication of the participatory approach is that there may need to be a variety of structures to channel participation. This is especially true for participation by clients, but it may also be true for lower-level employees who have not been as involved in decision making as is envisioned in this approach. As governments have begun implementing programs of participation for both clients and workers, a variety of councils, advisory groups, and the like have come into being. As with so many issues surrounding contemporary administrative reform, a number of points about the involvement of clients in organizations remains open for contestation.

Fundamentally, who are the clients? This is a question analogous to that asked about customers in the market approach. Are they only the individuals who are being served directly by the program, are they all the people who are indirectly affected by the program, or are they the public at large? Obviously, each of these possible definitions, all of which have some validity, imply different structures for channeling the participation. In many countries there are already well-developed mechanisms for handling the input from the immediate clients of programs, although to some critics these remain oriented toward top-down explanations of policies and decisions rather than being authentic input from the clients. At the extreme, however, clients increasingly are being empowered to manage their own programs, thus ensuring that at least the direct "customers" of programs do have influence (Clarke and Stewart 1992).

Second, it is interesting that much of this definition of the rights of participation, albeit defined as citizenship rights, in practice means the rights of consumers of public services. This characteristic again brings the participatory approach closer to the market approach than might be expected, given the political ideologies of their typical adherents. The development of charter rights, even for consumers, may be especially difficult to bring about in transitional and developing societies in which there is not a strong tradition of involving "customers" in government decisions or even of the right to complain about decisions once they have been made. Even among the developed democracies there may be marked differences in the more participatory cultures of North America and the more quiescent public consumers in Europe.[17]

A third point about the participation of clients is that most existing programs of participation in the public sector operate as ex post rather than ex ante controls over government. That is, government is much better organized to deal with the complaints of citizens about the poor quality of services than it is to involve the public in the design of programs (Lewis and Birkinshaw 1993; Griffiths 1988). Although it is difficult to argue against the desirability of effective complaint procedures in government, it is also difficult to accept on democratic grounds that this is the most desirable form of participation. This is especially true when dealing with services, e.g., health care, that produce outcomes that may be difficult to reverse.

The Citizens' Charters in the United Kingdom are an example of a mechanism that operates largely ex post (Doern 1993; Connolly, Mckeown, and Milligan-Byrne 1994).[18] These statements of consumer rights for government services are mainly about the redress of grievance, as are devices such as alternative-dispute resolution (Solovay 1994), the ombudsman, and administrative tribunals. The Citizens' Charters were even promulgated with much input from citizens about what they wanted from the services but were actually top-down instruments (Tritter 1994). There have been increasing attempts to involve citizens in the creation of charters in Britain. This has been particularly true for the growing number of local charters put forth by individual hospitals, schools, community-care facilities, and the like (Department of Health 1994).

Some devices, e.g., public hearings, public inquiries (Barker 1994), and *remiss* proceedings in Scandinavia, do permit greater public involvement at the policy formulation stage, but these devices are less prevalent than those designed to handle administrative failures. As important as the redress of grievance is, certainly it would be better for a democratic government to prevent the grievances in the first place. Further, the redress of individual grievances may not address fundamental design problems in public programs, so that administrators may become the scapegoats for the poorly designed programs they must administer.

A further implication of this approach to governance has been the creation of a number of new participative structures that complement, or circumvent, traditional structures of government, especially local government. These tend to be concerned with a single policy while local governments tend to be multipurpose. The reasoning behind the single-purpose authority is that it can focus attention on the issues in the one policy area more effectively and will not get bogged down in issues that cut across policy domains. Moreover, single-purpose authorities involve people in the community who might not be interested in the total array of public issues but who do care intensely about a single issue, very often education or the environment.

There may be political reasons as well for wanting to circumvent control by existing local authorities. For example, in the United Kingdom, many local authorities have been controlled by the Labour Party even during the long period of Conservative dominance at the national level. Therefore, creating new single-purpose authorities may reduce the political control of those local services by the opposition party as well as making the performance of the single-purpose authorities easier to identify and measure. Similarly, the creation of quangos and other bodies permitting appointment by central government also permits evasion of controls by powerful local authorities.

MANAGEMENT

The participatory approach to governance contains somewhat more obvious implications for public-sector management than it has for structure. The basic premise is that government organizations will function better if the lower levels, and perhaps the clients, of the organization are included more directly in managerial decisions. At one level this involvement might be considered manipulative, with top management exchanging a little bit of participation for greater productivity and loyalty from workers. Though early "human relations" management had some of this manipulative character, the contemporary advocates of participation have been more ideological and believe in the human as well as the organizational importance of participation. Even then, however, there can be something of a manipulative element in thinking that overall social governance can be enhanced through permitting and encouraging greater social "discourse" in the process of making decisions.

Perhaps the most important feature of the participative approach is its attempt to involve social interests in governance explicitly. We should remember, however, that these managerial ideologies are by no means the first theoretical justifications of enhanced participation. The neocorporatist and corporate pluralist literature represents another strong strand of thinking about how to gain the advantages of the knowledge, and quiescence, of social groups (Olsen 1986). The difference may be that this level of legitimate involvement of social interests is now becoming popular in countries with an Anglo-American political cultural legacy as well as in countries with a continental legacy. Thus, while the market model may denigrate the role of the citizen and exalt that of the consumer, the participation model tends to enhance the role of the citizen and attempts to facilitate democratic participation in means other than voting.

The participation of clients may extend to managing a program directly. Rather than depending on professional and bureaucratized structures to manage services such as local schools or housing projects, governments have been permitting groups of clients (parents in the case of schools) to assume that responsibility themselves, albeit within guidelines established from the center. This change in the manner of service delivery may save money, permit greater adaptation of programs to local demands, and create greater political efficacy among the public. Of course, there are programs that the clients might never be able to manage, given that they require making difficult decisions about individual eligibility and amounts of service to be provided, but experiments in debureaucratization have shown promise.

POLICYMAKING

There are several implications of the participatory vision of governance for policymaking, to some extent because of the internal differences in the approach itself. One of the more obvious implications is a preference for a bottom-up versus a top-down version of the policy process.[19] That is, this vision does not assume that governments can govern best by making decisions in a centralized fashion and then implementing them through laws and relatively rigid hierarchies. Rather, the vision, like that of the market to some degree, favors decentralized decision making. This is true both in the sense of the lower echelons of organizations having substantial, if not determinate, impact on policy decisions and in the sense of the organizations themselves having a great deal of control over the decisions that determine their own fates. The assumption is also that decisions made in this manner will be objectively better, given the presumed higher levels of information possessed by these lower levels of the organization. In this emphasis on decentralization, the participative approach shares a good deal with the theorists, if not always the practitioners, of the public-choice approach.

Given its concern for involving lower-echelon workers, the participative approach is almost silent on the involvement of top-echelon bureaucrats—those usually referred to as at the "decision-making" level—in policymaking. One possible implication would be that political leaders, having greater involvement with the public, might be more suitable conduits for participatory inputs than would be senior public servants. On the other hand, if communication within organizations is even moderately efficient, the lower echelons should be able to send messages that then influence policy through their organizational hierarchies. In either case, one must question the design for participation: how can those employees usually excluded from decisions influence them? There is no simple answer. The other perspective that the participatory model may have on policymaking is the descriptive statement that lower echelons of the bureaucracy do have a major impact on policy in almost any political system (Lipsky 1980; Adler and Asquith 1981). Most decisions that governments make are not made by their political leadership, or even by the upper echelons of the civil service. Rather, by far the greater number of policy decisions are made by the lower echelons—the policeman, social worker, tax collector, and other street-level bureaucrats—who must make numerous decisions about particular cases every day. The available evidence indicates that these lower-echelon workers already possess a great deal of discretionary power when making decisions about individual clients, so that there may be little enhancement necessary.

The level of discretion available to street-level bureaucrats is especially evident in settings such as welfare offices, police stations, and sometimes schools, where the clients themselves have little power. The argument has been advanced in these settings that policies are designed and implemented to control disadvantaged members of the public instead of assisting them (Piven and Cloward 1993). Therefore, rather than concentrating on empowering lower-echelon officials in these organizations, some critics instead search for additional means for holding them accountable. One essential difference between the public and private sectors is that in the public sector the client usually has some capacity to appeal against decisions as a matter of right.[20] If lower-echelon workers are empowered too much, they may be able to escape the legal constraints on their ability to act in an "arbitrary and capricious manner."[21] Thus, there is a need to balance administrative discretion with appropriate levels of accountability and responsibility.

Not only are those decisions crucial for the actual determinations of citizens' claims for services, but they are also crucial for popular perceptions of government. For most people, government is the policeman, or the tax collector, or the safety inspector, and the interactions between citizens and state representatives shape the public's ideas about what government does and what it thinks about its citizens (Rouban 1991). Thus, more participation may make government more popular with clients, if not necessarily more efficient in delivering services.

One of the prevailing ideas about reforming public management is that the public will be better off if there is greater decentralization of existing hierarchies. Market reformers want these new organizations to be entrepreneurial and responsive to market signals. Participatory reformers want to permit clients and employees greater involvement in decisions affecting them that are made by public organizations. Decentralization may mean different things to different people, but to most contemporary critics of the public sector, two of the basic aspects that require attention are its centralization and hierarchy.

The market approach, with its recommendations to create many small and possibly competitive organizations to provide services, clearly creates coordination problems. These may be exacerbated by the simultaneous invocation of participatory ideas. If workers in organizations are empowered to make more of their own decisions, the probabilities are that they will be more variable than if there were more concern about hierarchy and the imposition of a common pattern within the organization. This in turn will make coordination and coherence even more difficult to achieve. Even if decisions made at the lower level are uniform, if each organization has greater freedom to make them, then coordination becomes more unlikely.

Furthermore, if the ideas about "dialogical democracy" are implemented, then coordination of programs and organizations will become even more problematic. If there is wide-scale consultation about decisions, then once they are made they will be difficult to change. Coordination among organizations, however, often requires that the organizations involved be able to bargain among themselves to produce a package of policies that all the relevant actors can accept. This in turn requires some flexibility among the leadership when they negotiate with one another. In short, although consultation and dialogue may produce greater happiness within an organization, they may in the end produce increased incoherence within the universe of policymaking organizations and simply move the locus of imposed, as opposed to bargained, decisions to another level within the political system.

Following closely then, if workers and clients do participate in making policy for the organization, through devices such as Total Quality Management, then the decisions reached will have ideological as well as just practical importance. That is, by virtue of their being created through an open political process established as a result of the participative methods of management, decisions become the collective property of the organization. Coordination with other organizations that may not share the same view may become more difficult, even if the organizations serve the same clients. For example, studies of coordination point out that organizations with different values or different orientations toward clients—even if existing within the same policy areas—have difficulty coordinating (Gray 1985).

Further, organizational change and policy change may also become more difficult if there is a collective commitment to a decision. This observation is reminiscent of some of the arguments by the new institutionalism (March and Olsen 1989; see also Selznick 1957), in which institutions invest their own processes and the decisions that emerge from them with particular meaning and thus resist imposition, or even bargaining, from the outside. If, as in the world of communitarianism, a number of groups and individuals are co-opted into programs, then they will have even more internalized meaning attached to them and change will be even more difficult.[22] In short, participation can be a great strength, but it is also a weakness when flexibility and rapid adaptation to a changing environment become important.

There appear to be several ways to address this coordination problem. Chisolm (1989), for example, argued that there could be "coordination without hierarchy." He has argued for coordination in the context of transportation systems that, to serve the public well, needed to be well coordinated. Unfortunately, the formal structures providing these services were themselves not well coordinated. Chisholm discovered, however, that informal mechanisms of coordination developed to compensate for what the formal structure could not do. In this case the relatively decentralized structures, instead of the developing cultures that were internally directed, developed cultures that were more service oriented and that hence solved the interorganizational problems rather than exacerbating them. The question then is the extent to which this is just a fortuitous outcome or is (or can be made to be) a general feature of the cultures existing in more decentralized, empowered organizations.[23]

Similarly, Scharpf (1989) argues that there are mechanisms available for producing coordinative outcomes among any set of organizations, although he places a great deal of emphasis on unanimity rules that appear most likely to emerge as the basis of interorganizational bargaining.[24] These rules in his "confrontational style" present real barriers to effective coordination. In his "problem solving" style, however, Scharpf argues for the presence of positive-sum games that can be used to create more positive forms of coordination (see also Mayntz and Scharpf 1975, 145–50). Even in the confrontational style, however, there would be options for side payments and issue packaging that could ameliorate some of the barriers of coordination, a style that can at times be observed within the context of the European Union.

THE PUBLIC INTEREST

The participatory state assumes that the public interest is served by encouraging employees, clients, and citizens to claim the maximum involvement possible in policy and management decisions. This involvement can occur through at least four mechanisms. First, and basically, citizens and employees should have the right to complain if they believe that they have not been served properly by government or if the system as a whole does not appear to be functioning properly. In order for this right to be effective, they also need to know first what is going on in the public sector. Thus, one of the requirements for effective citizenship and participation may be more open government, not necessarily in the radical sense of the dialogical theorists but at the more basic level of making policy-relevant information available to the public and even to other formal decision makers (Overman and Cahill 1994; Ashton 1993).

Many countries have already made substantial strides in opening their governments to greater participation. In particular, the Scandinavian countries have had extremely open political systems for a number of years. The Swedish Press Law, for example, permits access to almost any government document that is not explicitly classified and also makes classification of documents difficult. The United States passed the Freedom of Information Act in 1966 and, despite some limitations and difficulties in implementation (Cate and Fields 1994), this has been a landmark in opening government to greater scrutiny by the press and the public. Other countries, especially those derivative of the British tradition, have found creating open government to be difficult, but it may be a prerequisite for meaningful participation (Plamondon 1994). And as governments begin to employ market thinking as a part of reform, information may become less available as it is subjected to a variety of user fees or privatized outright (Victor 1995).

One aspect of openness often overlooked is that for many services the public may not know what to expect and what actually constitutes "quality." It is easy to tell if the trains run on time, or if garbage is collected when it is supposed to be. For more complex services, such as medicine or education, however, is the average citizen capable of determining what high-quality service is? Even for the more mundane services it is still difficult to say what is "good enough." Circumstances will inevitably cause some trains to run late. In fact, if the trains are late for safety reasons that may be a higher-quality service than if they are on time but inordinate risks are being taken. Also, good services for some citizens (travelers wanting to get through customs quickly) may not be good for all citizens wanting protection against smuggling. How do members of the public tell when they are being served well by the public sector?

A number of attempts are being made by government to establish standards for adequate performance by public services. In the United Kingdom, for example, the Citizens' Charters (Doern 1993; over twenty separate charters now exist) are means of enumerating service standards that then permit citizens to identify when the standards have not been met. The citizens are thus able to complain and perhaps receive compensation. At the very least, these standards can function as diagnostics for the behavior of public organizations. They serve as a kind of substitute for the signals generated by the market that are used to guide decisions in private-sector organizations. Numerous other countries are implementing or considering programs (Rhodes 1995) designed to be like the citizens' charters, but several of these programs contain almost as much about the duties of citizens as they do about the service-delivery responsibilities of government.

One interesting aspect of citizens' charters and a number of other similar participatory mechanisms is that they have been mandated from the top down (Hood, Peters, and Wollman 1996) rather than coming from the bottom up. An uncharitable characterization of this practice would be that citizens are being told what quality they should expect by public officials in whose self-interest it is to have them not expect very much. This is not, however, just a critique of the Citizens' Charters in the United Kingdom but is true for almost all similar exercises in drafting service standards for the public sector (Barnes and Prior 1995). Public involvement tends to be permitted and encouraged only after the basic issues—what the goals of the service should be—have been decided rather than while the more fundamental questions are being asked.

The second mechanism for involvement is that for employees of public organizations, effective participation can occur through their enhanced capacity to make independent decisions and to influence the policy directions taken by their organizations. This concept of governance is sometimes discussed as a means of conferring power on street-level bureaucrats and of making policy-making a bottom-up as opposed to a top-down process (Peters 2001). This openness to influence from the bottom is assumed to make the decisions of government objectively better, given that they will reflect the knowledge of participants in the organization who are most closely in touch with the relevant environment. Even if the decisions are not objectively superior, they will "feel" better to the people who made them and that at the least their implementation should be smoother.

But again, who is the public in this version of the public interest? I have asked this question in other contexts, but it keeps returning. Most adherents of participation tend to define the public very narrowly as the direct producers and consumers of the benefits of the program instead of as the public at large. For many citizens—and especially the communitarians and deliberationists—this narrow conception of public involvement would most certainly not be an acceptable definition of the public interest. They, the taxpayers, would be required to fund the programs but would no longer be able to exercise control through the mechanisms that are expected to function in a democracy.

For the average taxpayer, this constrained version of participation would not be seen as a democratic process but as a rationalization for continuing to serve special interests. It could be, in fact, that this clientelistic approach to governance might be a retrograde step in terms of how democratic systems are managed. At the extreme, it would become almost a re-creation of the patron-client relationships about which Western analysts have commented in such unfavorable terms concerning the less-developed world (Roniger and Ghuneps-Ayata 1994; Crook 1989) or some parts of the industrialized world (Meny and Della Porte 1998). Thus, for many of the definitions of participatory democracy currently in vogue, there should be a means through which the public at large can scrutinize government decisions, whether it be political (oversight) or administrative (auditing).

The third meaning of the public interest in the context of enhanced participation in decision making is more political. This version of the participatory state argues that public decisions should be constructed through a "dialogical" process permitting ordinary citizens to exert a substantial influence over policy (Linder and Peters 1995). In this conceptualization the public interest will emerge through creating processes that enhance the rights of citizens to say what they want from government. Further, citizens should be capable of bargaining directly with other citizens who have different views about appropriate public policies as well as bargaining directly with government bureaus. This "discursive" view stands in clear contrast to the "decisional" approach more characteristic of traditional representative and bureaucratic government institutions (March and Olsen 1995). In the decisional view the capacity to produce decisions, rather than the ability to create consensus, is the mark of governance capacity.

The final meaning of the public interest within the participatory approach depends upon citizens themselves being involved in making many choices about policy and even in delivering those services. In this way the participatory state is similar to the market state, given that both broad strategies for reform recommend allowing citizens to make more consumer choices and giving them more direct control over programs. The manner in which consumer choices would be exercised in the participatory state is, however, more political than that of the market approach. Rather than voting in the marketplace with dollars or vouchers, citizens would vote through a political process. This voting may be in referenda on policy or it may be through localized political structures, as exemplified by parental involvement on school management committees in Chicago (Vander Weele 1994) and in the United Kingdom (Levacic 1994). One fundamental point is that for advocates of greater participation in governing, better decisions (procedurally if not necessarily substantively) are reached through public participation instead of through relying on bureaucracy and technocracy.[25]

The United Kingdom has gone perhaps further than most other industrialized democracies in institutionalizing mechanisms for choice within the public sector. Although critics of British government, and especially local government, point to its seemingly undemocratic nature along some dimensions, it has been able to implement a number of direct participatory mechanisms within particular policy areas. For example, in education, the capacity of schools to opt out of local-authority control and attain grant-maintained status gives school governors (often parents) more real capacity to control the type of quality of education provided (Leonard 1988). It must be said, however, that this decentralization is occurring in the context of the simultaneous imposition of greater central controls over education funding, a new national curriculum, and an increasing impact from the school inspectors that minimize the real autonomy of the school governors.

The housing sector has been opened up for enhanced participation and self-management in the United Kingdom and Denmark (Malpass 1990; Sorenson 1997). The United States has engaged in some experiments with tenant management of large public housing projects (Hula 1990), but the efforts in the European countries have been more extensive. Though the scheme for Large Scale Voluntary Transfers in the Local Government and Housing Act of 1989 is in many ways just one more form of privatization, it does permit tenants some control over whether their housing estates will be transferred from local-authority control to alternative forms of management. In at least two instances, tenants have been successful in blocking proposed transfers (Pollitt 1995).

The coproduction of public services (Hupe 1993; Gurwitt 1992) and the use of voluntary action as a complement to, or substitute for, government activity is emerging as a mechanism for thinking about the public interest. To some extent coproduction is not a new idea at all but reflects old traditions of community involvement and participation in public-service provision. These ideas have been displaced by professional public services in most industrialized democracies but remain in operation in some. For example, corporatist political regimes often use interest groups to implement the policies they previously helped formulate (Cox 1992). The "militia bureaucracies" of Switzerland are examples of the widespread use of the public and of organizations as means of effecting policies and involving the public in government (Germann 1981).

Communitarians tend to consider voting and other political forms of participation as necessary but insufficient to change the nature of governing in what have become highly bureaucratized service-delivery systems. A more fundamental requirement, they argue, is a shift toward greater personal involvement in the life of the community. This involvement could be through helping out in school, or at the extreme doing homeschooling. Communitarian participation would mean not counting on government to care for the homeless and needy but engaging in cooperative efforts to feed, house, and reintegrate those fellow-citizens. Many people consider several ideas of communitarianism utopian, but its advocates argue that theese approaches are the only way to recapture society from alienation, bureaucracy, and, ultimately, decay.

The participatory model is not as clearly articulated as is the market model of administrative reform. Actually, the problem may be that it is too well articulated, with a number of different versions of the one basic approach competing for attention among political activists and the concerned public. Even with the internal differences, it is possible to extract several common implications of this vision for the role of the civil service in governing society as well as for the nature of governance processes themselves. This approach is ideologically quite different from that of the market model and from the public-choice concepts that undergird market interventions into public management. Moreover, the participatory ideal is built upon very different assumptions concerning human behavior within organizations. Perhaps fundamentally, this approach assumes that individuals are motivated in their organizational and political lives by "solidary"—participation—incentives rather than by "material"—pay and perquisites—incentives (Clark and Wilson 1961).

Even with those differences, the prescriptions for institutional design coming from the two approaches are not all that dissimilar. In particular, the principal prescription is for decentralization and some transfer of power to the lower echelons of organizations as well as to their clients. Further, most versions of the participatory model recognize the central role of the bureaucracy in making public policy, just as does the public-choice approach, although the advocates of participation consider this involvement more positively than do champions of the market alternative. If nothing else, the bureaucracy can provide a channel for participation by interest groups, the general public, or both, whether that participation is designed to bolster the position of agencies or not.

Although some prescriptions from the participatory approach are not dissimilar to those from the market model, the meaning attached to those designs for governance are markedly different. Rather than creating competition among service providers so that a market can develop and function, decentralization in the participatory model is intended to channel control to a different set of bureaucrats or perhaps to the clients of organizations. This outcome could be thought to be the very "regulatory capture" that the public-choice model seeks to avert (Macey 1992). Likewise, involvement of those lower-level bureaucrats in decisions is considered positively in the participation models, with the alternative being domination by upper-level bureaucrats, not political leaders. In this model these elites are considered equally antithetical to the interests of clients instead of as competitors for power, as in the usual presentation of public-choice perspectives.

4

Flexible Government

The third alternative to the traditional model of governing will be characterized as the flexible government model. This alternative is the least clearly articulated of the four, yet it captures several important realities of both public complaints about government and contemporary reforms. At a more basic level a flexible government is simply one that is capable of responding effectively to new challenges and of surviving in the face of change. A number of governments in Eastern and Central Europe, as well as many others in the developing world, have failed that simple test in the past few years. At a more refined level of analysis, flexibility refers to the capacity of government and its agencies to make appropriate policy responses to environmental changes rather than merely responding in their habitual ways to what are inherently novel challenges. These adaptations may involve structural changes as well as substantive policy choices.

The responses of flexible government can also be considered as the antithesis of common patterns of public-sector management in the recent past. Joining a government organization has been conceptualized in many countries as accepting a lifetime occupation (Walters 1992a), assuming that the individual wants to remain in public-sector employment.[1] Likewise, forming an organization in the public sector conventionally has been thought to be creating a permanent entity, no matter how transient the rationale for forming it may appear (Kaufman 1976). The permanence of both public employment and organizations frequently is overstated, but these suppositions still tend to shape a good deal of thinking about the formation and management of public-sector organizations. In particular, government leaders, the media, and the (moderately) informed public have begun to advance proposals for decreasing the permanence of budgets, organizations, and employment in the public sector as a means of addressing perceived deficiencies in governing.[2]

The dysfunctions of permanence in government, both for individual employment and for public organizations, are widely recognized. Governments have begun to address those dysfunctions even though permanence and institutionalization are more familiar as solutions than as problems, especially in transitional regimes. Despite the absence of clarity of some of the ideas to be discussed, this approach to reforming governance makes several viable proposals about changing the status quo in the public sector. Flexibility also represents a pragmatic alternative to the more ideological approaches, such as the market or participation. Further, despite the apparent lack of specificity in its recommendations, the ideas and suggestions about practice that are derived from the basic assumption about permanence in the public-sector do appear to be emerging in a number of governments.

As they do with most other diagnoses and prescriptions, the critics of permanence in government have somewhat conflicting views about the dynamics of the problems and therefore about the remedies required for producing a better public-sector. On the one hand, permanence has come to be considered as the source of excessively conservative policies and of the commitment of employees to their organizations rather than to the policies being administered by the organization.[3] Individuals may be more concerned with keeping their jobs and keeping the organization healthy in budgetary terms than with doing anything in particular about public policy. On the other hand, however, the presumed conservative consequences of organizational permanence may be to institutionalize the liberal social programs of the past.

Besides presenting management problems, a commitment to the existing organizational structure of government tends to institutionalize prevailing conceptions of public policy, and even of what the "real" policy problems are, so that policy change becomes ever more difficult (Hogwood and Peters 1983; Rochefort and Cobb 1993). This immobility of ideas exists even when the objective environmental conditions that the organization and its policies confront change radically. The organization provides a conceptual lens and a largely stable and sufficient resource base that permits its members to ignore or simply to repudiate those environmental changes if they desire to do so.

Some of the more extreme versions of this conservatism have been encountered in military and international affairs, e.g., the persistence of the horse cavalry into the twentieth century and the failure to learn lessons in foreign affairs (Etheredge 1985). But the same sort of locking into the ideas of the past is also encountered in domestic organizations. For example, agricultural policies appear locked into a model of a highly regulated and subsidized market while most other industries have been privatized, deregulated, or both (Skogstad 1993). Similarly, most public organizations responsible for labor-market policy continue to operate as if the phenomenon of globalization had never occurred (King 1995). Few organizations (public or private) are willing to invest in change while they are still viable, and the conceptual lenses provided by the organization may even distort collective perceptions of viability.[4]

Although it is conventional to think of organizational permanence as something of a mortmain on creative, activist policy initiatives and an assurance of incremental change (Hayes 1992), some critics from the political right believe that the same fundamental characteristic of the organizational universe has rather different policy effects. In particular, the political right tends to consider virtually all existing public organizations as committed to "big government" and to the perpetuation (and even expansion) of programs developed during past liberal regimes (see Aberbach and Rockman 1976). These continuing programs have produced (at least in the eyes of their critics) the "excessive" public spending perceived as characterizing contemporary mixed-economy welfare states (Cook and Barrett 1992; Taylor-Gooby 1985). The programs are also blamed for other problems, such as continuing public-sector deficits.

The critics of public bureaucracy tend to conceptualize existing organizations as defending their policies not so much from interest in their clients or "customers" but more from their own self-interest as the producers of services (Egeberg 1995). In this now familiar negative view of bureaucracy, the institutionalization of government structures has produced a perpetuation of policy priorities and governing styles that have had serious negative consequences for the society. These self-perpetuating structures are claimed to be especially out of touch with the current mood of most industrialized democracies in which the public is seeking mechanisms to reduce the size and influence of the public sector.

This conservative conceptualization of government is similar to that of Niskanen and the other market advocates already mentioned, but in this case the principal dynamic force (if this is not an oxymoron in this context) creating difficulties for the public sector is permanence.[5] In budgetary terms, a permanent organization may be a source of increasing expenditures, even if spending increases only gradually and incrementally.[6] Some earlier techniques for reforming government, such as Zero Base Budgeting (Schick 1978), have attempted to eliminate the upward pressures on expenditures associated with permanence, but for a variety of reasons they have been unsuccessful. So long as government organizations exist they will require care and feeding, and if politicians are incapable of making the difficult decisions required to terminate them (Bothun and Comer 1979), then there is likely to be an ever-increasing public budget.

Thus, from the perspective of critics of permanence, the easiest and most effective way to generate a significant transformation of the public sector and its policy priorities will be to shake up the organizational universe that makes and implements those policies. Reforms such as Next Steps in Britain and the "corporatization" of government in New Zealand clearly had their major intellectual roots in the market, but they also had some justification in the simple desire to force the system of government to change (Boston 1991; Hogwood 1993). Some advocates of administrative reorganization, as well as some advocates of reorganization for firms in the private sector, have argued that change can be in itself positive (Hult 1987). In the case of these reforms, however, there were clear policy targets ssociated with the desire to transform the organizational universe.

THE UTILITY OF STABILITY

We should not be too quick to dismiss the virtues of stability and permanence in either public or private organizations, however. As well as imposing a mortmain on positive changes, long-standing organizational structures can help to guide policy choices along positive, if well-trod, routes. The assumption that all old policies are bad is almost certainly as fallacious as an assumption that all existing policies are good.[7] The challenge then is to identify mechanisms for identifying and discarding the overly mature policies while retaining the effective ones. This choice of which ones are excessively ripe and which ones are still useful is, of course, dependent largely upon policy values (Mansbridge 1994) rather than on the existence of unambiguous standards for measurement.

The negative characterization of stability also assumes that the civil servants who are members of public organizations desire only a quiet life and lifetime employment. It may be, however, that these employees actually are professionals (Guy 1985), whether self-defined professional administrators or members of other more well-defined professions such as engineering and medicine. With this background the employees will maintain contacts with professional organizations and generally attempt to improve the policies they administer, often in the face of political opposition. In the present conservative political climate, such policy advocacy—whether for professional reasons or only for reasons of institutional protection—may be considered even more negatively than excessive stability, but advocacy by professionals does point to the need to avoid overly facile condemnations of permanence.

Organizational stability is an important source of organizational memory, and with that memory comes some of the institutionalized capacity of organizations to avoid expensive error (Stein 1995; March 1991). Ministers may resent (Theakston 1992) being told that "we tried that before and it didn't work" when they have a bright idea for a policy innovation (at least to them), but this simple statement by their (permanent) civil servants may save the public a good deal of time and money. The policy process requires important judgments about whether the persistence of memory serves to hinder needed change or preserves some necessary stability during times of rapid social and political change.

It is clear from a more theoretical perspective that the organizational memory is simultaneously a repository of prior learning and a potential barrier to future learning (Olsen and Peters 1995) for organizations. There is always the danger that organizations (or individuals) may learn one set of lessons too well, which may then inhibit their learning newer and more relevant ones (March 1991). Similarly, if it is at all possible, memory and routines press an organization to encode any new events and challenges as merely repetitions of older happenings. This characteristic of memory to enable the organization to use existing responses can remain appropriate. The inability to recognize the new or novel for what it is also inhibits the ability of organizations to adapt.

ORGANIZATIONAL PERMANENCE—
FRUSTRATION AND FUTILITY

Despite some obvious and important attractions, permanent government structures present significant problems for effective and efficient governance, at least in this one view advocating flexible governing. The dinosaurs that still roam the landscape of government are a source of expense and may constitute barriers to policy innovation. Many existing policies and programs are valuable, but none should be allowed to persist without effective testing and evaluation. Further, some politicians and scholars believe that making government organizations less permanent has virtues as a goal in itself, regardless of how well or how poorly they may be functioning. Simply forcing organizations to rethink their values and their policies on a regular basis may be a spur to more effective government.

The changing nature of problems of governance has produced movement away from permanent structures. First, an increasing number of the significant problems governments confront are "crosscutting" and fall between the stools of existing organizations. In some cases these issues produce only "simple" coordination problems among many organizations doing approximately the same thing. For example, although the United States has a Drug Enforcement Agency, a large number of other agencies—the Coast Guard, the Department of Defense, the Customs Bureau, the FBI, and state and local government police, among others—also are involved in the War on Drugs. This type of coordination is conceptually simple but is often politically extremely difficult, even with a drug czar to try to bring it about. Being willing to engage in that coordination may imply a loss of turf by one organization in favor of another, and with that a loss of budget, prestige, and perhaps even organizational survival.

In other cases, the coordination problems are more complex. For example, in making drug policy, law enforcement actors often must become involved with the health and education dimensions of the problem, and treatment confronts law enforcement as the best remedy (Sharp 1994). These coordination questions are conceptually more difficult because they require some fundamental thinking about what the policy of the government is, and what it should be. Such exercises also involve some turf fights, but the encounters are more often so fundamental that the turf issues become subsumed under questions about the nature of the problem being "solved" (Rochefort and Cobb 1993). Shaping the nature of the issues and policy problems is a fundamental aspect of the policy process, and the most fundamental coordination issues arise from conflicts over ideas rather than just from organizational interests.

This widened involvement of multiple agencies in almost all policies has created a fourth or fifth or nth branch of government that attempts to coordinate and control existing organizations and policies (Fournier 1987; Derlien 1991). The "policy space" and the organizational space for governments are already well populated (Hogwood and Peters 1983), and there is a rapidly increasing need to coordinate actors and actions within that policy space. Because of real changes in policies, changes in the international environment of public policies, and greater awareness of the multiple interactions of policies in the society (Peters 2000), these coordination problems appear to have become exacerbated over the past several decades. For example, no longer is economic policy a concern just for economists and central bankers, but it must also involve departments responsible for education, unemployment assistance, agriculture, labor market policy, international affairs, and probably many others.

Further, the Zeitgeist for contemporary administrative reform is to devolve the functions formerly performed by one large department into a number of smaller organizations, bearing names like "executive agencies" or "special operating agencies." Though there may be some efficiency gains from the disaggregation of larger organizations, there may also be significant losses, including losses in overall efficiency within the public sector. One of the more important sources of efficiency losses is a reduction in coordination. Although these executive agencies have been designed to some degree to be flexible and creative themselves, they, like any other organization, quickly become permanent (or at least begin to feel and act as if they were permanent). Hence, they quickly require some form of coordinative action from above. This need is even more evident, given that these organizations were designed to be creative and entrepreneurial. This matches the market motif of their formative ideas rather well but makes the governmental character of their activities more difficult to reconcile with traditional values, such as elimination of redundancy and enforcing accountability.

Moreover, the need to coordinate across the range of public organizations may itself vary across time. For example, at a particular time economic policy departments may have a paramount need to coordinate with foreign policy departments over issues of trade. That problem may be solved, or at least slide lower on the agenda (Downs 1972; Peters and Hogwood 1985), and those same economic policy departments may then need to coordinate more with education, training, and unemployment insurance departments. In this example, having created a permanent coordinative structure for the first problem might represent an inappropriate locking-in of priorities, and a more flexible structure would, in practice, be more appropriate for the needs of the public-sector. There may then be a role for the coordinators of coordinators if government cannot respond more creatively to its needs for coherence in policy and programs.

It should be noted that the idea of using temporary organizations in the public sector is hardly new. These have been a common means for addressing the rapidly expanding and contracting administrative needs of wartime and other emergencies. All governments have from time to time developed task forces or other (presumably) temporary organizations. Governments in France and Germany, for example, have used formats such as the *projets de mission* and *Projekt- gruppen* to address policy areas that they believed could be solved by short-term but intensive governmental action (Timsit 1988). Those efforts to generate quick solutions were far from universally successful, but these structures did represent an effort to prevent creation of more permanent organizations.

Some scholars have argued that organizational permanence borders on futility instead of presenting a real problem. The formal structure may remain the same, they contend, but their capacity to control the society is not sustainable. The argument is that society is "autopoetic" (in t' Veld 1992), or self-organizing. Likewise, other scholars talk about organizations becoming self-designing systems (Kiel 1989). As government organizations institutionalize their instruments of control, the regulated segments of society will find ways to minimize their effects. Thus, a flexible approach to regulation and a set of flexible organizations ultimately will produce better outcomes than will a more rigid and permanent structure. Further, this form of governance structure will be more legitimate, so it is argued, because the regulated will believe that they have more influence over policy outcomes.

TEMPORARY EMPLOYMENT

So far we have been exploring primarily the perceived need to make organizations less permanent. The other pressure creating impermanence in government organizations is the fundamental transformation of the labor market in most industrialized societies (Borjas 1995; Dicken 1992), in part a result of profound technological change and in part a function of internationalization of economies (Savoie 1995c). With those changes have come much less full-time and permanent employment and increasing levels of part-time and temporary employment. The assumptions that most workers have held about being able to prepare for one type of employment that would then last a lifetime simply do not hold true any longer. Most people can now expect to change jobs several times during their working lives and also to be retrained for different types of employment during that time.

Government has already begun to adjust to these broader economic changes and has found offering part-time employment to be a way of saving money and enhancing organizational flexibility. There may be no reason, at least in efficiency terms, to keep employees who are needed only for peak workloads or for emergencies. Some government organizations, e.g., parks and recreation and conservation organizations, have always operated in this manner but could depend on a stock of interested, and even dedicated, temporary employees available on a seasonal basis. Other public professions, such as teaching, have reserves of employees who tend not to be employed on a seasonal basis but who fill in for full-time employees who must be absent for a day, a week, or a term. In these instances professionalism and commitment have been able to substitute for continuing attachment to an organization and its values. It is not clear if that model is generally applicable, however.

Further, advocates of the role of the market point to the need to use outsiders in government to eliminate its separation from other actors and values in society. One standard complaint about government is that its employees are unaware of the problems of the real world and thus make decisions that appear nonsensical to business or other private-sector actors. If there were greater rotation of personnel through the public sector, then perhaps public employees would understand better the needs of the rest of the economy and society.[8] Some governments, e.g., that of the United States, have always been more open to temporary employment,[9] but that model is now being considered in a range of other countries (OECD 1990).

Thus, even when there is a permanent public organization, its members may themselves be transients. This is certainly a shift from the tradition of government employment, and the permanent civil servant would no longer be the backbone of government. This change has important managerial and policy implications. Even more important, it would have implications for public accountability and the ability to make the public-sector more responsible and responsive. Strict economic efficiency is but one of many values that government should seek to uphold; and flexibility, especially in employment, may undermine many other important values.

THE IMPACTS OF THE FLEXIBLE MODEL

We now have an idea of the problems that the model of flexible government is intended to ameliorate. As with the other three emerging models of governance, the flexible model has a number of specific implications for how government is, and should be, practiced. These implications are perhaps less well articulated and integrated than those arising from the other three perspectives, but they are nonetheless interesting and important. They provide a somewhat different perspective on how to push the public-sector to perform better. If nothing else, this approach to reform requires some collective thinking about why specific public organizations exist and why government employs as many people as it does as a part of the career public service. The market model assumes that feedback from society will make that determination, but this approach appears to require a somewhat more "rational" consideration.[10]

Structure

The fundamental advice that this approach offers is for alternative structural arrangements within government. Rather than relying on traditional departments, agencies, and bureaus that perceive themselves as having virtually a permanent claim on a policy space, this approach seeks flexibility and frequent termination of existing organizations.[11] This frequent termination is intended to prevent the ossification that often can afflict permanent organizations. Further, greater flexibility might allow government to respond more rapidly to changing social and economic conditions. There might be less resistance to creating organizations to respond to novel circumstances, for example, if there were some assurance that they would be terminated when their task was completed.

The ability to create and destroy organizations easily appeals to fiscal conservatives who argue that permanence and bureaucratic monopolies create excessive costs along with policy rigidities. In fact, the organizational universe emergent from the flexible approach might not be too dissimilar to the agencies already being created by market advocates. However, the agencies can attain an air of permanence about them rather quickly while organizations created through an attempt to enhance flexibility would be subject to rapid change. Further, the market approach tends to want to use market tests to evaluate performance of programs and organizations, but the flexible government approach tends to look at flexibility almost as a benefit in itself. Therefore, advocates of flexibility want to establish the principle of uprooting organizations instead of relying excessively on evaluations that can always be rigged in favor of an existing organization.

Another organizational option appears to be the extension of the quango state (Wilson 1995) that is already being created in the United Kingdom, with analogous structures apparently spreading in many other political systems (Kettl 1993; Hood and Schuppert 1989; Masa 1990). Though exact definitions and classifications differ (Hogwood 1995), the basic concept here is that under pressures to reduce the apparent size of the public sector, governments have begun to use increasingly nondepartmental bodies and quasi-governmental organizations to conduct their business. Given their somewhat less formal structures and small staffs, these organizations seem to be a viable means of providing public services while maintaining organizational flexibility. In practice, however, they appear to have substantial survival power themselves. There may therefore be no simple structural answer to the problem of permanence but a need to address the perceived problems with procedures, management, and political will.

As well as being structurally impermanent, these organizations might not be populated to a large degree by full-time employees who (at least in the United States) would spend most or all of their careers within the same organization. This change in career patterns is already occurring in government. For example, the proportion of total work hours put in by federal employees has been gradually creeping up since the 1960s and appears likely to continue to increase. The predictions of almost all studies of the labor market are that the trend toward temporary employment will continue in almost all segments of the economy. This trend may be applauded by fiscal conservatives who want to save money in the public sector, but it potentially does damage to other conservative values about the accountability of the civil service and its stability as a source of advice and values in an otherwise rapidly changing government.

The discussion to this point has focused on the structure of "line" organizations actually providing public services. Another aspect of creating flexibility is in the management of coordination and the interfaces among organizations. Some countries already have a well-developed system of committees and task forces that coordinate existing agencies and ministries. France, for example, has coordination devices existing at three levels within its administrative apparatus (Fournier 1987), and the central agencies such as prime minister and cabinet (Australia) and the *Kansli* (Sweden) perform these coordinative tasks in others (Painter 1981; Larsson 1986). The problem is that central agencies tend to be even more ossified than the organizations that they attempt to coordinate so that the *coordinative* structures can outlive their utility even more readily than the *coordinated* structures.

Virtual Organizations

Central agencies usually can evade hierarchical controls that would tend to force their own reorganization, with the major exception of elections and new governing political parties. Therefore, they must find methods for institutionalizing their own responses to change or they become barriers to effective governance. One possible solution to this problem of reforming the reformers is the idea of the "virtual organization" (Bleeker 1994). This idea is based on the common observation that almost any formalized structure that is created has the tendency to attempt to perpetuate itself. This may be exaggerated in the public sector, but it seems to be present in private-sector organizations as well, as several classic studies of voluntary organizations have demonstrated. Therefore, to the extent that organizations can become virtual, as opposed to formalized, structures, then there is a greater possibility of their being more adaptable to external change.

It is difficult to identify exactly what is meant by a virtual organization. For example, when the Gore Commission (NPR) completed its formal work and was dissolving, it created what it called a virtual organization (Peters and Savoie 1994). This was to be a group on the Internet designed to keep members of the NPR project in contact with one another and to serve as an instrument for advocating the ideas of the report across the public-sector. The development of technologies such as electronic mail have made the creation of loose, informal organizations of this sort very easy. Other ideas include the creation of one-time, ad hoc organizations to attempt to solve a specific question, or the creation of loose networks of like-minded individuals existing within and between other organizations while the individuals retain their own membership in the constituent organizations.

These conceptions of virtual organizations are only slightly more formalized versions of the interorganizational network thinking that is by now rather common in organizational theory (Benson 1982; Hanf and Scharpf 1978). The basic logic is that any policy area, or almost any area of human endeavor, will be characterized by the existence of a host of organizations that interact to constitute a social institution, if not a formal institution (DiMaggio and Powell 1991). These networks will develop their own informal, if not formal, rules and a set of norms that will guide their actions. The members also tend to share a number of values and commitments. In short, under this definition, a huge number of virtual organizations are already in existence. The task for government may be to tap into this rich organizational life and make use of it for policy advice, implementation, and coordination of programs.

Further, we can think of the virtual organization as a means of managing government at the systemic level rather than at the organizational level. As analysts have pointed out for years, the organization is the basis of much of the behavior of the public sector (Seidman and Gilmour 1986; March and Olsen 1984). This is in some ways a strength, providing identification for the members of the organizations (and for clients) and also linking programs with structures (Rose 1984). Yet the organizational basis of political life can also be a decided weakness in the system, with rigidity and excessive identification with the organization resulting.[12] The concept of the virtual organization could be a means for overcoming the barriers to change that more formal organizations present, although we may first have to find a way to overcome the probable resistance to the idea.

Ranson and Stewart (1994, 140–42) talk about the problems of managing government at the systemic level. They point to the fragmentation and interorganizational dependence that exist in all contemporary governments and the importance of structuring systems so that the difficulties generated by those features are ameliorated, if not eliminated. Though their focus is more on service delivery, especially at the local level, the same problems arise when policy is being formulated. Creating multiorganizational structures to cope with these problems will involve providing some overall direction to the institutional apparatus of government as a whole and, as Theodore Lowi (1972) has phrased this problem in a very different context, shaping the environment of behavior rather than the behavior itself. That is, it may be easier to create the circumstances in which flow of information and influence make certain types of decisions probable than it is to command other decision makers to adopt those same decisions. Here, then, are the fundamental questions about virtual organizations: will they look and act any less permanent simply because they do not convene in a single place or because they are not really formalized structures? Will not their shared commitment to their policy goals and their continued association over time produce the same desire to maintain the institution's existence that is found in other forms of organization? Indeed, may not the very informality of such forms of organization make them appear less dangerous than permanent structures of other types and thus permit them to persist even in the face of desires to trim down the organizational universe of the public sector?

Management

The manifest managerial implications of the temporary state are clear, but the latent implications are perhaps more interesting and more important. At the manifest level, this approach stresses the ability of managers to adjust their labor forces to match changing demands. This flexibility can be used to save a good deal of money for government as well as mitigating some of the public perceptions of waste and empire-building by government organizations. Further, this style of management may have some benefits for the personnel themselves, given the number of employment issues such as the impact on families of both parents working and all the other stresses associated with the contemporary economy.

Further, flexible personnel management may permit governments to respond more quickly and effectively to crisis or to rapidly increased demands for service. The potential service-delivery benefits tend to be discussed less than the cost-cutting benefits. If managers can add to their workforces without the fear of having long-term commitments to the employees, then coping with emergency and unanticipated needs is much easier. Even when it appears that the new level of demand may be permanent, maintaining flexibility is always a virtue for public managers. Of course, in many settings this style of personnel management is already practiced, but an even greater loosening of the traditional system may produce real benefits.

The latent implications of this approach are some diminution of the commitment of employees to their public employers, and with that, a potential threat to public-service values and ethos. It now appears excessively idealistic to discuss the commitment of civil servants to their organizations and to principles of public service. Yet there is substantial evidence that civil servants have been motivated by these values and that many would like to continue to be motivated by service values rather than "just money" (Zussman and Jabes 1989). For many public employees, joining the public service was not the economic decision implied by the market approach; rather, it represented a commitment to achieve certain policy values through their careers in government (Peters 1994).

Making more public-sector jobs temporary and part time will almost certainly diminish the commitment of employees to their jobs and also will tend to minimize their motivation for excellent performance. The flexible approach is therefore to a great extent antithetical to the ideas of the participatory state, given that temporary employees are unlikely to be interested in real involvement with the organization or capable of such participation (see Daley 1988). Thus, just when some of the management literature (public and private sector) is touting teams and employee involvement as the panaceas for all that ails organizations (Korsgaard, Schweiger, and Sapienza 1995; Berman 1995), workers are being told that their organizations have little or no real commitment to them as individuals. This appears to be an extremely mixed set of messages to be sending to employees.

Further, temporary employment may make civil service values of probity, accountability, and responsibility even more difficult to enforce. Despite attempts to socialize temporary or part-time employees, they may not have any continuing interests in any one organization and little reason to invest their energy in complying with traditional public-service values. The values of temporary employees are more likely to be the self-interested ones prevailing in the marketplace.[13] In short, one could argue that a good deal of conventional value may be sacrificed to gain some reductions in expenditures.

Policymaking

The "temporary state" approach to questions of governance appears to have little to say directly about the role of the public service in making public policy. However, we can explore the logical implications of this approach to governing concerning an active policy role for the civil service. These implications appear to be potentially contradictory, with some pointing toward an enhanced role for the civil service and others seeming to reaffirm the older wisdom of the political dominance of the elected classes over policy, with civil servants being in a subordinate position.

On the one hand, by placing so much emphasis on the fragility of government organizations, the traditional sources of organizational power in a common culture and commitment to existing policies would be diminished. The old bureaucratic structures had both the advantage and disadvantage of stable personnel and stable policies. The permanent personnel provided a great deal of direction to policy and provided an experiential knowledge base for construction of any new policy initiatives. On the other hand, stability has been a barrier to innovations that would extend beyond the conventional wisdom about what is "feasible" in the policy area (Majone 1989, 69–94). This absence of a mortmain may permit political leaders to have a stronger role in altering policies than they might otherwise. A group of radical reformers, such as the Thatcherites or Reaganauts, would be pleased to have less organizational inheritance to counteract.

All the pressures from this approach, however, do not have the effect of making the life of political leaders easier. By removing the anchor of large, stable organizations, the elite of the civil service may be able to develop their own policy ideas more autonomously. To some extent the conception of the Senior Executive Service in the United States was that of a free-floating resource that could be used in a variety of managerial and policy-advice situations. Without large, permanent organizations to encumber them in the exercise of their own conceptions of good policy, these senior officials may in fact be able to be creative forces in policy development, clearly a circumstance that would be opposed by most contemporary political officials.

In addition to its implicit advice about the role of the civil service in governing, the "temporary state" approach has some profound implications for policymaking. If indeed permanence is a problem, then impermanence may be a virtue, and with it, experimentation in policy becomes much more possible. Governments are often reluctant to take chances on policy. This is in part political; they do not want to be seen as wasting public money when they are unsure of the effects of their program.[14] Further, to have a program passed by the legislature often requires overselling the program, with admissions of uncertainty being an almost guaranteed way to assist critics of the program in causing its defeat. Thus, the dynamics of politics tend to push programs toward appearing, if not actually being, permanent.

As a counter to the ideas of permanence and the mortmain of existing policy understandings, several scholars have advocated a more experimental conceptualization of policy. In particular, Donald T. Campbell (1982; 1988) has long advocated the "experimenting society," in which government would quite explicitly try innovative policies, not always knowing whether they will work or not. Rather than always arguing that a program is the solution to a problem, an experimental approach would have the appropriate humility and honesty to say, "We don't really know if it will work or not, but we think it is important to try." Campbell's argument is that all policies (even well-established ones) are in essence theories (1982) about the capacity of government to alter behavior and outcomes and therefore deserve to be treated in an experimental manner rather than with any certainty.

In a similar vein Yehezkel Dror (1986; 1992) has advocated the concept of "policy gambling," in which policymakers must recognize quite explicitly that they are taking risks when they embark on any new venture.[15] Dror was speaking primarily in the context of foreign policy, but the same logic can be applied equally well for domestic policy changes. His point is that policy makers may make better decisions if they accept the uncomfortable fact that they really do not know a great deal about the context within which they make policy or even about the nature of their own policy "tools." Therefore, if they think about their policies as little more than gambles, whether against an actual adversary or simply against nature, then they will make better decisions than if they presume too much knowledge and too much control over outcomes. Thinking about policies as gambles may produce excessively conservative choices, or at least choices that have a "minimax" character, but governments also may be able to avoid massive and irreversible errors.[16]

Real-world politicians have also been willing to adopt a more experimental approach to governing. For example, President Franklin Roosevelt, when assuming office during the Great Depression, openly advocated trying a number of alternative approaches to the economic problems of the time, in the hope that at least some of them would be successful. He perhaps more than any other president believed in flexible government, creating and destroying dozens of federal organizations while he was in office.[17] More recently, former president Bill Clinton (1994) has advocated that governments of the developed economies should engage in a variety of experiments to attempt to solve the continuing problems of unemployment and underemployment. He said quite forthrightly that no government really knew the answers to these problems, so that experimentation was perhaps the only way to find out what interventions could work. Linking scholarship and practice, former secretary of labor Robert Reich (1983) has argued while in office and in academe for a progressive and experimental approach to government and especially to problems of employment policy.

The continuing devolution of authority over policy in the United States, and to some degree in other countries, can be seen as a series of policy experiments. In some instances the call for social experimentation is quite explicit. In welfare reform, for example, policy makers do not really know how to alter the behavior of clients, and some states are already embarking on a series of experiments in producing behavioral change among program beneficiaries (Lampe 1995; Katz and Nixon 1994). The use of the states as the "laboratory of democracy" has produced a number of significant policy changes in the past, including trials of programs that eventually evolved into social security at the federal level.[18] At the present time, other significant experiments at the state level are under way in providing health care to all citizens (Leichter 1992), an undertaking that so far has proved to be impossible at the federal level.

Institutionalizing some form of flexible government (another oxymoron?) makes adopting an experimental approach more palatable to political leaders. If politicians or administrators can be certain that when they initiate a program it need not be a permanent fixture on the public landscape, but can be terminated rather easily, then that experimentation is more likely to occur. The history of creating and (infrequently) destroying public organizations might lead a politician to be skeptical about the real capacity to produce rapid change in the organizational universe. Even organizations designed to be "temporary" sometimes persist for a very long time.[19] Still, writing more explicit terminations into legislation, placing limits on budgetary authorizations, and/or using sunset provisions (Opheim, Curry, and Shields 1994) can be means for creating a more flexible organizational frame, and a more flexible frame of mind, within government.

Even if the explicitly experimental approach implied by the model of flexible government is not adopted, an emphasis on flexible employment arrangements may generate some de facto experimentation. If there are a number of employees with limited training making decisions about cases and with little or no connection to the collective memory of the organization, then there will almost certainly be substantial variance in their decisions. In some ways this variance may be a positive outcome, if the differences can be monitored and if the error is primarily in a direction preferred by the organization. That is, staff members may be instructed that when in doubt they should err on the side of granting benefits to the client, or on the side of saving money for the government, or whatever. This more random pattern of decisions, however, will almost certainly lead to the need for greater hierarchical supervision. Thus, there would be some loss of autonomy by workers throughout the organization, so that managing participatively may be difficult.

Budgeting

The budget process is an important part of the policymaking process, and ideas about flexible government have some potential implications for the allocation of public funds. The concept of flexibility would help to overcome what some analyst of budgeting regard as the principal barrier to rational allocation of public funds, incrementalism (Hayes 1992). A number of attempts at budget reform such as PPBS and ZBB in the United States (Draper and Pitsvada 1981); PESC, PAR, and their successors in the United Kingdom (Thain and Wright 1992a; 1992b); envelope budgeting in Canada (Savoie 1990, 63–67); and RCB in France were justified at least in part by their capacity to reduce or eliminate commitments to existing organizations in favor of a more comprehensive evaluation of spending priorities.

Other analysts have argued that incrementalism is, in fact, a rational way of making spending decisions (Lindblom 1965; see Rubin 1997). They argue that the magnitude of contemporary public budgets is such that it is almost impossible for decision makers to consider priorities comprehensively. Therefore, the shortcuts provided by the marginal analysis in incrementalism are an aid to rational allocation of public funds. Thus, having to recast the budgetary bargain anew each year, or even having to consider thoroughly a number of program terminations and reallocations, may reduce the overall efficiency of the budget process. Still, central financial organizations are faced with the necessity of finding some sort of workable balance between permanence and flexibility, between incrementalism and synopticism, that will permit government to allocate funds efficiently without creating excessive disruption of services or imposing too heavy an analytic burden. Wildavsky (1978) has argued that the traditional budgeting system is just that sort of compromise; it does not work particularly well, but neither does it do anything poorly.

Other changes in contemporary public budgeting appear to enhance flexibility within government but with the loss of some degree of central financial control. I will discuss these budget reforms at greater length, but the shift to bulk budgeting and the ability of organizations to retain "profits" for future use deserve some mention here. As one component of the new managerialism in the public sector, government organizations are being granted the right to retain any unspent funds from one budget year to use in subsequent years. This budgetary flexibility, while making the time horizon of the public manager more like that of the private manager, reduces the control of central agencies, and hence the public, on the actions of these organizations.

THE PUBLIC INTEREST

As flexible governance is the least clearly articulated of the four alternative models, it follows that it also contains the least clearly articulated concept of the public interest. One obvious component of the implicit concept of the public interest contained in this model is that lower costs for government are beneficial for society. If using more temporary employees will reduce the costs of government, and less permanent organizations prevent wasteful expenditure on "dinosaur" programs, then the public as a whole, it is argued, could benefit through lower taxes. This is seen as true even if particular clients of government services are potentially disadvantaged by being served by less knowledgeable and committed public-sector employees. This basic premise about the public interest is not different from that of the market model, although the causes for excess cost and the logic of remedying the problem are different.

A second implicit concept of the public interest within the flexible approach is that the public will be better off with a more innovative and less ossified government. One standard complaint about government is that the organizations within it represent special interests outside the public-sector. These organizations fight for their programmatic turf on behalf of their clients and attempt to preserve themselves, whether or not there is any real justification for their continued existence.[20] The conventional wisdom presents a somewhat exaggerated interpretation of the reality (Peters and Hogwood 1988) of the permanence of government organizations, but there is still some truth in it. If change could become as much a part of existence in the public sector as is permanence, then there will be some chance of greater creativity and, perhaps again, some opportunities for saving the public money.

There is, of course, a reverse argument to be made in defense of permanent structures as an institutionalization and a representation of the public interest: the weakest interests in society have the most difficult time having their interests embodied in organizations. Thus, if the existence of organizations is regularly brought into question, then it is just those representing the most disadvantaged that are most likely to be terminated.[21] For example, amid all the organizations and programs in the federal government, the ones most commonly threatened with dissolution are those serving the poor. The Republicans' Contract with America sought to eliminate a number of programs of this sort, and even President Clinton, a Democrat, had sought to cut back or even terminate several of these programs.

Even if the organizations serving the most disadvantaged members of society are not necessarily terminated, any broad-scale attempt to create greater organizational flexibility is likely to generate uncertainty among their clients. Although some politicians assume that uncertainty is a positive incentive for both employees and clients, too much of a good thing can be extremely dysfunctional. One of the virtues of bureaucrats, as opposed to politicians, is that they can adopt a somewhat longer time perspective on policy and do not have to think about the next election. If bureaucrats must spend all their time thinking about the next budget and its effects on them, they are more likely to engage in the same short-term thinking that characterizes politicians and thus produce policies that may be suboptimal in the long term.

Another argument for the virtues of permanence, or at least against the virtues of impermanence, is that our evaluations of programs are at best inadequate, especially in the short term. Therefore, any attempt to make judgments about programs and to terminate those that are "unsuccessful" may terminate the wrong programs for the wrong reasons. The evaluation literature is filled with examples of programs with "sleeper effects" (Salamon 1979; Rossi and Freeman 1989, 350–71). The benefits of these programs did not become apparent until after they already had been terminated.[22] The loss resulting from too rapid termination was not only what had been invested in the program but also the potential benefits that might have been generated. Providing programs ample time to prove their worth, therefore, appears to be a logical strategy although analysts do not yet have any agreed-upon means of deciding just how much time is "ample."

Another implication of flexible government for the public interest is that although in general policy coherence is a good thing, it is difficult, however, to determine a priori just which substantive dimensions of coordination and coherence will be most important at any particular time. For example, at one time an economics ministry may require extensive coordination with social service (unemployment, education) organizations in government while at another time foreign trade issues make the foreign ministry crucial. At still other times agriculture and forestry may be the most important concerns for coordination. Therefore, any formalized structure designed for coordination may solve an immediate problem but may actually misdirect policy makers' attention when the next issue arises and hamper solving that issue. The obvious answer is flexibility, but achieving that in a world of government more accustomed to permanent organizations is difficult.

Given this fluidity of external influences on policies, therefore, the public interest is best served not only by the individual service-delivery organizations being more flexible but also by having a control superstructure on top of them that can create some predictability of outcomes. That superstructure usually will be in the form of central agencies that are now under pressure themselves to become more supple and agile in meeting changing external demands and tensions. The problem here is that central agencies tend to be the least reformed parts of the public sector and probably are also the most resistant to change of any sort (Savoie 1995b). Those central agencies may persist in implementing the coordinative structures and ideas that have served them well in the past, despite the vast changes that have since occurred within the public-sector.

The concept of flexibility tends to bring into question the fundamental point that governing is often about absolute rights rather than about more flexible programs and policies. Although efficiency is important, the protection of the basic rights of citizens is even more so for a functioning democracy. Flexibility and the defense of rights may well be incompatible, even when those rights are economic and programmatic, e.g., entitlements to social benefits. Designers of policy and administrative regimens must be careful to match those systems with the policies being administered and the clients being served.

SUMMARY

The old stereotype of government organizations as permanent and inflexible is not totally true, but it is certainly not totally false, either. There is no market to force government organizations out of business or to assist them in midcourse corrections that might enable them to make their programs more effective. Therefore, some critics of the existing arrangements in government have argued that the presumption of permanence should be shifted to a presumption of impermanence. The danger in some of this discussion appears to be that, as with so many reforms, there is the hazard of creating excessive impermanence as the cure for excessive permanence. The real answer is to find the appropriate balance between the ability to force organizations out of business and the ability to sustain them. Identifying and then achieving that balance of stability and movement is difficult in any set of organizations, however, and not least among those in the public sector.

The dangers of impermanence appear more pronounced for employees than they do for organizations. One would argue that almost any organizational framework, peopled by individuals with a strong commitment to the public service and to achieving policy goals, might work effectively. Yet even the best structural arrangement inhabited by employees with little or no commitment to public service would find it extremely hard to perform its tasks efficiently and "in the public interest." It is difficult to expect that individuals who have only minimal commitment to public-service values can perform their jobs in the public's interest, even if using temporaries does save some money. We must be cognizant of important values that transcend simple economic efficiency when we begin to manipulate public-sector organizations and the individuals working within them.

Although the actual programs motivated by each set of ideas may be placed into effect at the same time, this model of reform and the participation model appear fundamentally at odds with each other. This is especially true for their treatment of personnel management. The participation model requires strong commitment from public employees, and perhaps even from clients, but the flexible government approach appears to treat employees rather shabbily. Flexible government assumes (much like many significantly older conceptions of management) that employees are almost interchangeable cogs in the vast machine of government and that they can be replaced almost at will. Similarly, the flexible approach assumes that organizational values and the civil service ethos are of little importance and indeed may be an impediment to good government rather than a potential source of it.

This model, however, appears compatible with the market model, as does the participation model with deregulation. Therefore, as with so many other issues encountered in administrative reform, there is a fundamental trade-off of values implied here. The flexibility and responsiveness of this approach to governance can be bought at the price of substantially less organizational memory and less commitment from employees. The selection of one set of values over the other may then become a contingency question: under what circumstances should the clever manager or political leader opt for one or the other of these approaches (or for the other two) as the principal guide to reform? Most of the discussion of reform in government and even in the academic literature has tended toward the simple "one size fits all" approach to change, but that is almost certainly an oversimplification of the complex dynamics of the public sector and the efforts to make it work better.

5
Deregulated Government

The final option for reforming government has been to unleash the potential power and creativity lying within the public sector by "deregulating government" (Wilson 1989; Barzelay 1992; DiIulio 1994). This term (like others we have discussed) has been used in several different contexts and with several different meanings. In this context deregulation is not concerned with economic policy but with the internal management of government itself. Thus deregulating government could be seen as almost the complete antithesis of the politics of the 1980s, which attempted to reduce the activity of government and severely control those actions that remained. The politicians of the 1980s appeared to have a special dislike and distrust of the public bureaucracy and sought to curtail its powers over public policy.

IDEAS MOTIVATING DEREGULATION

The fundamental assumption of the move toward deregulating government has been that if some constraints on bureaucratic action are eliminated, government could perform its functions more efficiently. As the National Performance Review reported, the problem is not the people in government, the problem is the system, meaning chiefly the rules and regulations that inhibited swift and effective action. In addition, government *might* even be able to undertake new and creative activities to improve the collective welfare of the society if some of its shackles were removed.

This perspective on reform through deregulating the public sector was expressed well by Constance Horner (1994, 87): "Deregulation of the public sector is as important as deregulation of the private sector, and for precisely the same reason: to liberate workers' entrepreneurial energies. We need a lean, resolute civil service able to decide and to act, rather than wait and see." It should be remembered that Horner was a high-ranking official in the Reagan administration and might not have been expected to be advocating such an apparently activist position for government. However, the implications of the deregulatory approach clearly can be to unleash the energies contained within the public sector and to produce higher levels of government activity. Yet presumably, with the removal of the constraints of internal red tape, that activity would be more creative, more effective, and more efficient. Further, conservatives sometimes assume that any activity created through deregulation will be in the direction of doing things they will approve rather than in making social and regulatory programs more generous for the poor and more restrictive on industry.

Deregulating government may simply be another version of the market model and its managerialism, however. In the marketized version of deregulation, the principal purpose of removing the internal controls is to advance the power of public managers to manage. So long as managers are constrained by the public-sector apparatus of personnel rules, budgeting rules, purchasing rules, and the like the true possibilities for enhanced efficiency through managerialism can never be achieved. Therefore the deregulation and market models can be seen as complementary approaches to reforming government. In particular, removing internal constraints over personnel management, purchasing, and similar functions will enable public-sector managers to act much like their private-sector counterparts, presumably making the public sector more efficient.

Further, the deregulatory version of reform contains a number of the elements of the participatory model within it. Just as the latter argued in favor of involving workers more completely in making the decisions for their public-sector organizations, advocates of the former believe that exercising individual discretion is superior to rules and regulations for producing effective public action. As James Q. Wilson, one of the intellectual fathers of the deregulatory approach, has written (1989, 369): "Most people do not like to work in environments in which every action is second-guessed, every initiative is viewed with suspicion and every controversial decision is denounced as malfeasance." The difference from the participatory model is that advocates of deregulation consider this style of reform to be linked almost entirely to enhancing efficiency rather than to values such as self-actualization and participation itself.

In these three conceptions of and justifications for deregulation the enemy under attack is essentially the same: a public sector that has become increasingly bureaucratized (in the pejorative sense) and constrained by its own rules and its own red tape.[1] The argument of the deregulation advocates is that the internal regulation of government prevents it from achieving its purposes as efficiently or as effectively as it might. Because of the distrust that politicians often have of the public bureaucracy and also because of the even greater distrust that the politicians' constituents have of it, control after control has been piled on public-sector managers. As a natural consequence of those controls, the managers believe they do not have sufficient latitude to do their jobs as effectively as they could.

In most instances it is not the bureaucracy itself that is the root of excessive internal regulation. Rather, it is the perceptions of the bureaucracy and its dysfunctions held by the public and by their elected representatives that appear to be the source of this managerial problem. Members of the bureaucracy themselves are often as frustrated by the internal regulations imposed on them as are its clients. These administrators rarely have been capable, however, of convincing their political masters that the controls being imposed on them are actually counterproductive. On the contrary, imposing additional rules and controls on the bureaucracy is rarely bad electoral politics, while any politician who becomes too cozy with the civil service becomes suspect in the contemporary antigovernment political climate. For example, the 2000 presidential race in the United States appeared to require bureaucracy-bashing even by Al Gore, who had been a central political figure in some initial deregulation (Wolfe 2000).

The rule-bound nature of public administration slows action and reduces flexibility in a number of areas. Before initial deregulation, the civil service system itself had become a labyrinth of rules designed to protect public employees from abuse, to ensure more equitable hiring, and to prevent patronage and political exploitation of government positions. Other rules, such as Veterans' Preference in the United States, may prevent government from hiring the best candidates in favor of achieving other goals and serving other constituencies (GAO 1995). In the midst of achieving those laudable, if ancillary, goals, civil service rules were also supposed to be able to fulfill their principal purpose: to assist managers to hire, reward, promote, and terminate employees. Many public managers find the rules anything but helpful, and experiments with alternative methods of management appear to produce better outcomes (Feller et al. 1995).

The rules surrounding procurement and purchasing developed during the post–World War II era were even more restrictive than the personnel rules, requiring elaborate bidding procedures for even small purchases and preventing government from making purchases in ways that ultimately would have saved public money.[2] A history of corruption and preferential contracting may have justified those purchasing rules initially, but they appeared to have long outlived their usefulness. Budgeting rules also imposed restrictions on agencies, for example requiring them to return money to the general fund if it was not spent at the end of the budget year, a rule designed to save money. These budget rules, it can be argued, also tended to *cost* the public money in the long run by promoting unwise spending and limiting the initiative of public managers.[3] Further, constraints on use of budgeted funds tended to restrict the capacity of managers to make the most efficient use of the money available to them.

There are cross-national differences in the extent to which rule-bound bureaucracy appears to present problems for people in government. This complaint has been most prevalent in the Anglo-American countries, and perhaps for good reason (but see Reichard 1994; Gibert and Thoenig 1992). In part because of the comparatively low regard in which citizens in these countries have tended to hold their public services (Goodsell 1995, 49–75; Peters 2001), there has been a tendency for legislatures and central agencies in the Anglo-American countries to heap rule on top of regulation in order to control the public sector. The legislature has been a particular problem for public administration in the United States. Congressional "micro-management" (Gilmour and Halley 1994; Wilson 1994b) of individual programs, as well as of the public sector as a whole, has limited the flexibility and adaptability of federal programs, with the blame then being placed at the feet of the bureaucracy.

Countries operating within the Germanic and Napoleonic traditions (Loughlin and Peters 1995), however, tend to be burdened by much less specific sets of rules controlling actions in public organizations; general statutes seem to be sufficient in those legalistic regimes. Further, the public tends to evaluate their public services more positively in continental systems than they do in the Anglo-American world.[4] As a consequence, the rules that have been imposed on the continental governments appear to constitute much less of a burden and to produce less inefficiency than in the Anglo-American countries.[5] Therefore, the major action in deregulating has been in the United States and other Anglo-American countries, although some of the ideas have spread to others, including Scandinavian countries, which usually are less hostile to state involvement in society (Olsen 1991).

Although there is still a great deal of ongoing advocacy of the deregulatory approach to changing government, a substantial amount of movement in that direction has already occurred. In some cases, as with the Glassco Commission in Canada, advocacy of deregulation began decades ago (Canada 1962). More recently, for example, in the United States, the federal Office of Personnel Management (OPM), with great fanfare, has thrown out the ten thousand–plus pages of personnel regulations that had been amassed over the decades. OPM is now attempting to operate a highly decentralized and flexible personnel system in place of the more rule-driven system and to devolve a good deal of personnel policy to individual agencies (Feller et al. 1995). Most other industrialized countries also have been in the process of deregulating their personnel systems, with individual contracts rather than standardized pay and grading systems becoming the most common approach to personnel issues.

A number of countries have discarded many of their purchasing rules and are permitting departments to purchase most materials and services on their own, albeit subject to auditing and other scrutinies after the fact (Kelman 1994; Haves 1993). Budgeting has become much more deregulated, with central finance agencies in Australia, New Zealand, Finland, and Sweden now willing to grant departments "bulk budgets" or "frame budgets" as well as the latitude to decide how to use money within broad categories. The managers are held closely accountable for their actions but do have the freedom to act and to spend money in what they consider to be the most efficient and effective manner (Schick 1988). These changes provide managers a great deal of room for action but raise a number of important questions about accountability.

Perhaps predictably, many government organizations have found the newly deregulated world somewhat threatening. Internal regulations and procedures clearly provided some certainty and predictability of action for both employees and clients. The individual civil servant did not have to take too much personal responsibility but could depend on hierarchy, rules, and regulations for guidance. Avoidance of responsibility is the stereotypical behavior pattern of public employees and could easily become pathological and self-protective (Crozier 1964). Therefore, it is also not surprising that some organizations have sought to reestablish the old, comfortable regime. Thus, for example, soon after the Office of Personnel Management had abolished its old personnel rules, many agencies within the federal government adopted the same set of rules as their own. Undoubtedly, as new needs and issues arise, these agencies will each add to their own stock of personnel rules and will do so in different ways, with the consequence that the federal government may in effect become even more negatively influenced by rules than before deregulation simply because there is no common and understood set of rules that can guide actions across the service.

In the United Kingdom there appears to be some incompatibility emerging between the dominant market-based approach to reform and attempts at deregulation of the public sector. For example, although the Treasury has been arguing that it is decentralizing and deregulating itself, many aspects of its financial management and government purchasing seem to have become even more rule-bound (HMSO 1995; Hood et al. 1999). This expansion of regulation is being carried out with the good intention of saving public money. The purpose of deregulating is also to save money and to permit government to move more quickly, and even creatively, in procuring goods and services. The United Kingdom experience, however, seems to be the paradoxical case of deregulatory intent being accomplished through highly regulatory mechanisms.[6]

Levels of Government

Central governments have had some success at deregulating themselves, but the performance of subnational governments in ridding themselves of excessive rules has been even more impressive (Light 1994). Much of the now famous Osborne and Gaebler book (1992) on reinvention can be seen as descriptions of state and local governments in the United States deregulating themselves, albeit discussed under the rubric of reinvention. Despite the reforms that already have been undertaken at the subnational level, there is advocacy for even greater deregulation. For example, the Winter Commission (Ehrenhalt 1993) proposed significant deregulation of state governments, including changes in personnel, purchasing, and budgeting rules.

As well as deregulation of the internal management in state and local governments, the U.S. intergovernmental system has become increasingly deregulated. One of the few components of the Republican Contract with America that
could be passed during the first year of the Gingrich-controlled House of Representatives was a call for an end to unfunded mandates from the federal government. That is, many federal laws had required state and local governments to do
certain things, e.g., comply with clean drinking-water standards, but had not provided them the money to meet those standards (Posner 1998). These mandates
imposed substantial costs on subnational governments but are now being
reduced, if not eliminated. Further, first through the waiver process and then
through welfare-reform legislation, the federal government is permitting the
states to experiment more with social policy (Pear 1995).

Although less fabled in print, local governments in many other countries,
e.g., Canada, have been engaging in the same processes of change, reinvention,
and deregulation (Borins 1995a). For example, although the unitary governments
of Scandinavia have always permitted a good deal of autonomy for their local
governments (communes), the "free commune" experiments of the 1980s and
1990s are allowing them much greater local freedom in making policy and in
implementing national policies (Baldersheim 1993; Stromberg 1990). At the
other end of the spectrum of local-government autonomy historically, France
now is providing much greater latitude for its local governments (Loughlin and
Mazey 1995).

One interesting case of lack of movement toward more deregulated management for local government is the United Kingdom, where local authorities
remain under tight central control, despite the major administrative reforms
occurring in much of the rest of British government (Elcock 1994). If anything,
central-government controls, especially financial controls, were tightened during
the fifteen years of Conservative rule (Rhodes 1992) and may be tightening even
further under New Labour. Certainly there have been some managerial changes
in local government (*Public Money and Management* 1994), but not to the extent
that might have been expected, given the pace of change elsewhere within the
British public sector. Further, much of the managerialist change that has occurred
in local government has been imposed through that central control instead of
being adopted from below. In this one case, therefore, deregulation has come
about through intergovernmental regulation.

The observed differences among levels of government are predictable. It is
in most instances substantially easier for local governments to deregulate themselves than it is for central governments to eliminate the procedures that structure their activities. Local governments are generally of a more manageable size
than any central government so that managerial control can be exercised without
the need for impersonal rules. Further, the tasks that local governments perform
(streets, sanitation, and so on) tend to be more readily measurable than do the
tasks performed by central governments; thus, exercising managerial control

should be easier. A danger arises, in fact, in assuming that the experience of lower-level governments is readily transferable to central governments (Savoie 1995a). Even within the same country, the differences in tasks and managerial styles among levels of government may make the transfer of ideas difficult so that the enthusiasm with which Washington greeted the Sunningdale experience may have been misplaced.

Deregulation and Error

A final general point to be made about deregulation of the public sector is that if this model is selected by governments, then a certain amount of error will have to be accepted. Part of the logic of deregulation in the public sector is to make public servants become risk takers to an extent not previously seen in government. Human beings, even when highly motivated, ethical, and highly skilled, will make mistakes, and some of them will be embarrassing for government. The likelihood that any mistakes made will be exposed to public view is now greater than ever before, given the increased activity of the media, the increased openness of most governments, and apparent public glee whenever any failures in the public sector are brought to their attention. Errors are almost inevitable in any administrative system, especially ones as large and complex as those of contemporary governments; the question is, what should administrative and political leaders do when those errors occur?

One natural reaction for politicians faced with obvious and publicized errors in their departments is to retreat from the brave new world of deregulation and attempt to reassert the ex ante controls. This reaction may be especially common in Westminster systems, with their traditional conceptions of ministerial accountability, even if those concepts now appear to be honored more in the breach than in the observance (Sutherland 1991; Marshall 1989). This political reaction to error reflects, to some degree, the history of the huge collection of internal regulations that existed prior to attempts at deregulation, and it would be easy to see a circular process of deregulation followed by reregulation emerging (see Müller and Wright 1994; Hood et al. 1999). Though it is difficult for politicians to deny the demands of their constituents for greater ex ante controls over bureaucracies, political leaders will have to exert some real leadership to maintain the gains (if the leaders conceptualize deregulation as that) that have been achieved.

Another point concerns policy design (Linder and Peters 1995; Ingram and Schneider 1991). Policies may have to be designed to minimize certain types of error while permitting other types more readily. For example, given the current political climate in many countries, it may be more palatable to design programs in which the a priori decision is to deny social welfare benefits to applicants rather than to grant them. Though this strategy may well be morally repugnant to many people, the political fallout will probably be less than that from designing programs in which there are numerous examples of ineligible applicants receiving benefits.[7] Other types of programs such as veterans' benefits, albeit similar in many ways, may best be designed with the opposite assumptions about desirable errors, given that their potential clients enjoy a higher status in society. Careful initial design of programs may make it possible to maintain internal deregulation even in the face of relatively high rates of errors in judgment by the public bureaucracy in making decisions about individual eligibility.

EVALUATING THE MODEL

As with the other three models of governing, we will look at the implications of the deregulated models for four aspects of life within the public sector. As this is the last of the models to be surveyed, I will be making a number of references to the way in which this model corresponds, or does not correspond, with the other three. One of the major points of this book is that the numerous strands of reform being implemented currently do not constitute a coherent model of governing but four potentially contradictory and mutually negating views. Further, there are internal contradictions even within this one view of reform (as with participation) that should be discussed, given that the same terms may be used to advocate very different types of change within government.

Structure

The structural implications of the deregulation model are rather sparse. Although its advocates would not say so directly, structures appear to be much less important in their thinking than are the rules and procedures used to control public organizations and the people within them. It may also be that in their concerns about the ability of governments to act effectively, traditional hierarchical structure is less an anathema than in other, more "modern" conceptions of organizations. The premise that bureaucratic structures are almost inherently undesirable has become virtually the conventional wisdom in public organizations, but proponents of the deregulation model argue that they are indeed acceptable, and even desirable, in certain situations.

Hierarchy is more important, and a more positive value, in the deregulatory model than in the other models for several reasons. First, most other mechanisms for internal control of personnel will have been removed through deregulating. Second, part of the reason for deregulating (like some aspects of the market model) is to unleash the creative energies of managers. If that is to be the case, then those managers need to be able to produce concerted action within their organizations, and hierarchy would be the most practical way to do so. Therefore, unlike the participatory model, which seeks to gain action through involving the lower orders within organizations, this approach tends to place somewhat greater emphasis on the role of leadership.

Another possible structural implication of this model is that the control agencies developed by political leaders at the center of government are less desirable than they generally have assumed. The administrative history of many countries, perhaps especially the Anglo-American democracies, can be written in terms of changes in central agencies and their relationships to line departments (Heclo and Wildavsky 1974; Campbell and Szablowski 1979; Savoie 1995b, 1999). Governments have invested a great deal of effort attempting to develop ways for central agencies to control spending, personnel, and purchasing, presuming that centralizing these decisions would produce more efficient government, eliminate redundancy, and prevent waste. Advocates of deregulation, however, tend to argue that the controls created waste instead of minimizing it, if for no other reason than that they require a large staff to manage them.

In the deregulated model, de-emphasizing centralized control structures would permit the individual organizations to develop and implement more of their own goals than would be true when central agencies (Campbell and Szablowski 1979) exert more control. Despite frequent protestations to the contrary, central agencies do exercise substantive policy control as well as simply managerial oversight. This is true even in the devices that they may propose to use when deregulating their relationships with line departments. For example, an emphasis on mechanisms requiring quantification of outputs by departments advantages programs with clear and unambiguous indicators[8] while disadvantaging programs with "softer" outcomes.

A highly regulatory system from central agencies should be able to fulfill one of the goals of managerialism by letting the political leaders have enhanced control over policy. Domination by central agencies, however, obviously tends to lessen the capacity of managers to manage and thus weakens one of the other managerialist goals. Internal regulations by central agencies can be used for a variety of purposes, with their actual impact being determined by the intentions of the "superbureaucrats" in charge of exercising the control and the direction provided to them by their political masters.

The continuing reforms of the British Treasury represent one major attempt to deregulate a major central agency and to change its habits of imposing control on other organizations. The White Paper on the Treasury, "Continuity and Change" (HMSO 1994a), seeks to initiate a new era of deregulated management within government. Although some of the initial changes have been structural (e.g., delayering at the top of the organization), there is also a need seen for changing the culture of control that exists within the Treasury (Norman 1994). Indeed, it is argued that the changes appearing in the White Paper represent only the beginning of the process of making the Treasury into a more user-friendly organization. The long decades of Treasury power over the details of personnel and expenditure may make that image a difficult one for many civil servants to accept.

Although a number of changes have been imposed on the Treasury during the past decade, it has also maintained its central control position and indeed may have strengthened it after Labour returned to power. Central agencies have, in general, if not withered away, become less central under deregulation, and other organizations will have to become more central to governing. If we assume the desirability of maintaining responsible democratic regimes, then there must be some means of holding organizations accountable. Central agencies to some degree have done this by imposing their vision—and presumably that of the political leaders of the system—on policies *before* they are implemented or even while they are being formulated. This practice is less permissible in a deregulated government, and therefore evaluation and controls *after* the policy is put into effect become the crucial means of enforcing accountability. Thus, if governments are able to pare down their central control agencies, they must in turn beef up their central evaluation agencies.

This shift also implies that the central evaluation agencies will have to continue in the direction that they have already begun to go, i.e., becoming increasingly policy analytic rather than being merely accountancy organizations (Rist 1990; Gray, Jenkins, and Segsworth 1993). Further, this trend will tend to place pursuit of the deregulated model more directly at odds with the market model, at least as it has been practiced. One ironic feature of many of the administrative reforms that have been implemented over the past several decades is that with all the talk of efficiency and effectiveness there has been some tendency to dismantle the analytic capacities of government (Aberbach and Rockman 1989). For example, the Government Performance and Results Act in the United States (passed in 1992) stresses results but does so with inadequate resources and methods to measure those resources (Kimm 1995). There is little institutionalized way of knowing whether government is indeed now more efficient than in the past or not.

Many of the market reformers have assumed that they were correct in their general interpretations of the problems and the solutions for what ailed government and implemented their reforms with little or no formalized means for evaluating them. Further, to the extent that evaluation "shops" remained open in government, they were at the center rather than in the agencies (Aberbach and Rockman 1989; but see Mayne 1994), in part because the market reformers did not trust the results they might get from agency-level evaluators who obviously would have had a vested interest in the outcomes.[9] Thus, if deregulation is to be successful, it will have to re-create the analytic capacity that has been lost. This will to some extent be true for central agencies such as the General Accounting Office or the National Audit Office and for decentralized evaluation activities.

The further structural implications of the deregulatory model are not too dissimilar from those derived from the market model. If bureaucratic organizations are not really that bad in the context of a deregulated model, then the active, entrepreneurial agencies being developed as a result of the market model, e.g., "Next Steps" in Britain, might be even better. Not only would internal controls over "proper management" be weakened or eliminated, but the exposure to more real or potential competition might create even more effective deregulated organizations. The fundamental point is to encourage government organizations and their managers to use all available skills and energy to achieve their goals.

Unlike the participatory model, however, the deregulatory model appears to be much more compatible with hierarchy, or at least with strong leadership from the center in organizations. That being the case, the control that is exercised through hierarchy will mean that flatter organizations with middle-management levels removed may not be particularly congenial to deregulation. The organization may operate in a more fluid environment, but the individual employees may remain under control from above. Further, the logic within this approach appears to be that of deregulating managerial activities in the pursuit of predetermined goals, rather than of encouraging employee participation in setting those goals. Thus, although individual civil servants may be freer to perform their tasks, they may not have any more real control over the policies they administer than they would have had within the conventional models of administration.

Management

The managerial implications of the deregulation model could go in two quite opposite directions, largely because management does not appear to be one of its central concerns. In one approach, deregulation maintains that traditional forms · of structure and management may not be as bad as some contemporary critics argue. This being the case, it tends to find hierarchical management acceptable and even desirable. This style permits policy entrepreneurs who presumably are in positions at the top of the hierarchies to generate action throughout the organization. This practice, in turn, would depend to some degree on a common culture within the organization that supports the policy direction advocated from above.

Deregulated government will place a heavy burden on managerial leadership within public organizations to reach its goals. This leadership is not, however, the simple managerialism advocated in the market model (Behn 1991). Under this conception of the public sector, public managers must be not only the entrepreneurs required in the market model, but they also must have some elements of the democratic leaders visualized in the participatory model. Further, they must be able to be moral leaders and create a climate of honesty, commitment to the public service, and accountability within their organizations if so many of the ex ante controls are to be removed successfully. This is a large set of responsibilities for these leaders, especially given the lack of respect from the public, and even from politicians, with which they are commonly confronted in the very societies that are stressing deregulation.

The alternative managerial implication would be for a pattern similar to that advocated in the participatory model. If the creative powers of government are indeed to be unleashed, then that goal may be reached most easily by involving all levels of the organizations, not just senior managers. Indeed, the constraints of rules and regulations within government have been more stifling for lower-level employees than for the more senior positions. If those rules are eliminated and their jobs can be done in a less constrained manner, the employees should generate a burst of energy and commitment, or so the argument goes.

Thus, if government wants to be effective and creative it will require the commitment of all its available resources, and most important, of its employees. This logic is much in line with that of the participatory model and is in sharp contrast to the flexible model, which does not assign any real importance to involving public employees in the performance of their agency. As with the participatory model, the assumption in the deregulatory approach is that individual public employees do want to do their jobs as well as possible. Further, it is assumed that if employees are allowed greater freedom, they will use it for the benefit of the organization and its clients.

Generally, the deregulatory approach is quite compatible with the market approach, but in some important managerial issues they appear to clash. As managerialism has come to be practiced in many governments, it has begun to impose more procedures and internal management practices rather than fewer, all in the name of good management. For example, in the United Kingdom attempts to improve the internal management practices of the National Health Service have produced claims, at least in Labour Party campaign materials, that service providers have been replaced with accountants. Similarly, imposing resource accounting (HMSO 1994b) across the public sector may require a huge amount · of accounting work and internal controls, all in the name of improving management and enhancing performance (Kemp 1994). The merging of procedures and controls, based on output (results) rather than input (budgets), actually may structure behavior more directly than did the old ex ante regulations, given that individual careers become more contingent on adequate performance on the new performance indicators.

Management and managerial tools in government have become something of a "cargo cult" for reformers (Hood 1991; Pollitt 1990). Their prevailing assumption appears to be that the simple copying of devices that are used in the private sector will almost certainly make the public sector more efficient. The deregulators, however, might see many of the same barriers to action in the private sector as they identify in the public. Further, mechanisms such as resource accounting may make sense in the private sector, because of more clearly identifiable costs and revenues, than they would in the public sector. The deregulators, therefore, would argue that imposing different rules, especially where inappropriate, is really no better than keeping the old rules.[10]

Furthermore, the deregulatory reforms can succeed only within the context of a dominant civil service ethos. The values of the civil service—providing faithful service to any political master, fiscal probity, fairness, and so forth—are just the values that would make a system with fewer ex ante controls on civil servants a viable alternative to the status quo. The new public management, on the other hand, tends to denigrate this culture and to laud (implicitly and sometimes explicitly) people who have rejected this value system and who are more committed to an individual, entrepreneurial one. It may therefore be self-defeating, or dangerous, to attempt to implement some of these ideas simultaneously.

Policymaking

The implications for policymaking are somewhat clearer than the other implications of the deregulatory model. Indeed, this model is primarily concerned with the procedures by which decisions are made and laws implemented. In the traditional view of policymaking in government, to some extent reinforced by the "new managerialism," it was the prerogative of political leaders (Wright and Peters 1996). The deregulatory model would appear to assign a somewhat stronger role to the bureaucracy in making policy. The logic is that these organizations tend to be major repositories of ideas and expertise and hence should be allowed to make more decisions. To the extent that this also implies that the lower echelons of the organization, because of their expertise and close contacts with the environment, should have somewhat more influence, this model has implications similar to those of the participatory model.

This characterization of the deregulation model should not be taken to mean that it argues that policymaking powers should be entirely abrogated by political institutions in favor of the public bureaucracy. Rather, it is intended to mean that policymaking is likely to be better on substantive grounds—if not in terms of democratic theory—if there is an active role permitted for the bureaucracy. The positive role of the civil service may be especially evident for developing societies in which a large proportion of the available expertise is located in the public bureaucracy (Peters 1995a). The broad policy criteria it uses to guide decisions must be made to serve the goals of political leaders, but successful policies are unlikely to be adopted without an active role for career public servants.

Budgeting. One of the important dimensions of deregulation of government has been budgeting and the allocation of public money. Most efforts at budgetary reform in Western democracies have been attempts to balance competing values of "rationality" and political control over expenditures (Savoie 1990). Reforms such as program-budgeting (PPBS in the United States and RCB in France),[11] the Public Expenditure Survey (PESC) in the United Kingdom, and "reconsideration" in the Netherlands (Van Nispen 1994) tended to place a larger burden on analysis and less on raw political power to guide the spending decisions governments make. Although analytical in character, these efforts were implemented, however, in the context of a top-down regulatory style in which the central financial organization—Treasury, Treasury Board, Office of Management and Budget, or whoever—would make the final determinations about how much to spend and how best to use the money available.

Indeed, most of the budgetary reforms undertaken in the 1970s and 1980s tended to diminish the discretion available to agency officials in determining their own budgets. Even under the more analytic schemes used earlier, the agency could negotiate on the basis of the outcomes of policy analysis, but the decisions were still taken at the top. Other mechanisms such as cash limits in the United Kingdom (Thain and Wright 1992a; 1992b), Gramm-Rudman-Hollings and the Budget Enforcement Act in the United States (Kettl 1992), the "main alternative" in Sweden (Ericksson 1983), and even the envelope budgeting system in Canada tended to diminish the capacity of managers to make financial decisions on their own. The common strategy was to replace judgment with formulas (Hanuschek 1987) and to use them to drive down public spending.

The rather crude first round of reform under the market-oriented, antistate approach is now being replaced with a more deregulated style of financial management. The basic idea of the more contemporary approaches has been to permit managers to make decisions, albeit still within relatively firm overall program parameters. Further, by going toward multiyear budgeting and capital budgeting, the emerging financial system permits a manager to make longer-term decisions than would be possible under traditional budgetary systems. These long-term decisions may themselves become a form of internal control, however, as spending commitments made in one year constrain flexibility in subsequent years.

Coordination. I have discussed the impact of several of the other models of administrative change on coordination, and there appear to be some potential effects for this approach as well. Coordination seems to be an increasingly significant factor in policymaking for industrialized democracies. The increased impacts of the external socioeconomic environment and the need to generate better coordinated responses to an international political economy that is itself often incoherent in the pressures it places on domestic policymaking (Savoie 1995a) demand more consistent government responses. Further, political demands for cost-containment and efficiency mean that redundancy and overlap are even less permissible than they have been in traditional public administration.

As with the market approach, the deregulatory approach to reforming government apparently makes coordination and policy coherence more problematic. Deregulation may make policy within each organization more coherent and integrated, given that presumably greater authority will be granted to policy entrepreneurs and managers to shape those policies and to implement them throughout the organization. The problem is that this internal coherence may well exacerbate the tendency of individual organizations to work in isolation from one another and to pursue their own goals and organizational self-interest at the expense of the greater collective good. Managers would have little or nothing to gain in a deregulated environment by investing money and effort in pursuing goals that did not directly benefit their organization.

From the perspective of coordination, the worst of all possible worlds may be the simultaneous acceptance of the structural ideas of the market model and the

policymaking ideas of the deregulated model. Market reformers have been tend-
ing to break government down into a large number of smaller organizations, each
with a single purpose or a limited range of purposes, e.g., Next Steps in the United
Kingdom. The market model tends to assume some entrepreneurial freedom for
these organizations, albeit acting within the context of signals sent from the marketplace to guide policymaking. The evaluative standards in the deregulated
model are less clear, although there certainly is an idea of ex post performance
evaluation. If the leaders of the decentralized organizations are granted substantial latitude, weak evaluation mechanisms, and few ex ante controls, there may be
severe problems in making government work as an integrated set of organizations.

The Public Interest

The deregulatory model by its very nature would substitute alternative forms of
control for the rules and regulations that are usually employed as the means for
producing accountability in the public sector. These differences are related to the
distinction that William Gormley (1989) refers to as "muscles and prayers." He
has pointed out that most mechanisms for enforcing accountability depend on
"muscles," or direct controls. He instead argues on behalf of catalytic controls
that would encourage members of the public sector—elective or nonelective—to
act in ways that would enhance public accountability. Although written well
before the bulk of the deregulatory literature was conceived, Gormley's argument clearly points to means for having an accountable public sector without
excessive ex ante controls. Although that approach is appealing, it may be difficult for governments to overcome the temptation to use their "muscles" when
confronted with apparent malfeasance.

The Civil Service. The deregulatory model appears to assume that the public
interest can be served through a more activist, and a perhaps less accountable,
government. The latter characterization is perhaps unfortunate, given that there
are more differences about the best forms of accountability than there is agreement about the need for some form of that important component of democratic
governance (Day and Klein 1987). The assumption of most attempts to control
government through structural and procedural devices is that without them the
public bureaucracy will either behave abusively toward the public, or (somewhat
contradictorily) will do almost nothing. The participatory model, on the one
hand, places an increased emphasis on the role of the public and public participation as the best means of controlling the public sector, with grievance procedures being crucial to the success of this form of governance.

   The deregulatory model, on the other hand, assumes that the civil service is
composed largely of dedicated and talented individuals who want to do as well
as possible in serving the public. The view here is if the putative controllers will
get out of the way, albeit with a number of ex post controls still in place, then the

system will probably function fairly well. This debate between participation and deregulation is, in many ways, simply a restatement of the familiar Friedrich/Finer debate over accountability (Gruber 1987). It is a debate over whether formal rules are really capable of preventing the dishonest civil servant from engaging in corrupt activities or the inept civil servant from making mistakes. Are not the only real defenses against those problems more ethical and more competent public employees rather than formal barriers?

The most important difference here is between ex ante and ex post controls over the public service. The traditional regulated public sector depended heavily on ex ante controls, although there certainly were a number of ex post controls, e.g., auditing, in place as well. Personnel, purchasing, and other sets of rules were designed to stop public employees from doing something illegal or unethical and to provide a basis for punishment if the rules were violated. The problem was that following these rules almost became an end in itself rather than the means to other, more purposive ends.[12] Further, the detection of any loopholes or ambiguities in the rules as employees attempted to make the organizations function tended to be met with the imposition of even more rules, and with them greater rigidity.

To the extent that the current spate of reforms in the public sector is concerned with evaluation and control of program performance, the mechanisms imposed are almost entirely ex post. Indeed, there have been substantial growth and development of central monitoring organizations in most industrialized democracies. For example, organizations such as the Auditor and Comptroller General in the United Kingdom, the Auditor General in Canada, Riksrevisionsverket in Sweden, and similar bodies in other countries have expanded their activities to include more extensive efficiency and effectiveness in auditing (Power 1994). In the United States, the Inspectors General are charged with monitoring internal conduct and exposing administrative malfeasance (Light 1993) and have added another avenue of redress for clients and employees.

These auditing and oversight organizations can be described under the general term of counterbureaucracies (Gormley 1993). They are organizations designed to control other organizations, ranging from central agencies responsible for overseeing public finance to monitoring administrative performance. In each case, counterbureaucracies represent another form of control over bureaucracy, although most tend to be ex post. The democratic pressures associated with enhanced participation, however, do tend to press for some enhanced ex ante controls in areas such as economic regulations and public spending.

We find once more a fundamental contradiction between several approaches to reform. Many of the efforts at imposing market reforms appear to require greater monitoring of programs, employees, and their behavior. This tendency is seen most clearly with the monitoring of the economic and social regulations issued by public organizations. The market model requires that these regulations meet market standards, e.g., that they create more economic benefits than costs for the society. This is obviously a great deal of ex ante regulation over the actions of bureaucracy. Although both approaches talk about efficiency, their conceptions of that idea are different in this context.

The greater dependence on ex post controls over the public sector as a result of deregulation could impose a number of significant burdens on public servants (Wehrle-Einhorn 1994). In particular, deregulation would force them to make decisions without the guidance they would have had before it. Those rules may have stifled some creativity among civil servants, but one person's creativity may be another person's malfeasance. Similarly, one person's red tape may be another person's procedural due process (Kaufman 1977). It is not clear that in systems of democratic accountability we really want civil servants to be extremely creative. Even without extensive deregulation, we have not done a very good job in specifying what the appropriate limits of their action and discretion should be. Until we can do so in more operational terms, perhaps the ex ante controls are desirable.

Further, using the deregulated model, without ex ante controls civil servants would almost certainly be held accountable for the decisions that were made. In this regimen the increased freedom of employees would mean that they probably would be held more personally accountable for decisions than in the past. This may then produce exactly the opposite reaction of that intended by the reformers. Although the advocates of reform may assume that civil servants want to take responsibility and work in a deregulated environment, that may not in fact be true for many of them, especially in the lower ranks.[13] Often the anonymity and protection afforded by large, bureaucratic structures are preferred to personal exposure and personal liability, no matter how "empowering" those changes might be. The net result of deregulation, therefore, may be to produce "buck passing" and other familiar bureaucratic pathologies instead of leaner and more effective organizations.

No matter how it is phrased, the adoption of a deregulated conception of governance will do some violence to traditional ideas, such as ministerial accountability (Marshall 1989). If decisional competence is devolved to lower echelons within an organization, then the capacity to hold ministers accountable for all actions within their organizations becomes even more of a fiction than it has always been. In fact, in a deregulated (or even a market) model of the public sector, such lack of direct involvement of the top in policy becomes a virtue rather than a vice. In this conception of governing, lower-level officials should make more of their own decisions and be held accountable for them personally, not as a part of an organization headed by a minister. What this will mean, then, is that a fundamental rethinking of accountability will be required.

Government and Society. As well as making assumptions about the role of civil servants in governance, this model also appears to make a statement about the role of government in society. And that role would be quite different from the one assigned it by most successful politicians during the 1980s. The assumption appears to be that the public interest would be better served by a more active and interventionist public sector and that collective action is part of the solution, not part of the problem for contemporary societies. Deregulation is far from a knee-jerk reaction in favor of "big government" but represents a recognition that many of the most important problems facing society can be solved only collectively. Moreover, it recognizes that this solution in turn requires a major role for the public bureaucracy. Further, that involvement can be effective only if the bureau-cracy itself is capable of swift and efficient action.

What this deregulatory model does not appear to have figured out is how to mesh a deregulated civil service with empowered clients and with political lead-ers who want things done their own way, not the bureaucracy's way. Most of the rules that govern administrative practice arose because politicians demanded greater control over the way in which bureaucracies did their jobs. Some of these rules were to protect the public from excessive discretion; others were to protect the public purse from "fraud, waste and abuse"; and still others were designed to ensure control of policy by elected officials. Those are laudable goals, and it is not always clear how a more deregulated government is to guarantee the public interest without some of these external controls in place.

Goals Beyond Efficiency. Some of the other implications of deregulating gov-ernment for the public interest are more subtle but are nonetheless real. For example, in the United States the Office of Personnel Management, with great public fanfare, abolished SF-171, the form that had been used for several decades in the process of hiring new employees. It was discarded as being "excessively bureaucratic," with the argument that deregulating the recruitment process should make it more user-friendly for people unfamiliar with federal government practices (see Agresta 1994). The actual effect of deregulation on personnel selection, however, may be quite the opposite, and it may make finding employ-ment more difficult for people who are not already familiar with how govern-ment functions. The old bureaucratic form, for all its embodiment of the internal regulations of government, also created a relatively level playing field for indi-viduals seeking jobs in the federal government. With the abolition of the stan-dardized form, experienced insiders may have a pronounced advantage over people coming from outside. They may not be aware of what personnel managers within the system need to know about applicants and what particular information may make the prospective employee appear attractive. This disadvantage may be especially significant for minority candidates. They often lack the resources to use specialized employment agencies or may lack the informal networks to advise them about how to write the most effective résumé. The net effect of this particular deregulation may be to institutionalize the old-boys network in the Washington community rather than to weaken it, as was one of the intentions of the reformers. One should not overplay the significance of this particular change in internal controls, but it is indicative of the potential effects of a variety of deregulatory reforms.

Besides advantaging some groups within the public sector, the deregulatory approach may benefit certain groups within society at large. It is likely that these changes will have the same negative redistributive consequences in society as they did in the bureaucracy itself.[14] For example, if general purchasing rules such as open bidding are altered, or virtually eliminated, then the provisions that have served groups in society such as minorities and women may also be eliminated. Claims about the effects of minority set-aside programs and similar regulations in the United States vary (Mills 1994), but their general effect has been to encourage the formation of minority enterprises and to provide them with some means of making a start in the world of business.

Therefore, the search for efficiency within the public sector may deny government the capacity to use its powers to promote other worthy public goals. These are not just goals of minority recruitment and the formation of minority businesses. Other goals, e.g., environmental improvements, can be pursued through the internal regulations attached to public programs and through the provisions imposed when awarding government contracts. The real question for governance, then, may not be so much whether rules within the public sector are good or bad per se, but whether they are pursuing the most appropriate goals or not. Rules that promote efficiency, e.g., competitive tendering, are now considered appropriate within the public sector, but rules that promote other goals, e.g., ethnic and gender equality, are now less valued.

The ability of government to purchase goods, hire people, and dispense grants provides it with a huge set of levers to achieve public ends, and it may in fact be inefficient to abrogate that range of possibilities. As well as being inefficient in a strictly economic sense, such a denial of the possibility of using regulations may be inefficient in a political sense. There certainly has been substantial political furor raised over the issue of affirmative action (LaNoue 1993; Orlans and O'Neill 1992). Despite that, however, the use of rules associated with purchasing, hiring, and so on may be less obtrusive instruments for reaching certain policy goals than would be other, more direct, approaches. Therefore any politician interested in achieving these goals would be well advised to pursue them through the internal regulations of the public sector rather than through a more visible and intrusive means.[15]

SUMMARY

This fourth model of reform has some interesting points of similarity with the other three as well as some equally important points of dissimilarity. The deregulatory model may be seen as containing some elements of the other three models but also as containing some important contradictions to each of the others.

Despite its being "marketed" by some academics as a relatively distinct approach to change, is deregulation of the public sector really so distinctive, or is it merely a restatement of some bits and pieces of the other models, dressed up in language that is appealing, especially for civil servants? If it is not distinctive, is anything gained by approaching it as a unique manner of changing government?

The deregulatory approach is distinctive simply because it emphasizes a unique set of problems within the public bureaucracy. The market model tended to emphasize the negative consequences of monopoly, the participatory model hierarchy, and the flexible state model organizational permanence, but the regulatory approach to reform emphasizes internal regulations within public organizations as the principal source of dysfunctions so often observed within the public sector. Many, if not most, of the numerous "bureaupathologies" identified (Caiden 1990, 127) within the public sector can be laid at the doorstep of internal regulations.

Further, the reformers of the past have tended to pile new rules on top of old ones as the preferred means of producing a better public sector (March and Simon 1957). Whenever anything went wrong in administering a program, the common reaction was to develop a new set of rules and procedures that would prevent it from occurring in the future. Inevitably, new problems would arise that would require even more rules, and each set of internal regulations would create negative, unanticipated results that were "solved" by yet other rules. The argument of the deregulators is that internal rules for controlling the public sector are not the solution to the problems of governance; they are the fundamental problem.

Given that the diagnoses of the four models are different, the prescriptions offered for successful reform must also be different. In particular, the deregulatory approach, as that name implies, tends to focus most of its attention on changes in procedures within the public sector rather than on structures or the nature of the personnel who occupy administrative positions in government. The underlying assumption is that if the internal regulatory bonds that constrain its actions are loosened, then the bureaucracy will have the capacity and the willingness to make government function better. This assumption is seen as especially true for rules that cut across the entire administrative systems, e.g., civil service codes, but is also to some degree true of all internal controls within public organizations. The reason that rules developed within a single organization tend to be privileged is based on the assumption that they will have been selected to meet the particular needs of that one entity rather than being designed to serve some central control purpose.

Reformers, no matter how committed to their goals, should not expect government to become fully deregulated. Such a complete transformation is not going to happen, given the legitimate demands of the public for accountability and the real need of managers for some mechanisms for measuring and evaluating performance of their subordinates. There are two real questions then: how far can deregulation be extended, and what are the consequences of going down this road of change? There also may be important cross-national differences in how far deregulation can be extended. In Anglo-American countries, for example, the continuing distrust and skepticism about the public bureaucracy may make such changes in the public sector difficult. Yet these are just the countries that may need the changes the most. On the other hand, the Germanic systems may find this change relatively easy, given the limited amount of specific regulation imposed on the public sector and the capacity of the general code to handle most issues, but unfortunately these are the countries that can profit least from such changes.

Further, these deregulatory reforms must be considered in light of numerous other reforms that also are being implemented in the same countries. Although these different types of reforms are sometimes advocated by the same people and appear similar to other types, at least on the surface, the changes proposed actually may be contradictory and antithetical. Wise reformers therefore must understand how their preferred administrative reforms correspond to the others being implemented. Moreover, advocates must understand how the one set of changes might be made to correspond even better with the others. These same wise reformers must find the political means to have all these reforms accepted in the manner they desire or to find ways of developing appropriate packages of changes. None of these tasks is easy, even for the most skillful politician or manager.

6

From Change to Change: Patterns of Continuing Administrative Reform

The basic dimensions of reform occurring in the public sector during the 1980s and much of the 1990s were extremely impressive. Many of these changes persist into the current century. As dramatic as some of the individual reform programs have been in the industrialized democracies, the cumulation of changes over the two decades in these public bureaucracies is perhaps even more impressive; perhaps still more remarkable is that the interest in administrative change continues in almost all countries.[1] Despite those changes, almost no national government would argue that administrative change has now been completed or that the public sector has been put into good working order. Rather, the observer can easily identify continuing attempts of actors in the public sector, as the Gore Report (NPR 1993a) has described it, to make "government work better and cost less."

There have been several spates of administrative reform in the past, and several of the attempts at changing public administration during the 1960s and 1970s were perhaps even more significant that those that were implemented during the 1980s and 1990s.[2] The real difference from previous periods of change in the public sector is the ongoing nature of the change and the seemingly endless attempts—tireless tinkering—of a variety of actors to improve performance of the public sector in their countries. Reform fatigue is commonly assumed to be the reaction to pressures for change, but during the past decades there have been continuing efforts to reform and a succession of reforms that build upon (and in some cases counteract) those previous ones.

THE PROGRESSION OF CHANGE

Although each country has had its own distinctive pattern of reform, there are some general patterns that can be discerned in almost all the cases.[3] The dis-

cussion thus far has been to illustrate the point that although the New Public Management is often discussed as a single entity, it is actually a variety of different approaches to change, some of which are contradictory and mutually exclusive. The various meanings of reform and the various reform strategies can be seen clearly in the first rounds of change. The reforms that have been implemented have profoundly altered the public sector in most countries of the industrialized world and also have to some extent set the stage for subsequent rounds of change.

The reform process that is continuing appears to contain two fundamental types of changes, although those two are themselves closely related. First, some of the same types of reform continue to be adopted and implemented. The particular instruments being selected tend to be refinements of those used during the first rounds of change, or they represent alternative mechanisms operating within the same general approaches to governing. Market instruments have moved from rather simple acceptance of the market as an unquestioned exemplar of good policy and management to more sophisticated conceptions of the ways in which market principles can be used to produce more efficient and effective, and at times even more equitable, government. The more widespread acceptance of market principles in a variety of societies has made the debate over their use less ideological. For example, the Labour government in the United Kingdom has persisted in using much of the market approach to increasing efficiency in service provision, especially for local government services (Geddes and Martin 2000; PAC 2000). This shift in the climate of opinion toward acceptance of market-based solutions also means that the debate over reform initiatives has become directed more at ameliorating policy and managerial problems, including those generated by simple-minded acceptance of market principles, instead of just implementing a program because it is market-based.

The second type of change being implemented during the early twenty-first century represents direct reactions to these earlier attempts. In some instances these reforms represent responses to problems generated by earlier reforms and may at times involve returning (implicitly or explicitly) to older patterns of public administration. In other cases the more recent round of reforms constitutes more novel developments in the style of public management, albeit generally operating within the managerialist conception of how governments should function.[4] Few of these changes are so completely novel as to represent startling innovations in the way in which the public sector is managed—that level of innovations has indeed been evident during the first round of reform. The current round, however, does constitute important additions to the repertoire of would-be reformers. Some novelty in the reforms arises from combining principles that undergirded the earlier round.

Table 6.1. Characteristics of Second Round of Reform

	Coordination	Accountability	Reregulation	Performance Management
Diagnosis	Excessive disaggregation	Inadequate control	Excessive autonomy	Poor quality services
Structure	Return to hierarchy	Institute control structures	Create regulators	No particular recommendation
Management	Require consultation	Create personal responsibility	Impose ex post	Focus on performance
Policymaking	Consider collaboration	Use external mechanisms for control	Measure outputs	Assess quality
Public Interest	Policy coherence	Accountable bureaucracy	Control *with* autonomy	High quality services

ADMINISTRATIVE REFORM: ROUND TWO

The nature of change in the contemporary round of reform can be identified by using the same set of variables used to characterize the directions of change in the earlier round (see Table 6.1). Just as I argued that there are a range of diagnoses that guided reforms during the 1980s and 1990s, there is also a fundamental idea of what is presently wrong in government that is guiding the more recent reforms; and that diagnosis is crucial for understanding contemporary reforms.

This exercise of identifying a diagnosis and set of remedies will be done in two stages. The first stage is to identify some generic features of this second round of reforms that I believe is being implemented at the beginning of the twenty-first century. Then I will identify some of the more particular versions of these reforms and provide some analysis of their nature and likely consequences.

Central to the generic diagnosis of problems in the public sector is that the New Public Management has created conditions within government that produce much less predictability for the average citizen. The conception of the citizen as a consumer of public services that formed one part of the NPM may lead to government serving the public better, but the latitude granted agencies and managers might actually have a number of less desirable consequences for the public (Hogwood, Judge, and McVicar 2000). Further, governments may have substantially less public accountability for their actions than they did prior to reforms, and many actions may be less transparent than in the past.[5] Some of the problems motivating more contemporary reforms represent unresolved problems from "old-fashioned" government, but much of the diagnosis to be discussed here represents a reaction to the reforms implemented as components of the New Public Management.

The diagnosis of the difficulties in the contemporary period of change in the public sector is somewhat more diffuse than those diagnoses of the past, in part because clear, consistent ideas (especially those of the market) are not motivating this round of changes. Therefore, the specific recommendations for reform are also somewhat more diffuse than most of those implemented during the previous round of changes. For example, although the structural recommendations appear rather specific about returning to some degree of hierarchy in management, there seems to be little if any interest in returning to the strict hierarchical systems that characterized traditional public administration. The question therefore becomes one of balancing the positive benefits of NPM concepts with some of the virtues of traditional management. The problem is that specifying the exact nature of that balance is more difficult than adopting either of the more extreme positions.

The same requirement for balancing important values in the reform process also is apparent in many other contemporary recommendations for change. The management of personnel can now be seen as requiring some balance between the deregulation of the NPM style and the rigidity characteristic of a more conventional civil service system. The deregulation of personnel systems that has been implemented in many governments, including opening of many former career positions to competition from people outside the public-career structure, has tended to reduce organizational memory and hence may increase error and reduce the predictability of outcomes for citizens. This internal deregulation of the personnel function may also have reduced the commitment of many individuals holding public office to public-service values, such as impartiality and fiscal probity (Chapman 2000). The very process of recruitment itself has become less transparent than it once was, given that its formalized, rule-based systems have become substantially devalued and individuals are hired on contracts not available to public scrutiny. This system of external recruitment may produce good managers for government, but perhaps at some cost.

Since many contemporary managers have been recruited more to manage programs in the style of the private sector, rather than necessarily to serve the public interest, their activities may have been enriched by some old-fashioned values (see du Gay 2000). The previously described reforms of the public sector have tended to stress efficiency over procedures, but that term has in some cases meant expediency rather than efficiency per se, with arrangements being reached outside the procedures designed to ensure probity and protection of the public interest. In many cases managers recruited outside the career public service do not recognize that they are violating procedures and even formal laws—it is just business as usual. Likewise, the entrepreneurial role of public servants in the New Public Management may well be tempered by greater commitment to "neutral competence" and a willingness to follow the directions of political superiors (see Peters and Pierre 2001).

Ultimately, the public interest appears crucial as an issue in the continued reform of the public sector. Accountability has emerged as a problem as a result of the initial reforms, and many of the traditional mechanisms for enforcing it have been devalued through these reforms (Aucoin and Heintzman 2000; Peters

2000). More than anything else, the conventional means of using political mechanisms of accountability—ministerial responsibility within parliament, for example—have been depreciated by reforms that have loosened the control of ministers. These reforms appear to make many organizations in the public sector virtually as autonomous as any private contractors providing public services and hence are equally difficult to hold accountable.

The autonomy of agencies and other bodies of that type created in the process of administrative reform (Bovens and Plug 1999) is in many ways a useful fiction for both politicians and managers. It provides politicians the capacity to dodge accountability and to avoid blame, even for agencies for which they are officially responsible. In almost all governments agencies are "sponsored" by a ministerial department, but ministers may be able to forget that point of detail at convenient times. Likewise, managers can claim the autonomy to act more like a private-sector organization, including having salaries and perquisites with few controls, yet can attempt to flee behind the political accountability of the minister should there be any troubles. Thus, in many cases a game of avoiding and shifting responsibility for action has developed around the quasi-autonomous organizations.

In fairness, the reforms that have been implemented have some alternative forms of accountability embedded within them, but those means also have some notable weaknesses, especially from a democratic as opposed to a managerial perspective. The logic that managers and organizations are responsible through contracts for their performance, with little or no external assessment, or can employ self-defined values to assess how well they are doing their jobs is alien to conventional ideas of political accountability. In particular, these more market-focused approaches to accountability present little opportunity for involvement of elective officials in the process of holding individuals and organizations to account and therefore appear to deny the democratic nature of accountability.

The other dimension of accountability that has to a great extent been devalued during the initial period of reform was the importance of a code of ethics (formalized or not) that guided civil servants when making decisions (Chapman 2000; CCMD 1998). Opening positions within the public bureaucracy to non-career employees—especially at the senior levels—may well have enhanced the management capacity of government. Yet it may also have diminished the commitment of the average manager to the values of the public interest that usefully guided officials for some years. Those values actually have been denigrated by politicians of the right and left in almost equal proportions, but it has become apparent that those values also have had substantial beneficial features in maintaining the probity and responsibility of those officials. Without that internal moral compass, it will be more difficult to make sure that programs are indeed administered in the public interest.[6]

In summary, there is a continuing spate of reforms occurring in the public sector. They lack some of the ideological basis that had motivated the earlier round, but they still do have a great deal of coherence and represent logical reactions to the problems of governing that have been emerging after the first round. This contemporary series of reforms is intended in large part to restore some significant features of more traditional styles of governing lost in the first round, at the same time that several other aspects of the NPM reforms are being extended and improved. These reforms are an attempt intended to return government to the traditional, Weberian style of governing, but these are only partial efforts to resurrect the past; and even those seemingly retrograde steps are being adopted in light of the major changes already brought about through the New Public Management

THE NATURE OF THE CONTINUING CHANGES

Moving from the generalities of change implemented in the second round of reform, four dimensions within those reforms can be identified. Each of these dimensions to some extent addresses the generic issues just discussed, although accountability emerges as a concern in general as well as in the more particular reforms. Perhaps the dominant concept motivating contemporary administrative reform is that of "performance" and the associated idea of providing "service quality" in the public sector (Pollitt and Bouckaert 2000; OECD 1997). These ideas can be related in part to the now-familiar market ideas for reform, given that they emphasize improving the effectiveness of public programs (albeit perhaps not so much their efficiency, as in a strictly market regimen). Advocates of quality, however, need not rely completely on the market to achieve their purposes. Quality actually can be achieved through using conventional hierarchical methods of administration, as it is in some administrative systems, although devotees of the New Public Management might refuse to admit this possibility. Therefore, the reforms have now begun to be concerned even more directly with what governments *do* rather than with the means by which they do things.

In practice, the concept of service quality contains a participatory component in addition to the market component. One of the important means of measuring the quality of services being provided is to permit the clients of the programs, and perhaps the public at large, to make those assessments. This participatory idea is consistent with the concept that members of the public are the "consumers" of public services and therefore have many of the same rights to expect high-quality services and to complain about poor quality that consumers of private-sector goods and services would have. Beginning with citizens' charters in a number of countries, the public has been given the opportunity to evaluate their public services and perhaps to receive redress for poor services. Part of performance-driven reforms, therefore, is to transform the expectations that citizens have about the services that they will receive from government and lead them to expect and demand better service.[7]

The other three patterns of reform to be discussed represent more or less direct responses to the last round of reform. First, the process of deregulating the public sector has engendered a process of reregulation, with government finding that it needs to reinstitute some of the controls that had been abolished previously (see chapter 5). Second, the numerous structural reforms in the first round, particularly decentralization and deconcentration, have created the need for enhanced coordination and coherence in the public sector. The concept of virtual government as one organizing feature for reforms attempted in part to address the coordination issue but has proven far from adequate to produce the desirable level of coherence, and further change is required. The need for improved coherence is increased by changes in the policies being administered and in the political environment. Third, much of the reform implemented during the last round had negative consequences for accountability, and governments are finding that they need to return to that old but still significant value if they want to maintain their legitimacy. Further, accountability is also important as a means of feedback for both politicians and administrators and therefore fuels the emphasis on performance management.

Just as we did with the four ideas central to the first round of reform, we will look at several fundamental aspects of each component in this next round. These descriptions will not be as detailed, partly because these ideas are neither as detailed nor as intellectually coherent as those of the first round.[8] Still, each concept does offer a basic diagnosis of the problem(s) that the reform is meant to address. Further, each approach to reform contains some ideas about the operative mechanisms for bringing about the changes. These reforms, however, appear to be more about pursuing particular goals than they are about the methods for achieving those goals and therefore often lack the recommendations for more detailed changes.

It must also be said that it is somewhat more difficult to identify the emerging patterns of change in the public sector, in part because they are indeed still emerging. Reregulation within government, for example, can be seen very clearly in the United Kingdom (Hood et al. 1999), but the process is somewhat more amorphous in most other countries. There are, however, some inklings that any number of other countries will find it necessary to reestablish control over public-sector activities through creating new rules or reviving old ones. That having been said, however, the four important directions of change in public administration that I have identified are being implemented during the first few years of this century in a number of countries, and they do require some detailed attention. These reforms represent to some extent continuations of patterns of change that were already well established, albeit with different points of emphasis or slightly different goals. Other reforms go in newer directions, so the differences from the past are subtle but nonetheless real.

Performance

Performance, along with the closely allied concept of service quality, is a direct successor to several strands of reform implemented previously; its emphasis is a logical consequence of them. The idea that the public sector should be concerned with what it does, and how well it performs those tasks, was already becoming popular during the 1980s, with some attention given to ideas of benchmarking to other organizations and across time (Helgason 1997) and to other mechanisms used for performance management (see Pollitt 1986). Likewise, the idea of the citizen as consumer began to grow popular during the first rounds of reform, with the implication that the consumer should be able to receive the best possible services (Hood, Wollmann, and Peters 1996). The notion that government should be concerned with its outputs, rather than with the procedures through which they are produced, has been part of the drive to change government for some time[9] but has come to be perhaps the dominant component of the reform processes in the late twentieth and early twenty-first centuries. To some extent public management is now becoming "quality management," and with that comes a particular conception of what needs to be changed. The basic diagnosis motivating the performance-based reforms is that government programs and organizations may not perform as well as they might, and there should be ways of making them perform better.

It is difficult to be opposed to high-quality programs or to excellent performance in the public sector, but one needs to inquire what these terms may come to imply in practice, and which political actors will be given the power to define their meanings. The notion of performance is simply that demonstrable standards and measures should be employed to assess how well government is performing its tasks and that performance (and its analog, service quality) should be a central, if not the central, means for assessing management capabilities and organizational achievements. When applied fully, performance can be linked almost directly to budgets and to management contracts that are increasingly motivating the behavior of public-sector managers. Therefore, some objectivity is needed as to the extent to which standards are defined appropriately and levels of performance are monitored effectively.

This view then is somewhat in opposition to more traditional normative views about administrative behavior in the public sector. That traditional view stressed *process* rather than performance criteria and often appeared to consider the absence of manifest problems or complaints as an indicator of adequate performance. Organizations and their managers increasingly are being assessed on the basis of what they produce for the public rather than on the procedures they use to conduct public business.[10] This response is not only an interesting shift from traditional public administration, but it is also a shift from the market model of administration, which has become dominant. The emphasis on performance stresses some aspects of effectiveness of public organizations, but it may be as much concerned with the nature and the quality of the outputs as with the economic efficiency of their production. Indeed, the manner in which performance is treated—quality versus efficiency—may become a crucial management and political question.

Performance is both a vague term and one with a great deal of normative content. Given the absence of a clear bottom line in government, measuring performance may have a number of subjective elements and therefore is difficult to demonstrate in an unambiguous manner. In some ways the normative content and the apparent vagueness of these elements can be virtues. The normative content does mean that building coalitions to support these programs is less difficult than it might be to build support for other aspects of the managerialist agenda. Both the political right and left can favor high-quality public services and good per- formance by the public sector, if perhaps for different reasons. For the political right, enforcing performance is a means of ensuring efficiency and perhaps even reducing costs. For the left, both performance and quality can be a means of ensuring that citizens receive the services they need and deserve and perhaps a way of loosening some of the fiscal constraints that have become common in the public sector.

The use of performance measures as guides for management is one way to counteract some of the excesses arising from the first round of public-sector reform. In particular, employing standards for performance is a means for coun- teracting the possible loss of political control through deregulation of the public sector. For example, loosening control of budgets, through substituting "frame" or "bulk" budgets for traditional budget presentations, generally implies a sig- nificant loss of control over programs for legislatures and even for political exec- utives. Managers are provided the latitude to use their budgets more independently under frame-budgeting systems, but with performance manage- ment they are then held accountable for the quality of what they produce and the efficiency with which they perform their operations. This approach to monitor- ing is indeed ex post facto but may be even more effective than the traditional forms of ex ante controls because of the use of performance measures to drive the assessment instead of the more diffuse standards that might be used in con- ventional budgeting.

Though performance management may counteract some of the market con- ceptions common in the earlier reforms, it may reinforce some aspects of the par- ticipatory ideas motivating the earlier rounds of change. To a great extent, objective performance measurement is a technical issue (see Hatry 2000), and there are indeed a number of crucial questions about how to move from an idea of performance to its practical application. An alternative way in which to address quality is to use feedback from the recipients of the services. Quality is to some extent in the eye of the beholder, or at least in the eye of the recipient, so using participation is a means of driving performance-based reforms. As with many questions of participation, however, defining the appropriate groups to consult to define adequate or excellent performance is difficult for most public- sector programs.[11]

Measurement. Perhaps the central question about using quality as the standard for the public sector is how one can measure it. There are significant problems involved in measuring quality within each program, and they become exacerbated when decision makers must compare performance in a number of agencies.[12] There are several technical issues involved in measuring quality in public programs that have been thoroughly discussed elsewhere (Halachmi and Bouckaert 1996). Rather than dwell on those methodological issues, I will focus more on the impacts that quality measurement can have on the politics of public programs and the manner in which officials can use performance (or have performance used against them) in making budget and policy decisions. The debate about performance and quality does have a technical dimension, but it would be mistaken to ignore the deeply political aspects of this approach to public management.

I will not dwell on measurement issues, but the choice of measurement does involve some fundamental assumptions about the definition of quality. Perhaps the basic assumption concerns the role of the public in the definition of quality. The widespread consumerization of public programs during the 1990s has created a number of means by which citizens monitor programs and can express their opinions about them (Hood, Wollmann, and Peters 1996). This populist definition of quality, while reflecting the triumph of some aspects of the participative approach to reform, may conflict with professional and even legal judgments about performance and quality (see Klages et al. 1995). This may be especially true in policy areas with more technical content, where the public may have expectations for outputs that exceed the possibilities of governments to produce.

The politics of quality, therefore, may to some extent revolve around the issue of popular versus professional assessments of quality and the role of the public in the process. The distance between outcomes and expectations, for example, may be a product of the actions of politicians and professionals in creating high hopes. This distance and the associated disappointments may be a result of the necessary politics of "selling" a program and creating the coalition required to have it adopted. Once those expectations are created, however, they may be difficult to dampen. This may be seen perhaps most clearly in policy areas such as health care, where scientific and technical advances may make it appear to the public that death has become negotiable; in reality, despite its advances, medicine remains imperfect, and not all cures work all the time.

The combined perspectives of clients are certainly one important measure of quality, but by no means is it the only one. For one thing, the clients of a program may have very different interests from the public as a whole, or even from the individuals responsible for managing the program. Travelers, for example, may like to get through the airport quickly and not be bothered by customs formalities, while citizens have an interest in preventing smuggling of dangerous drugs, and customs officials have a legal responsibility to ensure that there are adequate safeguards against smuggling as well as some responsibilities for generating revenue. How do managers and political leaders balance these three notions of what constitutes good performance by this organization?

The differences among the measurability and the immediacy of the outputs of programs can have a pronounced impact on the political success of programs.

For example, at the national level a program like defense, although popular with political conservatives and with many citizens, has outputs that are difficult to measure effectively (except perhaps in time of war). The diffuse character of the outputs of defense organizations, or some forms of social regulation (May 2001), may disadvantage these programs relative to programs such as social welfare or health, with more tangible consequences for citizens. Or the difficulty of producing benefits in many domestic programs may actually help those programs that do not have to change complex social processes but can depend on putative benefits accruing in case something else happens.[13] Paradoxically, the use of performance criteria may also disadvantage the central agencies that implement these programs, given that the outputs of these organizations are perhaps the most diffuse within government.

The same sort of argument is true for the differences between central and subnational governments. The majority of the services provided by subnational governments, and especially local governments, are tangible and measurable. We can count the potholes in local streets, or the number of times the underground train runs late, or the response time for fire departments and police departments (Hatry 2000). But central governments have programs such as defense, economic regulation, and foreign affairs, programs that are difficult to measure or even to identify in some cases. Therefore, local governments should be able to convince their citizens, or consumers, that they are providing the services of reasonable quality; the benefits of central government programs, however, are often more remote.

Linkage. A second question involved in using performance as a central component of management is how to link it with the intermediate variables that might be assumed to produce it. At its simplest, observers may want to use performance to guide decisions about the management of organizational leaders. But can they always attribute the failure or success of an organization so completely to its leadership? Performance criteria also could be used in budgetary decision making. But if this were to be done, would poor performance indicate that an organization should receive a smaller budget as a punishment or a larger budget to help it make up for its deficiencies? One can make a good case for either form of linkage, although the general pattern is to punish poor performance.

Rather than considering linkage on an absolute scale, it may be better to consider performance on a relative scale and to consider improvement and performance across time as the more appropriate way to assess linkages with other aspects of the political process. The most appropriate means of assessing the performance of managers or organizations is how well they do in one time period compared to how well they performed the same tasks in the previous time period. Thus, the notion of continual improvement is central for understanding the way in which performance and quality can be used to link the outputs of organizations and the rewards and punishments for organizations and individuals. Politically, this idea also makes it easier for central agencies responsible for implementing quality programs to involve the operating agencies. If the initial performance standards are sufficiently low, it is unreasonable for an organization to refuse to participate in the quality program. Once involved, however, year after year the standards of performance can be increased.[14]

In summary, in this version of administrative reform the public interest is assessed explicitly in terms of the outputs of government and implicitly by the efficiency with which they are produced. Most if not all of the process concerns that have dominated public administration are ignored in favor of focusing on what governments do and the extent to which they can improve their performance. This focus on outputs may be welcome when contrasted to the stereotypes of proceduralism and the red tape of more traditional forms of administration, but it also raises a number of problems. These issues are at once the product of other types of reform and have been addressed through a number of other contemporary approaches to reform.

In particular, performance management has an important influence on accountability regimens in government. Although it is a different form of accountability, the performance approach to management in the public sector does have an accountability notion firmly embedded within it. In some ways the conception of accountability is more viable than the traditional mechanisms associated with parliamentary democracy. The usual notion of accountability is that parliament is to identify any shortcomings of the government, no matter how trivial, and make the minister account for them in public. This can embarrass a government but often does little to improve the policies delivered to citizens. The emphasis on quality and performance, however, attempts to assess average performance of programs and to determine if that is adequate or not. Further, if the logic is extended, it can be used to drive government toward *exceptional* performance (see Miller 1984).

Another crucial aspect of the role of performance measurement in accountability is that this information is in a form that can feed rather easily into the policy and administrative process, while traditional forms of accountability were designed more for political forums. The thrust and cut of parliamentary life may be important for some aspects of accountability, but it does little for managers other than potentially to embarrass them. The information coming out of performance-management exercises may be embarrassing also, but it is directed more at what the manager is doing wrong (or right) and is closer to the needs of that manager for improving performance. That linkage may be far from perfect, and there are rarely clear answers about *why* performance was not what it should have been, but it generally provides more useful information than that coming from parliamentary debates.

Reregulation

Another reaction to the reforms that already have been implemented is a return to regulation within the public sector itself (Hood et al. 1999). The difference between the current round of internal regulation and the former pattern is that most of the current regulation is done ex post while the former was more ex ante. Rather than controlling what managers can do before they try to do it, the contemporary pattern is to monitor and assess after policies are made and implemented. The reregulation dimension of continued reform is closely related to the quality and performance dimension. Rather than using the rules of thumb, or political judgments, common in the ex ante controls, budgeting having performance criteria gives regulators in the center more reliable standards and (at least in theory) more information about what activities to regulate.

Another strategy for reregulation, closely allied with the quality movement in the public sector, is standard setting. For example, although educational management in the United Kingdom has in many ways been decentralized, the imposition of a national curriculum takes back a good deal of the freedom that appears to have been given. Even in the United States, with its long history of local control over education, there are some calls for national standards and even a national curriculum (Lofty 2000). Further, by establishing these central standards, the performance of each school (or hospital or whatever) is easier to monitor. There is no opportunity to argue that the school is trying to do different things or to achieve different educational goals—those have been established external to the school.

If anything, the regulations being imposed on public-sector organizations are more draconian than in the past, with the capacity for the central controllers within the system to do more than simply refuse budget or personnel allocations. Those constraints were, at the time, considered serious issues for an organization but hardly were so damaging to its continued survival as the current forms of regulation. For example, in the United Kingdom the pattern has become for central officials to "name and shame" organizations and local governments that are not performing up to the standards that have come to be expected of them. At the extreme, central agencies and ministries can assume control over those failing organizations and manage them centrally until they are able to manage themselves.

Even when central agencies do not use the "nuclear option" of taking over failing organizations, they may still intervene in situations that other managers may have thought were deregulated and decentralized. One of the numerous paradoxes of public-sector reform over the past several decades is that attempts to move authority from the center and to give it to individual agencies and even ministries has resulted in an actual strengthening of the center. Given that there are now fewer rules to guide decisions, central agencies often are able to exercise greater discretion, and with discretion comes power.[15] Thus, as Wildavsky (1979) has argued concerning health care, there is always some means of allocation to deal with scarcity, so that when rules are removed discretion comes into greater play.

To this point I have focused on inspectorates and their role in reviving control over the public sector. A more general phenomenon may be the "audit explosion" and the increased use of auditing in the public sector (Power 1994). Most governments have had a postaudit of their accounts for decades, but that has been largely financial. Beginning perhaps with the General Accounting Office in the United States (Mosher 1979), the green eyeshade image of auditing has been transformed into greater concern for performance and the best use of money, not just legal probity. The question now is not only was the money spent legally, but also was it spent in the most efficient manner possible. This concern requires auditing organizations to become involved with a much broader range of questions and perhaps also to become more political, given that their decisions are now more closely linked to policy issues.

These accounting organizations have become more central to the evaluation and assessment of public programs and feed their information directly into the policymaking process. Their reports constitute a different dimension of regulation and supervision over public-sector organizations than do the inspectorates, and they tend to be more concerned with correcting general faults in the policy process and in programs than in identifying individual organizations that are failing. This more general stance toward evaluation does not preclude their focus on the shortcomings of an individual organization, but the focus tends to be elsewhere.

Although the reregulation of government has somewhat different methods and purposes, its net impact can be rather similar to old-fashioned accountability models. Reregulation involves the upward flow of information that is largely gathered and interpreted within government itself, and the sanctioners are able to use the information for political as well as for managerial purposes. Of course, virtually anything that is done within the public sector is amenable to political use and interpretation, but this use may be more overt in the case of reregulation than for strictly performance-management programs. The "naming and blaming" characteristic of a good deal of the reregulation focuses attention on attempts of the government to improve the poorest performers.

While some of the conventional mechanisms for monitoring organizations continue to be crucial for the reregulation of government, there has also been a proliferation of new organizations that are used to exercise that function. The expansion of this type of organization can be seen most clearly in the United Kingdom (Hood et al. 1999). Since the early 1990s there have been some two dozen new inspectorates and similar organizations created within British government, most being responsible for supervising a particular policy sector and given powers to impose remedies if they find that organizations within their sector are failing to provide adequate services. Although central to the continuing reforms in the United Kingdom, the proliferation of inspectorates and commissions is also found in a variety of other countries.

The notion of reestablishing control over the public sector through the aegis of quasi-autonomous organizations such as inspectorates is new in the sense of the extent to which it is being used, but the basic concept itself is rather old. In France, for example, the Inspection des Finances is a creation of the Napoleonic era, with analogous organizations (the prefectoral corps to control local authorities) also dating to that period (Dreyfus 2000). In the United Kingdom, continuing organizations such as HM Inspectorate of Schools (1840) and HM Inspectorate of Constabulary (1856) were followed by other organizations such as HM Inspectorate of Prisons and that for the Fire Services (Rhodes 1981). In the United States, the Carter administration instituted Inspectors General in each executive department and large agency as a means of enhancing accountability (Light 1995).

In the United States the courts for some time have also played a role in regulating public-sector organizations, with that role waxing or waning depending on the activism of the courts at the time. For example, during the 1970s and 1980s there were a number of instances in which federal judges ruled that state prison systems were so bad that they violated the cruel and unusual punishment provisions of the Bill of Rights (Feely and Rubin 1998). The courts therefore appointed individuals as "special masters" responsible only to the court to assume control of these failing organizations and to put them back in proper order. This response is not dissimilar to the idea of inspectorates taking over failing school systems or other failing public organizations and imposing their own standards for proper administrations.

The idea of reregulation is obviously closely allied with the emphasis on performance in the public sector. The most important differences are first that reregulation is much more specific about the diagnosis—it is the absence of adequate rules and regulations within government that is the problem. Failing the creation of new general sets of rules that apply across all of government, such as those for purchasing or personnel in the past, it is assumed that the creation of monitoring organizations can impose control within particular sectors of government. Performance management can be "hands off" and border on the automatic, but the reregulation style of intervention is direct. A second important difference is that reregulation is more of an internal administrative tool for managing, using to some extent old-fashioned hierarchy to assess and then to punish malfeasance or nonfeasance by an organization.

Moreover, reregulation tends to focus more on individual organizations—the school, or the hospital, or perhaps the local government as a whole—rather than on the program. This is an important difference in part because it is related directly to the remedies to be imposed in the case of perceived failure. It seems here that the assumption is that the fault lies with the individual organization, or the individual manager, not with the design of the program. For example, if schools are perceived to be performing badly, even if as a group, the assumption is that individual controls are the appropriate route to rectify the problem. There is some of this same assumption in the performance approach as well, but it is even more manifest here. Thus, any recommendations about policy appear to be in the form of recommendations about implementation instead of about the fundamental issues of the programs being administered. Thus, although this style of reform may be able to capture headlines and demonstrate that government does care about what is happening to citizens, it may also be conservative and help to preserve the status quo in policy.[16]

The structural assumptions of reregulation follow from the comment that it is the individual organization that is the focus of performance and accountability in this view of reform. Given that focus on organizations per se, the structural assumptions behind the approach are of a large number of autonomous and quasi-autonomous organizations, not tightly coupled ministerial structures with hierarchically exercised control. The ministries do still exist, but they are no longer as central to the management process as they once were. This approach to the public sector therefore creates two lines of accountability, one within the ministry and a second through more or less autonomous inspectorates.

Further, the concept of the public interest contained in the reregulation version of reform is not dissimilar to that of performance models: in good government, public organizations do as good a job as possible and produce outputs as efficiently and effectively as possible. There is little wrong with this idea of good government, but it does leave unanswered some of the questions about procedure that may also be important in administration in a democratic political system. It does matter *how* programs are delivered. Old-fashioned public administration cared perhaps too much about the *how* question, but the New Public Management may care perhaps too little about procedure. Therefore, as some of the reregulation may involve government taking over programs from democratically elected local governments, or school committees, one must ask if performance is the only question of importance.

Besides implications for democratic control, reregulation raises other issues about quality and quality management. The idea of having a variety of formalized checks on the performance of public-sector organizations may produce a number of benefits for citizens, but there is also the distinct possibility of substituting political judgments for professional ones on how to deliver services (see Gosling 2000). The inspectorates that are developed to assess how well other organizations are performing may have sufficient expertise to make those judgments, but they may also have strong political motivations for making their decisions. Likewise, the auditing organizations may have developed substantial policy expertise but may not have the same level of expertise as the officials and professionals who deliver the services. Having invested heavily in the idea of creating quality in governments and in using reregulation as one of the methods, political leaders may find it difficult not to intervene when there are difficulties.

In summary, reregulation contains two important and to some extent complementary approaches to control in the public sector. First, some organizations involved in reregulation focus explicitly on individual organizations and their successes and inadequacies in providing public services as required by law or by contracts. These reviews of organizations generally focus on their management, with the assumption that this is the locus of failures. The obvious remedy when

failures are uncovered is to reform and/or replace the management of the organization in question, and, if necessary, for some other organization, often a central organ in the government, to assume responsibility for delivery of the
services. The second and related element involved in reregulation is the use of
performance and quality standards as the means of assessing performance. This
is a way to remove some of the subjectivity that might otherwise afflict the application of the standards.

Reregulation therefore does raise important questions about how to control
the activities of government organizations. There appears to be some general
agreement that some form of control is required and that attempts to deregulate
may have gone too far in freeing public organizations from democratic or legal
controls or both. That having been said, the substitution of ex post for ex ante
controls does not appear to have been a panacea for the public sector. Both forms
of control imply using standards other than those developed within the organization as the means of judging its performance; therefore, different evaluations
(political or legal) might be developed. Of course, some of these standards are
important for judging the behavior of programs and organizations, with the real
question being the balance struck among them.

Coordination and Coherence

This category is not so much a collection of particular reforms as it is the identification of goals for a wide variety of structural and procedural changes being
implemented throughout the public sector (see Peters 1999). For example, in the
United Kingdom the Blair government is emphasizing the need to create "joined
up" government, their term for a pattern of governing that is less fragmented than
patterns that have become standard in most governments (Cabinet Office 2000).
Any number of countries are launching other attempts to construct machinery for
policymaking and implementation that can coordinate programs and create
greater policy coherence. At times this machinery involves strengthening the
prime minister's office or central agencies such as the Ministry of Finance. In
other cases it involves creating interministerial bodies and working groups
responsible for involving the range of organizations.

Some of the absence of adequate coordination is a function of previous
reforms, especially structural reforms that have tended to disaggregate and
decentralize government. For example, in the United Kingdom the ministerial
structure had been extremely well coordinated through a strong central agency
(HM Treasury) and internal-management structures within ministries that permitted little autonomy for components within them. The creation of a large number of executive agencies, with over 75 percent of the civil service now
employed in these organizations, means that much of the activity of governing is
occurring at least nominally at arm's length from ministerial authority.[17] The
concept of agencies has become popular in other countries, including Japan and

to some extent Canada, as has been the creation of quangos and other quasi-governmental organizations that can deliver services at an even greater distance from ministerial authority.

In addition to the effect of structural reforms in the public sector, the increasing interest in performance management is also having some negative impact on the coherence of government programs. Most performance measurement has been confined to single organizations or often even to the particular services they provide. Therefore, managers need focus only on what their own organizations are doing in order to be seen as doing an adequate, or even exemplary, job. That focus makes coordination obviously more difficult, and it may even be a negative value if by coordinating, any possible performance within the particular policy domain of the organization is forgone. Therefore, if coordination is to be implemented successfully, the next round of developments in methodology may need to focus on broader issues. Some important moves have been made in that direction, but there is still a good way to go to have a workable set of measures that would enhance coordination.

The basic diagnosis of this set of second-round reforms is that government has become so decentralized that it is incapable of operating as a single entity. This represents more than a fear of untidiness; there are real economic and political costs involved in a failure to coordinate policies effectively. Programs that duplicate each other impose additional tax costs on the public. Duplicative regulatory programs also may require citizens to make multiple applications for licenses in order to go into business, or multiple social programs may require social service recipients to go to multiple agencies in order to get the full range of services required. The political costs result from public perceptions that government is incapable of managing effectively, reinforcing the native stereotypes that many citizens hold about the public sector.

Given the incoherence generated by the previous rounds of reform, the nature of contemporary governing, and the policy issues governments are confronting, coherence requires more concern. For example, the forces of globalization and internationalization place pressures on governments to better coordinate their activities at home and abroad. The increased impact of the international market, as another example, means that economic policy becomes defined broadly in terms of competitiveness. This, in turn, means that education and labor-market policies are no longer simply domestic policy programs. Rather, they are major components of economic policy, given that knowledge is now the basis of competitiveness for most advanced economies. Likewise, foreign-trade negotiations have become a crucial element of economic policy, and the organization responsible must coordinate its activities with a wide range of other organizations, e.g., agriculture, commerce, and foreign affairs, among others.[18]

The need to negotiate in a coherent manner in the international arena is especially evident for countries of the European Union (see Kassim, Peters, and Wright 2000; Kassim, Menon, Peters, and Wright 2001). These governments must first develop common negotiating positions within their home government and then take those positions into discussions with the other member nations. This involves either substantial bargaining among the actors or a powerful central agency that can produce a common position, if not consensus. That common position then may be maintained more or less acceptably by negotiators with other countries. Even with elaborate machinery in place to produce coherence, however, it is difficult to overcome the folkways of government, and many opportunities are still found to circumvent the coordination mechanisms (Mueller 2001).

The need for increased coordination within government is exacerbated by the declining trust and confidence of the public. The political drive for increased coherence in the public sector has arisen largely independently of that initial round of reforms, and indeed the consumerization ideas contained in them were designed to address some of the incoherence existing in the system. Still, persisting overlaps among social and regulatory programs present real problems for individual citizens and businesses. These overlaps make the public sector appear more inefficient and wasteful to the average citizen than it probably really is. Further, the acceptance of consumerization as a possible remedy to the problem of policy incoherence is one example of the externalization of the accountability system in contemporary government. If those in the public sector cannot design effective machinery for creating coherence, then they will let the citizen do the job for them, albeit after the fact.

Coordination and coherence are two of the oldest problems in the public sector (see Jennings and Crane 1994; Bardach 1998). That having been said, they have been exacerbated in the past several decades. Structurally, governments have created large numbers of organizations that were intended to make and implement policy more autonomously than in the past. That increased autonomy, then, makes coordination and coherence problematic. Those difficulties are exacerbated by the ideology of managerial entrepreneurship associated with the autonomy that justifies organizations following their own policy and management directions. In policy terms, the policy space in the public sector has become increasingly crowded, and therefore there is a commensurate need for governments to ensure that these policies do not bump up against each other too much and generate negative synergy among themselves.

Faced with a somewhat incoherent world of their own making, governments now are attempting to cope with the problem. One of the ways is to reverse the deregulatory trend and to reimpose direct controls over spending departments and agencies. Although a good deal of the reregulation is focused on individual organizations and their potential shortcomings, regulations can also be used to produce greater coherence. As governments have been faced with the need to be better coordinated, they have often installed procedures requiring vetting of laws and regulations through central agencies or potentially competing organizations prior to being adopted (Painter 1987). Further, the budget process may be reformed in ways that enhance the connections among organizations, or quasi markets may be used to facilitate exchange among them.

More direct political involvement may be another way of attempting to create greater coherence in government. For example, one aspect of the Blair government's attempts to create "joined up" government" is being carried out through the use of rather close personal and partisan supervision of ministries, agencies, and quangos. The structural separation of these organizations makes this coordination more difficult than it might otherwise be, so that appointments to positions of power within them becomes a crucial means of control. To some extent this has involved the re-creation of a politics of patronage in Britain, with thousands of positions on boards (as well as some managerial positions) being the government's to give (Skelcher 1998). Commitment to the goals of the sitting government among the managers of organizations then becomes the means of creating coherence. This may appear less intrusive than control from central agencies, but it still represents some loss of autonomy for presumably autonomous government organizations.

While ideas about public-sector reform implemented during the initial round of reforms were largely competitive and contradictory, I am arguing that there is at least some degree of overlap and complementarity contained in the second round. At a minimum, there is more complementarity in principle even if implementation of the ideas may as yet be imperfect. This possibility for linkage is evident, for example, in the connection between the emphasis on performance in the public sector and the desire for enhanced coordination and coherence of programs. Although a good deal of the emphasis on performance management is placed on individual organizations, there is also an increasing emphasis on the performance of the entire policy system, and that inevitably leads to questions of coordination and coherence. For example, in the United States the annual performance report issued by the Office of Management and Budget is an attempt to look at performance and quality across the political system (OMB 2000). Among other things, this report identifies the major policy challenges facing the federal government and presents an account of the actions that have been taken to address those problems.

Accountability

The familiar question of enforcing the accountability of public organizations has been returning to a central position in the assessment of public administration, partly as a result of its apparent degradation through earlier rounds of reform. Those earlier reforms had a variety of different consequences for it. The central argument that such issues have thus emerged indicates that the majority of these consequences have been negative, but some have been positive and also should be considered. For example, most older forms of accountability have tended to focus on the exceptional failures, their capacity to embarrass politically the sitting government, and perhaps to lead to its downfall. Many of the recent changes in the mechanisms of accountability tend to push the focus toward average performance and a more complete assessment of organizational and programmatic performance.

One of the most important reactions to changes in accountability comes from politicians who find that they are left with the political responsibility for delivering public services but have far fewer levers available to control that process or even to control the civil service. Deregulation of the public service and the increased autonomy for public and quasi-public organizations mean that politicians have reduced capacity as leaders to exert as much control over policy implementation as they might have had in the past. Those politicians are still responsible, however, in the public mind as well as legally in most instances, for what transpires in the policy domains controlled by their ministries. The imbalance between responsibility and control is a major problem for accountability. This is especially true, given that these changes were intended, at least in part, to rectify the situation in which political leaders had a large number of levers to control organizations but often were attempting to find ways to deny that responsibility.

One of the consequences of earlier structural reforms has been to make the lines of accountability less clear, especially for the numerous autonomous and quasi-autonomous organizations that were created to implement public programs (see Skelcher 1998). By being created outside the usual lines of public authority, these organizations are able not only to avoid some of the controls that might have inhibited efficiency but also to avoid the usual requirements for public accountability. For example, the reinvention exercises in the United States have resulted in many public activities being removed from the purview of the Freedom of Information Act (Roberts 2000). Likewise, private-sector accounting rules may be used instead of the more revelatory accounting typical of the public sector, permitting some evasion of transparency and accountability, although some forms of the latter are honored.

The problems of political accountability arise in settings other than those of newly autonomous organizations. Even in ministerial organizations that remain much the same as they had been in structural terms, the prevailing ethos of entrepreneurship and *managerial* autonomy have reduced the acceptability of direct political interventions in the day-to-day operations of public organizations. Lacking more subtle and graded means for exerting what they consider their right and duty to have some control, and of holding the organizations accountable, political leaders may have to resort to the more intrusive mechanism of dismissing managers and intervening directly into organizations that had come to think of themselves as autonomous. This "paradox of managerialism" (Maor 1999) is but one of the many unintended consequences of the first major rounds of reform that has spurred on additional reforms. The problem with many of the deregulatory reforms was that they did not establish clear limits on the freedom to be exercised by managers and organizations so that it became difficult to know what was appropriate and what was not.[19]

The rounds of reform following those of the 1980s have had as one goal

attempting to clarify and to strengthen the mechanisms of accountability, especially for those autonomous and seemingly unaccountable organizations. Some
of the attempts at reasserting accountability have been through traditional mechanisms such as parliament and the courts. Attempts also have been made to
implement accountability through quasi-legal mechanisms such as ombudsmen
and "commissioners" for a variety of service areas. These mechanisms are often
ineffective simply because a major portion of the logic of creating these
autonomous organizations was for them to provide services to the public at an
arm's length from the major political institutions, thereby presumably enhancing
their capacity for efficiency and creativity in implementing programs. Thus,
these organizations may rightfully claim that attempts to make them accountable
through traditional means may defeat the purpose of their current organizational
format. Further, the newer mechanisms often depend on public action to be effective, and although that outcome is quite likely for the more affluent and educated,
it is problematic for clients of many social programs.

To some extent the reforms implemented during the past several decades
have externalized the concept of accountability; and the responsibility to police
the services being provided in the public sector, and complaining about poor
quality, now often resides with the public itself. Instruments such as "league
tables" and "report cards" (Gormley and Weimer 1999) depend largely on the
willingness of citizens to use that information to place pressure on managers and
on elected representatives for better services. Likewise, the shift from procedural
to administrative justice toward an "uneasy mix of legalism and market forces"
(Johnson 1998, 161) in countries such as the United Kingdom puts citizens in a
more central place in enforcing accountability. That role may be reasonably
effective for middle-class clients who feel they have rights to complain and participate, but it may be more difficult for lower-class individuals and perhaps
almost impossible for some immigrant groups. Thus, accountability has come to
have somewhat different meanings and somewhat variable effectiveness, based
on the nature of the program and its clientele.

As well as parliaments and courts reasserting some traditional mechanisms
for accountability, political patronage has reappeared in some countries as a
means of ensuring political controls over public policy (Rouban 1998; Pierre
1997). In most Western countries the assumption has, or had, been that patronage appointments to public positions were an overt or covert form of corruption
(see Della Porta and Meny 1997). The American pattern of an incoming president being able to make a large number of appointments to important management positions that in other countries would be career civil service has long been
sneered at by Europeans (see Light 1995). Those Europeans, however, have been
finding that this and similar patronage devices, which they had assumed had been
abandoned decades earlier, are being revived and used to fill positions, especially
managerial positions, in quasi-government organizations (Skelcher 1998) and in
some cases to positions in the mainstream organizations of the public sector.

In addition to the (re)strengthening of formalized mechanisms for enforcing accountability through institutions, the more recent round of reforms in the public sector has been characterized by attempts to promulgate codes of ethics for public servants and in some instances also for politicians. It can be argued that the first rounds placed so much emphasis on the three E's of economy, efficiency, and effectiveness that there is a need to emphasize this fourth E of ethics. Moreover, the public sector has been opened to employees, often even in the most senior positions, who have not made their careers within government. Those employees have not been inculcated with values of public service probity and the "old bargain" between politicians and their civil servants (Schaffer 1973; Hood and Peters 2000) that had been an effective barrier against corruption in traditional administrative systems. There is consequently a need to formulate codes of practice and to use them as additional means of providing accountability for public action.

One of the important differences of the continuing round of reforms from the first major reform period is greater complementarity. This is especially clear in the linkage between performance management and accountability. As well as being directly concerned with the outputs of government, the concepts of performance and quality are strongly associated with pressures to ensure enhanced accountability of programs. The meaning of accountability has changed dramatically during the course of implementing the reforms already adopted. It is now perhaps conceived as more mechanical than political, but there is a return to accountability as a central focus for the policy process. Performance management requires that the leadership of programs and organizations identify their goals and then be held accountable for achieving them. This form of accountability will focus on the average performance of the organization rather than on the exceptional errors that may occur and hence may in reality produce a more meaningful set of controls over the way the organization functions.

Despite the complementarity found in the most recent round of administrative reforms, there are still numerous contradictions associated with them. For example, one possible consequence of enhancing coordination among government organizations is that the lines of programmatic accountability may become muddled. This is especially true when funds from a number of different sources are merged into a single program intended to provide services to particular areas or client populations. For example, one drive for improved policy coordination has been the need to provide services to groups such as women, immigrants, and the elderly, whose needs cut across a range of conventional ministerial structures (Peters 1999). These clients may be better served by combining funds and creating packages of services, but this strategy is not without its managerial, and possibly political, difficulties. How can public money used in this way be accounted for, and who is responsible if the program fails or goes badly wrong?

Through this example we can again realize that reforms of the public sector are interrelated and that one well-intentioned (and even beneficial) reform may quickly beget the need for another. Although the reform enhancing program coordination may create the "one-stop shops" that are so convenient for clients, it may also create additional accountability problems for government itself. If different streams of money and legal requirements are funneled into a single operational entity, tracking those resources and determining their best use may be difficult. This response is sometimes a bureaucratic argument against investing in the coordination of programs, but it is also a reality. Mingling money and laws often does create real problems in holding agencies to account—even in performance terms. Organizations may have to choose whether they will follow one or the other of the program guidelines and whether they will emphasize one or the other of the sets of goals over the other(s).

The growing concern over accountability in the latest round of reform has required public administrators and politicians to think again about "citizens" as well as about "clients." There has been ample evidence of citizens' loss of confidence and trust in government (Putnam and Pharr 2000), and the increased concern with accountability is one means of attempting to restore that reliance. The redevelopment of the institutional mechanisms for accountability and the creation of new ones, including performance management, represent ways in which governments can demonstrate to their citizens that the public sector is attempting to manage itself properly and to respond to the wishes and demands of the public. That having been said, however, the continual raising of expectations about performance may make restoring confidence even more difficult.

CONCLUSION

The earlier round of reform in the public sector produced a number of important changes in a number of governments in the industrialized democracies. Many of these consequences were extremely positive, and few if any analysts would argue that governments were less efficient and effective at the beginning of the new century than they had been twenty years earlier. Those same analysts might argue, and many did, that other problems had been introduced into these public sectors that themselves required some consideration and perhaps some additional reforms. Further, that round of reforms was perceived by many advocates of change as being only the beginning of a continuing process. Indeed, the concept of continual improvement appears to be firmly lodged in the thinking of many managers and reformers in government. Whether that idea will eventually lead to disillusionment as the possibilities for managerial improvements become exhausted has yet to be seen, as there appear to be ever more avenues for effective change.

Governments continue to reform and to attempt to become more effective, efficient, and accountable. Having already invested a great deal of time and political capital in the process of change during the 1980s and 1990s, they persist in their attempt to find new and better ways of governing at the beginning of the new century. In many ways this devotion to excellence is admirable, but it also may be the continued pursuit of a nonexistent philosophers' stone. Just as that stone was presumed capable of turning base metal into gold, many administrative reforms are directed at making essentially insuperable problems subject to quick, clean, technical fixes. That may not happen, given the complexity and the difficulties faced when administering programs within the public sector.

7

The Logic of Continuing Change

It is now time to inquire *why* there has been the continuing emphasis on change within the public sector. No matter how much a government may have changed its administrative system (see, for example, Halligan 2001), there appear to be numerous and persistent efforts to motivate the governance systems in most industrialized democracies toward even great change. I have pointed out that some of the more recent reforms represent direct reactions to the perceived problems (and some perceived successes) produced by the previous round, but the reasons for change seem to extend beyond that simple palliative exercise. Indeed, over the past several decades what is in essence an ideology of reform, with a belief in the possibility of continual improvement in the way in which public services are delivered (see, for example, Kettl 2000), has been developing and has become widely accepted. Although this idea of continual reform appears to be superior to the assumption that one particular change could fix government once and for all, a style that has often characterized reforming efforts, it does appear excessively optimistic about the capacity to produce one positive change after another in management.

A large number of reasons exist for the continuing changes in the public sector. They can be separated analytically, but they also are somewhat linked and reinforcing. For example, "administrative" reasons may motivate some of the political responses that have been identified and discussed. Further, some of the responses to previous reforms may be simply reversions to the status quo ante, and others are attempts to drive the reform process even further and to create even greater efficiency (as defined largely in market terms). Therefore, one must be careful in analyzing and categorizing the logic of continued public-sector reform. As I engage in this analysis, I will be particularly concerned with the politics of reform and the way in which political factors—bureaucratic as well as electoral—condition the behaviors of would-be reformers. It is easy to become captivated by the managerial ideas involved in reform, but one must always remember that this is reform in the public sector and that there is always a political environment within which change occurs.

ADMINISTRATIVE REASONS

The first set of reasons for the continuation of reform is labeled here "administrative." This group of justifications reflects the simple fact that administrative reforms have administrative consequences, and one round of reform often creates the opportunity, the necessity, or both, for subsequent rounds. This pattern of continuing reforms has been observed previously (Salamon 1980), but what appears to be different for contemporary reforms is that there has been such a short period of time between one change and the next. Governments hardly have time to assess the consequences of one reform before the next is being effected. Employees of the public sector thus often find that they have little time to adjust to one change in management practices before there are others, sometimes returning to the practices that had just been abandoned. This is a practical problem, but it is also an analytic problem in sorting out what, if anything, caused improvement or decline in performance in government organizations.

Disappointment

The simplest explanation for reform begetting further reform in the contemporary period, or any other period, is severe disappointment with the consequences of the initial attempts. Observers of the reform process commonly note that producing meaningful change is difficult at best in public-sector organizations (Caiden 1990; Loeffler 1997). Likewise, political actors are often reluctant to advocate or authorize reforms for fear of threatening the acquired rights and benefits of their constituents or of their favorite interest group. One consequence of the as yet inadequate theoretical and practical understanding of reform processes is that the outcomes of an administrative change are difficult to predict and often are quite the reverse of those intended (Hood and Peters 2000). Therefore, given the understandable skepticism that politicians and civil servants may have concerning any attempts at reforming administration, expectations may have to be inflated in order to overcome the inertia and the apprehension about the possible consequences of the reforms.

Given the problems of skepticism and resistance to change in government, to have any genuine opportunity of being adopted a reform must have *predicted* consequences that are so beneficial that the ultimate outcomes are almost certain to be disappointing. There was that same tendency to oversell the possible outcomes during the reforms of the 1960s and 1970s, simply to encourage reluctant politicians and members of the public to consider engaging in what might be a difficult process (Szanton 1981). During that earlier period, the same persistence of reforming was observed, at least in the area of budgeting (Schick 1988). Much of the overselling of reforms and raising of expectations may be unconscious, given the ideological commitment of many reformers to their enterprise. Some of this exaggeration, however, may be more conscious and motivated by more manifest political needs, with the need to generate some form of movement in the political system being one common justification of this sort. The experienced reformer will understand the difficulty of generating acceptance of changes and attempt strenuously to convince the relevant actors of the virtues of the change.[1]

The implementation of the Financial Management Initiative in the United Kingdom appears to be an example of disappointment producing even greater reform. The FMI introduced the concept of cost centers into the management of British government and was intended to make managers more conscious of the purposes for which public money was being spent. There were high hopes that this reform would create a more businesslike climate within the public sector in Britain and would thereby save it a good deal of money (Zifcak 1994). The FMI was supported by leading figures in the Conservative government of the day, who had great expectations of transforming the very nature of governing in Britain and devaluing the traditional power of the public service. These expectations were perhaps unrealistic, given the rather modest nature of the reforms themselves and the technical difficulties in allocating costs within many public programs. It was probably also unrealistic to expect significant changes in the deeply ingrained culture of administration in Britain from a primarily technical reform such as this, but its advocates certainly did act is if this were possible (see Brooks and Bate 1994 for a more optimistic perspective). Further, there was a mismatch between the disaggregated management implied by the FMI program and the maintenance of the unified ministerial structure within each department, with the consequence that this reform created managerial problems within each organization where it was implemented.

Still, the failure of this change to produce any significant modifications of behavior resulted in the search for even greater changes and ever greater gains in efficiency and economy in government.[2] The long tenure of the Thatcher government enabled it to create changes such as Next Steps by the time she and her successor, John Major, left office (Hood 1996). In particular, the Next Steps reform rectified the structural and managerial imbalances created by the FMI (Kemp 1994). This legacy of change continued with the implementation of accrual accounting (Resource Accounting and Budgeting [RAB]) into government toward the end of the 1990s, with some of the implementation coming under the Labour government. This late reform could be seen as the linear successor of the FMI and as completing some of the shift toward more businesslike managerial systems within the public sector.[3] RAB, too, is apparently "merely" technical but is also believed by its advocates to have the potential for sweeping impacts on government (Likierman 1998). In time, this reform may be only the source of another disappointment and another attempt at reform.

Disappointment with public-sector reforms is hardly a new phenomenon, and the history of planned change in government is one of numerous disappointments (Pollitt 1984; Raadschelders 1997). What is remarkable, therefore, is that governments continue to try to produce change and that political leaders continue to invest their scarce political capital in that extremely uncertain process. This dominance of hope over experience represents a continuing paradox of reform. As yet another of the paradoxes, given the generally low regard in which the public has tended to hold government during the past several decades (Norris 1998), there may be some sense that policy and performance in the public sector could not be much worse, so therefore reform has not been as threatening as it might otherwise be.

Success

Academic analysts of the public sector can reliably be expected to poke fun at the presumed naïveté of reformers operating within government and to assume that they are on some quixotic quest for an administrative Holy Grail, if that is not mixing metaphors too badly. What has been astounding about many of the administrative reforms observed during the past several decades is that they have been implemented and have worked. By no means have all of them been successful, but more have been so than we clever academics would have predicted, based on both the long history of their failure and the absence of any strong theoretical guidance for the reformers.

Given that there has been a reasonable number of successes, it may not be surprising that governments would continue to advocate reforms and to attempt to see just how far they can push change within their bureaucracies. The demonstrated capacity to produce meaningful change in administrative systems may have only whetted the appetite of contemporary reformers and may have made opposition on the grounds of impracticality more difficult to sustain. Bureaucrats and politicians who might in the past have been successful in resisting change now find it more difficult to argue that the reforms will not work, and they must find more compelling reasons to maintain that any proposed reform is impractical. Of course, saying that reforms in general are possible and practical does not mean that any *particular* reforms will be practical and successful, but the debate must be joined differently when there is less generalized skepticism about planned change.

Success, like so much else in administrative life, is difficult to measure or to demonstrate unequivocally and may be politically constructed as much as "real." This capacity to shape political reality enables governments who want to continue to drive change to find a good justification for their actions. If it can be argued that government has been able to be successful in reforming, then there is a reason to continue to change, thereby attempting to make government better and better. Politically, creating the belief that reform can be successful and can be brought about with a minimum of difficulty may be both advantageous and dangerous. On the one hand, such a belief makes continued reform in a desired direction more practical and can overcome some of the deep-seated resistance to change. On the other hand, creating this political belief will make reforms by any subsequent government, not of the same stripe, also easier and may therefore lead to the first round of reforms being undone.

One could argue that this culture of uncomplicated reform has to some extent been generated in many industrialized democracies, perhaps most notably the Antipodes, Canada, and some of the Scandinavian countries.[4] Such a shift of direction in reform has not happened in the United Kingdom, and the Blair government, if anything, has driven the administrative reforms of the previous Conservative governments even further and perhaps more vigorously. Similarly, in the Antipodes changes in partisan composition of governments has not been followed by radical shifts in reform strategies, but the potential is certainly there for change. In these cases, however, reforms were initiated by parties of the left rather than of the political right, as in the United Kingdom. Further, at least in New Zealand, there has been some backing away from the earlier firm commitments to managerialism and the market, as some of the unfortunate consequences of the earlier reforms have become evident (Gregory 1998). Acceptance of this backing away seems to be shared by all major parties.

Another version of success promoting further reform can be seen in the German experience of continuing incremental reforms rather than large programs, driven to some extent by "announcement politics" found in most other countries. Some analysts (Derlien 1995) have argued that Germany actually has reformed hardly at all in comparison with other European governments, and other scholars point to a continuing cycle of improvement of administration that has been in place since even before the major reforms began elsewhere (Jann 1994). Arguably, the incremental process should be expected to be more successful than the larger programs, given that the necessary smaller steps are more likely to require only minor deviations from the status quo. Success in producing major changes, however, may require a stable bureaucracy such as that found in Germany.

The interesting paradox here is that both success and failure can be conceptualized as reasons for continuing administrative reforms. Given that the two ends of a dimension appear capable of producing identical outcomes, there seems to be a need for additional variables to explain these outcomes. The more interesting question may be how political leaders who themselves deem their initial efforts at reform to be less effective than expected can still persist in advocating reform. The case of Margaret Thatcher and her persistent efforts at change is perhaps the clearest example. Her initial rounds of reform had rather modest goals and produced even more modest benefits than expected, but her personal commitment to change propelled the changes forward. Her tendency was to place the blame for failures on resistance within the bureaucracy rather than on failures of design within the programs, and that was perhaps an even greater source of motivation for continuing to drive the changes.

The other paradox of success is that some of the most successful reformers have been the most active in continued reforms of their public sectors. This can be seen most clearly in Australia and New Zealand, who have been world leaders in reforming their public sectors but who never seem satisfied with what they have produced (Halligan 2001). The paradox is especially clear in Australia, which has one of the smallest public sectors in the world but continues to press for greater economy and efficiency. Some of this continued reform may simply be that reforming gained a positive connotation in these political systems, and it became good politics to continue to change. Some of the continued drive for reform also seemed to reflect an almost ideological commitment to the ideas being used to guide the changes.

Perverse Consequences

One of the major reasons for the continuing pattern of change is that many reforms that appeared promising when considered in the abstract had rather perverse consequences when they were actually implemented. That is, rather than disappointment, these reforms produced outcomes that were directly opposite from those planned, or they produced negative side effects that offset any advantages the results may have produced. This has even been true for reforms that had been successful in one setting and then were shared with another government or even with another level of government within the same country.[5] For example, market-based reforms have been successful at lower levels of government in some countries, in part because of the more tangible nature of the services provided, but they create difficulties when applied in central government.

"Administrative science" is as yet hardly developed sufficiently to provide adequate advice that could be used to guide public-sector reforms (see Hood and Peters 2000). The predictive capacity of most of our knowledge about public administration is, to put it politely, rather limited, so that making those reforms is a question of judgment and experience as much as science.[6] Therefore, attempts at reforming the public sector may depend as much on intuition, experience, and good luck as on the capacity to predict outcomes, and therefore these perverse outcomes are to be expected (see Hood and Peters 2000). That failures and perverse outcomes can be expected, however, makes them no more desirable, and they may quickly produce yet more reform efforts.

The Grass Is Always Greener

Though many of the continuing processes of administrative reform are linear, adding one reform on top of another in a cumulative fashion, other reform processes have been cyclical, with reforms in one direction being followed (often quickly) by new reforms changing governing in the opposite direction or by returning to the status quo that existed prior to the first reform. This oscillation in the direction of change in government may be explained by the dualisms that exist for many important administrative issues[7] and the resultant inability to find any optimal strategy for organizing or reforming government (see Peters 1998). That is, centralization has some administrative virtues but so too does decentralization, and once reforms go one direction it is only natural that some of the benefits of the other approach will become evident. Reform may therefore be seen as a continuing search for the right balance of these and other factors that define proper administrative structure.

The organization and reorganization of several ministries in Denmark illustrate this pattern of change rather well. Denmark has been somewhat more agnostic about using the agency model for implementing programs than have its Scandinavian neighbors, but it has organized some public functions in this format (see Statens Information 1998). The Ministry of Education in particular, given that it supervises a significant number of largely autonomous institutions and organizations, had been organized with an agency model for some years. It then decided as a result of one round of reform in government to adopt a more unified structure from top to bottom within the ministry, although some institutions did retain autonomy. Then, after several years, managers decided to revert to the old structure (Krarup 2000) and to reintroduce the use of agencies for most of its implementation activities.

These changes within this one Danish ministry reflect the difficulties in getting the politics/administration dichotomy right, at least in its structural manifestation. On the one hand, separating implementation from policymaking may free the ministry from responsibility for day-to-day issues and enable the staff to concentrate on policy issues. On the other hand, linking implementation more closely with policymaking may improve the quality of both activities. The now familiar literature on "backward mapping" in implementation analysis (Elmore 1983; but see Linder and Peters 1987) demonstrates the potential desirability of making that linkage ever closer. No matter which choice a government has made, there may be good reasons for choosing the other organizational alternative.

Learning

These administrative justifications have described particular outcomes of reform and their possible interpretations as the principal forces driving additional reform efforts. In addition, however, there is a more generic process of learning occurring.[8] It tends to create among practitioners of public administration both an awareness of the possibilities of reform and a dissatisfaction with the outcomes of earlier processes. There is a great deal of learning about the reform process and its outcomes occurring across and within countries. The spread of information through a variety of mechanisms—international organizations, academics, consulting firms, and the Internet, among others—means that any one country will have numerous exemplars for change.

The spread of ideas and learning about reform has several interesting features. One is that adopting any particular reform may in fact make the country more likely to continue to change, given that it will then become part of a network of countries and/or other levels of government that have done the same thing. This is then apt to be a source of new ideas about fine-tuning the reform that has been adopted, with the likelihood of many small but perhaps still significant changes in the program. This appears to be especially true in relatively technical areas such as budgeting and financial management. The spread of ideas is inclined to occur within cultural and political groupings, with Anglo-American systems learning from one another and Scandinavian systems learning from one another, but there is still a continual process of change resulting.

This learning is relatively natural, with governments adopting changes in an autonomous fashion. In some cases, however, it may be characterized by a more coercive element, with governments being expected to adopt the ideas of managerialism in order to receive support from international organizations or donor nations. Many poorer and transitional countries are ill-suited for the introduction of this style of management, with the result that governance may actually decline as programs of "good governance" are adopted and implemented.

Another interesting outcome of the learning process can be termed "recursive learning," meaning that the originator of a style of reform may find it adopted elsewhere, refined (or at least changed), and then reimported. This was clearly the case with Total Quality Management, an idea first advanced by the American W. E. Deming, exported to Japan, and then reimported years later into both the private and public sectors in the United States. More recently, the idea of using agencies to deliver public services has been returned to a more prominent place in governments in the Scandinavian countries in a somewhat modified form after having become used commonly in much of the rest of the world.

TECHNICAL REASONS

The second set of reasons for changes begetting changes in the public sector will be discussed as "technical" ones. These factors may be considered a subset of the administrative reasons, but these several points do identify some of the inherent problems of measurement and conceptualization of reforms' consequences rather than factors that arise during the actual implementation of the reforms themselves. These categories, however, clearly do meet and overlap at their margins, so that categorization is to some extent for presentational purposes as much as it is for analytical clarity.

Measurement

One of the dominant technical problems in reforming government is in measuring what has been achieved—before, during, and after the reform. As reform proceeds, this problem can be observed along two dimensions. First, the economic question: how much money has been saved and how much has efficiency in service provision been improved? At least for some reformers, these financial questions are the dominant concern. As for the second question, how much have services delivered to the public been improved, and is the public more satisfied with them? Indeed, there are marked problems in identifying exactly how we can measure the quality of services in an unequivocal manner (see, for example, Bouckaert 1995).

To some extent the notion of continual improvement in government services is being institutionalized as the means of using measurement as a way to drive reforms. As governments begin to focus on performance management as the mechanism for assessing the need for changing their policies, administration, or both, the idea that programs can continue to change for the better becomes a set of ever higher hurdles facing public managers. This to some extent has been a political strategy for central agencies to co-opt organizations into the performance-management process; if the performance standards are set low enough at the beginning, managers cannot reasonably opt out of the performance system, and once they are in, the standards can be raised again and again.

Associated with accepting the concept of continual improvement in public management has been the institutionalization of greater evaluative capacity for examining and assessing the consequences of reforms for organizations and for the public (Holkeri and Summa 1997). Although this idea clearly corresponds to that of success or failure driving change, the institutionalization of evaluation means that there is less latitude for political and administrative actors to construct success and failure as they see fit. Of course, the measures employed in evaluations, especially of policies as potentially slippery as administrative reforms, are far from perfectly objective. Still, given the need to specify criteria for success and to provide measures that can be agreed upon by the actors, a more institutionalized evaluation system can help to depoliticize the assessment of reforms.[9]

What Are the Limits?

Following from the point concerning measurement problems for performance in the public sector, another technical problem in assessing the effects of reforms is that it is difficult to know just how far they can be pushed and if there are any absolute standards against which to compare the efficiency of public organizations. One perhaps extreme example would be whether the Swedish and Irish governments are able to continue to push their programs of reducing the operating budgets of agencies and departments by a fixed percentage each year.[10] Zeno's paradox aside, this process eventually would result in there being no operating budget for these organizations, so there is obviously some limit to these programs of cutting.

This example illustrates the point that in government one rarely can say just how much efficiency is possible, and how much public expenditure for each purpose is enough and how much is too much. These are of course political judgments, but they are also managerial judgments made in the absence of good measures of the value of what is being produced and the true costs of producing those publicly provided goods and services. The shift toward an emphasis on performance in government is helping to rectify some of those difficulties, but even the advocates of that approach to reform are conscious of the measurement problems and the absence of any clear standard.

POLITICAL REASONS

The dominant reasons for the continuing cycles of reforms in public administration are political, dominant meaning here the most powerful forces affecting the continuation of efforts at reform, albeit perhaps not the most frequently occurring. Some of the reforms discussed may actually have been initiated through the administrative agencies involved themselves, but the ultimate evaluation of the utility and the desirability of continued reforming will generally be done within the partisan political institutions. As in most matters of importance in the public sector, politics is trumps for administrative reform, and the continuing processes of change cannot be understood without understanding the political pressures that surround them.

"Political" should be understood rather broadly in this context and should include interorganizational politics as well as the partisan politics that usually motivates decisions of this sort. In particular, the administrative reforms introduced during the past several decades have altered the relative power distributions of organizations within government and therefore may have set up the need for additional attempts at change. To some extent the first rounds of reforms reduced the power of the central control agencies, and even some ministries, and have enhanced the power of the huge number of autonomous and quasi-autonomous organizations that have been spawned by the past reforms (Bouckaert, Ormond, and Peters 2000; Peters 1998). These politics may be vested with a partisan element, especially when the opposition can use these issues to embarrass a sitting government,[11] but many of their manifestations are purely organizational.

The Paradox of Quality

There has been a growing emphasis on the quality of services provided as a part of the reform process. The outcomes here appear somewhat paradoxical (see also Hesse, Hood, and Peters 2000). It seems that by raising the issue of quality in the public services, and by attempting to measure it, the apparent quality of services may have decreased even though it may in reality have been improving all the while. The political problem here (related to the preceding measurement problems) is that once the channels for complaint and for exercising other forms of "voice" are opened, then quality concerns become more difficult for sitting politicians to ignore (see Norris 1998).

The paradox observed here is that although the quality of public services has probably increased in a number of countries and in a number of policy areas, the creation of new mechanisms for the public to exercise voice may make it appear as if the services actually have deteriorated significantly. This perceived problem with quality, in turn, has driven the performance movement. This paradoxical outcome of reform appears to have occurred even in the Scandinavian countries that have had mechanisms for popular involvement in managing public services for much longer periods of time, and it has certainly been manifest in countries without those traditions, perhaps most notably in the United Kingdom.

The politics involved with the management of quality has been both organizational and partisan. Central agencies have been able to use the perceived shortcomings in service provision as levers to attempt to reassert some of their powers over policy and over organizations. The quality paradox is therefore linked both to accountability and to performance as second stages of reform, with central agencies to some extent crucial actors in both issues. For politicians, the accountability issue has emerged as the paramount concern. The (real or perceived) difficulties of public organizations in providing services to the public have meant a renewed interest in a means of holding them accountable, even if those means usually imply a reassertion of conventional ministerial accountability models (Aucoin and Heintzman 2000). This is unlikely to be the style of accountability that is most compatible with the reforms already adopted, but it is the form of best understood by politicians and therefore may be the form that is pursued most vigorously.

Changes in Parties and Ideologies

The most obvious political explanation for a change in reform priorities is that political parties change office, and with change in party comes changes in ideologies about government and the nature of the "good" public sector. As appealing as that explanation may be, the empirical record of reform experiences over the past several decades actually shows a remarkable degree of persistence of ideas about change in the public sector when parties change. In the political systems of Scandinavia and the Low Countries this persistence can be explained by coalition governments, consensus politics, and broad agreement within the society over the desirable nature of the public sector (Arter 1999). Even in the "majoritarian" government (Lijphart 1984) of the United Kingdom, however, administrative reform from Major to Blair has been almost a seamless web, with the Labour government if anything being more willing to "name and shame" failing parts of the public sector and to be more draconian in imposing their own views on organizations in both central and local governments.

Still, there often have been interesting transformations of reform strategies with changes in partisan control of government. One of the clearest cases is in France, where the Rocard and Juppe governments implemented rather different approaches to reform and to the public sector more generally (Bezes 2000). The socialist Rocard government, perhaps somewhat surprisingly, approached reform from a managerial and market perspective, adopting reforms such as the introduction of "responsibility centers" and attempting to make public servants more conscious of the costs of providing public services (Ministere de la Fonc-tion Publique 1994). Perhaps because it was a market reform being driven by a left-of-center government, these reforms are generally considered to have been successful.[12]

The Gaullist Juppe government that followed Rocard, however, sought first to enhance accountability by separating politics and administration and, in the process, reduced the power of the civil service while enhancing that of politicians and their appointees. It also sought to strengthen quasi-corporatist institutions already existing within French government. The Juppe reform program to some extent reversed the technocratic, strong-state vision of France and French gov-ernment that had been a central feature of Gaullist policy to attempt to promote somewhat greater democracy, both within public organizations and between them and the society (see Knapp 1994).

The interesting findings in these two reforms in France are not only that the change in political party did produce a significant departure from the patterns of reform that had been established but also that the directions of reform were far from predictable, given the ideologies of the parties involved. Indeed, the two governments adopted programs that might have been exactly the opposite of any informed observer's prior expectation of their preferences. There appears to be some felt need on the part of participants in a government of one ideological per-suasion, following one of another political cast, to reverse the previous reforms, or at least to water them down. This is true even if the reforms being reversed actually conform to the conventional program and policy of the party coming to office.[13]

Another version of the partisan drive in reform is that many of the changes implemented during the previous decades have tended to lessen the degree of control over bureaucracies available to other actors involved in the governance process, whether that accountability has been managed directly by political offi-cials or through other mechanisms for ensuring it (Aucoin and Heintzmann 2000; Peters 1999). With the familiar institutions of accountability having been deval-ued, politicians in many governments have returned to older, politicized versions of it in order to regain some control over the activities in organizations for which they, as political leaders, e.g., cabinet ministers, are nominally responsible. Thus, there has been a strong drive to make use of political appointments to positions that at one time might have been held by career officials.

Continuing to Run for Office

Another political justification for continuing to implement reforms is that political parties continue to run for office. In many countries it is politically profitable to run against the bureaucracy and to continue to suggest means for reducing the power of the public sector. In the United States, for example, even incumbents attempt to portray themselves as outsiders and attack the bureaucracy in Washington rather unmercifully. The reduction of public-sector employment and expenditure generally is acceptable if government is able to produce it without any reduction in the services rendered to the public, so the cost reductions must be achieved through efficiency. Even in countries that have a well-respected public sector and a commitment to providing public services, bureaucracy is not valued per se, and there is political mileage to be made by proposing to minimize it.

The continuing pressures to reform and to reduce the costs of government can be identified clearly in the experience of Dutch governments since the mid-1980s. Beginning at least at the time of Lubbers I, the Dutch governments embarked on a major and progressive series of reforms, and that behavior appeared to become a part of the expectations for any government. The pattern of reform continued through the Lubbers II government, into the "purple coalition," and even to the present, with no apparent end point in sight. Administrative reform may simply have become what governments in the Netherlands do. To some extent, the continuing reform process in Finland represents a similar commitment by successive governments to making government perform more effectively and efficiently. For over a decade one Finnish government after another has pursued goals of efficiency and effectiveness, and the quest appears to be continuing. The electoral connection may not be as clear as it is in other cases, but reforming has now become a component of popular expectations about government.

Going Too Far

Another possible explanation for continuing reform efforts is that their initial rounds may overestimate the possibilities and desirability of certain changes and thus go too far in pressing reforms or in proposing and implementing changes that are too extreme. This is perhaps another means of making the point that administrative science does not yet have the capacity to make unambiguous statements that can guide the initial design and reform of public-sector organizations. It may be clear that something is amiss within the public sector, but it is much less clear what exactly should be done about it. Further, even if it were clear what the problem is, it may be much less clear what the remedies may be.

The reregulation of government is one obvious case of going too far in one style of reform and then having to reverse the direction of that change. Deregulation, for instance, was one popular remedy for the problems of government, but it may have opened up the public sector both to unpredictability and corruption. Therefore, many new forms of internal regulation have been adopted, and some older ones brought back, in order to reinstitute some of that control. Interestingly, however, that reregulation has itself perhaps gone too far so that a discussion has emerged, at least in the United Kingdom, about relaxing (or perhaps redirecting) the controls that have been imposed (Hood et al. 1999).

The experience of the Dutch in implementing structural reforms illustrates the possibilities of going too far, too quickly, in changing the structural configurations of government. The government was interested in moving functions out of the ministries and rather early in the process created a number of quasi-governmental organizations that were to function at an arm's distance. These organizations—referred to by the Dutch acronym ZBO—succeeded in moving the functions out of the ministries but in the process created their own substantial problems of accountability. They were more flexible in responding to changing social and economic conditions but were in some cases sufficiently capable of doing so to ignore these very conditions.

The next round of structural reform in the Netherlands represented some backing away from the strategy of creating ZBOs in favor of creating organizations more similar to the agency structures that now have become familiar in the British public sector. These agencies are substantially more autonomous than would be the component sections of a conventional ministry, but they are also more closely linked to hierarchical political authority than most of the ZBOs have been. The use of the agency model still presents substantial problems of accountability within Dutch government, but they have been minimized by backing away from the more radical initial change. The initial reforms had clearly gone too far, and the government is engaged in a learning process about how to balance its autonomy and accountability goals.

Decentralization and centralization provide another example of governments going too far and then having to reverse their actions.[14] This dimension of organizational structures is an old and familiar one in the public sector, but the alternation between the two solutions can be seen in the reform process. For example, one strategy of change has been to decentralize control over purchasing. This was presumed to permit organizations to make more of their own decisions about what they needed to do their job and to match their purchases with local variations. Decentralization of purchasing was one aspect of the deregulation of the public sector, with central purchasing organizations (for example, the General Services Administration in the United States) being devalued and often disbanded.

Yet decentralizing the purchasing function ignored much of the economic advantage that a large organization, such as a government operating as a single entity, can obtain through purchasing in large quantities. This economic logic then calls for using a centralized purchasing function for at least part of the activities of government. That structural and procedural decision, in turn, implies that some forms of regulation over items that individual organizations can and cannot purchase will be introduced de facto if not de jure. These restrictions may not be as severe as in the past, but there will still be restrictions and standards. Denmark is an example of this pattern of change in purchasing, with initial attempts at decentralization being followed more recently by reintroduction of centralized purchasing for a large number of items. This then is yet another example of one style of reform (deregulation) being incompatible with, if not antagonistic to, another (the market).

Organizational Politics

Aside from partisan politics, there have been clear cases in which the drive for reform comes from real or potential conflict among organizations within government. These political conflicts often arise between central agencies that want to maintain, or now perhaps to recapture, their traditional dominance over budgets and management and that also seek to exert control over the newly created organizations in a more devolved public sector. The ministries that lost some control over devolved organizations will also want to recapture some influence. Similarly, the organizational products of previous efforts at reform desire to maintain and enhance their own autonomy, given that much of the logic of their creation was to be able to function with fewer controls. This rather natural conflict over power and autonomy therefore is one of the dynamics behind continued reforms, with each set of actors attempting to maximize its capacity to shape policy and to shape the budgets and personnel of the devolved organizations.

Somewhat paradoxically again, devolution of authority within the public sector has in many ways enhanced the power of central agencies rather than actually increasing the effective powers of lower-level organizations in government. This paradox results from the fact that after devolved organizations have been created, there is almost immediately a perceived need to coordinate their activities and to ensure that the more pervasive goals of government are being pursued by all, or at least most, public organizations. Given that ministerial controls over policy and implementation are often dismantled in the process of devolving powers to agencies or quasi-autonomous organizations, the major candidates for applying that control are central agencies, perhaps especially the financial ministries. Further, the types of indirect control that have been implemented as part of the managerialist reforms tend to be more suitable for manipulation by the central agencies than to being used by line ministers.

The role of central agencies is important for exercising control over autonomous and quasi-autonomous organizations and perhaps even more so for maintaining it over the increasing number of contractual relationships with third-party organizations responsible for providing public services (Fortin and Van Hassel 2000). These indirect controls available to central agencies may be the only realistic means of addressing the behavior of these organizations that are beyond the hierarchical control of ministries; and therefore central agencies—wielding as they do budgetary and personnel controls and often also having the capacity to review secondary legislation issued by administrative bodies—are the most logical sources of control. They can provide direction to a group of semiautonomous organizations that were created in their current form at least in part to evade other forms of control, such as that exercised by ministers in line departments.

Some aspects of this mode of reaction to previous reforms can be identified in the consolidation of financial and personnel management functions during the past several years. During the 1980s and 1990s the organizational fashion had become to create a number of separate organizations, all performing some aspect of the task of financial management within the public sector. For example, Sweden in 1988 had three economics ministries—Finance, Economic Affairs, and Budget—and a number of other countries had separated the budget function from finance or its equivalent.[15] Further, the pattern of having a separate personnel-management organization had been institutionalized in most countries.[16] The more common pattern at this writing is to have a single ministry exercising the full range of financial and personnel controls over a more disparate public sector. Likewise, in some cases the finance ministry or some other central agency has recaptured the personnel function that may also have been given to more autonomous organizations, again with the intention of unifying controls over management within government.[17]

The reregulation movement is another manifestation of interorganizational politics in the public sector and attempts to restore control from the center. Decentralization and deregulation created substantial autonomy for organizations and for their managers. Though perhaps creating some efficiency benefits, these reforms also have generated a number of problems, and central organizations have counterattacked by imposing regulatory devices. It is important to remember, however, that these devices are largely ex post facto, in contrast to the ex ante controls that characterized government prior to reform. Thus, this represents yet another attempt to get the balance of centralized control and organizational autonomy right, a search that is likely to continue as some of the excesses of reregulation become evident to managers.

Further, the creation of so many autonomous organizations within the public sector, and the increasing use of private-sector organizations to provide public services on its behalf, has created another form of interorganizational politics. Besides creating the demands for reregulation of the autonomized public organizations, their political need for support has led them to become more actively competitive and to seek more powerful mechanisms for influencing the budget and legislative processes. The budgetary process is almost inherently competitive (Kraan 1996), but the creation of more actors, and their increased linkages with the private sector, may make the process more competitive and the public sector more internally divisive. The consequences of those divisions may depend on several additional factors. On the one hand, if the autonomous organizations are closely linked with the private sector, then the capacity of central agencies to control them may be lessened.[18] On the other hand, if the organizations lack such linkages and are highly fragmented, the control capacity of the center may be increased.

CAVEATS

The idea that government can continue to reform and to deliver services in a more efficient and effective manner is now deeply ingrained in the public sector. The stated assumption of many programs of reform is that continued efficiency improvements are available on an annual basis and that it is the job of the public manager to find and implement them. This is a laudable manifestation of faith in public managers and in public servants, but one must question how realistic it is. It may well be that public programs have already been squeezed sufficiently and that they are operating at reasonable, or even exceptional, levels of efficiency. The economics and management sciences for the public sector do not as yet appear sufficiently developed to say when the point of diminishing returns for managerial changes has been reached, so that the only way of determining that is to overshoot and perhaps to harm some clients in the process. This is not necessarily an argument to stop seeking efficiency improvements, but it is a plea for caution and care when pressing managerial changes.

The possible strains the continued paring of administrative budgets may have for government present but one consideration. Another is that this emphasis on administration as the means of improving services apparently assumes that the programs being delivered are themselves appropriate and are conceptualized in the best manner, or at least adequately to meet the needs of the public. If the programs are not well designed, then an emphasis on management may only exacerbate the fundamental problems and make life worse for the clients. Of course, other aspects of the reforms—consumerization and public consultation, for example—are intended to deal with the ways in which citizens believe that they are being affected by existing programs, or lack of them. It does appear appropriate, however, for program designers and managers to consider the nature of their programs, the definition of the problems they address, the nature of the instruments they use for implementation, and their assumptions about clients that undergird the programs, along with considering management when they think about improved services.

The emphasis on citizens' problems resulting from poor administration is also a way that politicians can defend their own positions and their own possible inadequacies in the design and funding of programs. If education fails because of poor teachers and poor principals in the schools, then blaming school boards (and parents who do not vote for increased taxes for education in local elections) allows the politician an easy escape from being responsible for those failures (see Cohn 1997). There are, of course, poor teachers and poor school administrators; but there are also problems in education that go well beyond that level in the system, and these service providers can be made the scapegoats for other decisions. We also need to be concerned with the capacity of governments to assess and evaluate the consequences of the reforms they have adopted. Piling one reform on top of another makes such assessment more difficult. If there are positive or negative changes in the performance of an organization that has been reformed several times, which of those several changes is the cause, or is it the interaction of all the reforms that was responsible? The difficulties in evaluation are in many ways a boon for reformers, given that they can always claim success and place blame on other changes. Still, for political leaders and citizens alike, there should be some means of understanding whether the benefits claimed for a reform are indeed related to that change, and whether they are worth the (personal and financial) costs of the upheaval involved.

In assessing these administrative reforms, one must consider what the end point is toward which each reform is heading, or indeed if one is clearly identified. Are the implementations simply change for change's sake, or are there some superordinate goals that motivate the changes and move government services toward higher levels of objective performance and efficiency? The evidence to date is inconclusive and could easily support either argument. On the one hand, there has been some general movement toward government management that is more similar to the private sector in the way in which it allocates resources and manages its internal activities. On other hand, the reforms contain sufficient internal variation to say that there are no general principles and that different ideas are being grabbed in order to justify a movement from the status quo, often simply for political expediency rather than from any real commitment to improvement.

Further, one of the casualties of the initial rounds of reform has been the predictability that citizens and public employees once had from their governments. Citizens are probably better served through consumerization of public programs and the creation of a more service-oriented ethos within the public sector. They may lose some of the benefits of those changes, however, through the loss of uniformity and predictability that has occurred along with, and to a great extent as a result of, the more positive changes. This absence of predictability is in part a function of the empowerment of the lower-echelon service providers in bureaucracies (Peters and Pierre 2000) and the use of nongovernmental providers for many services. The variability in services available to "consumers" may in fact infringe on basic rights of citizens, with the services provided being different, based on factors outside program criteria. Moreover, employees may be empowered, but they must confront frequent changes in the requirements of their jobs and expectations about their performance. This constant change infringes less on the rights of the civil servants than on the treatment of citizens, but it does certainly present morale problems.

CONCLUSIONS

The progression of public-sector reforms is remarkable for several interrelated reasons. One is the simple magnitude of change that has occurred in administrative systems, which have a natural inclination to be static. Further, changes have been implemented virtually everywhere in the world, and the variety of types of changes is dramatic and unprecedented. Often there is a "flavor of the month" that defines reform at one point in history, but there have been numerous and often contradictory perspectives involved in this round of change. Perhaps only in time of war or major economic upheavals have governments attempted to reform themselves with quite this degree of zeal and over such an extended period of time.

Even when the results of administrative reforms have been disappointing to their advocates, or produced results directly contrary to those intended by their designers, many reformers appear to have persisted along the general routes that they were already treading. In the terminology of the historical institutionalist, there seems to have been a great deal of "path dependency" (Thelen, Longstreth, and Steinmo 1992) in these programs of reforming the public sector. Simple inertia, or intellectual commitment to particular styles of reform and particular styles of governing, has produced an apparent inability among decision makers to react to failure in ways other than to do more of what has already failed. Thus, no matter whether managerialist changes resulted in any definable benefits for government or for the public, elites involved in the process of producing change were likely to continue to implement yet more changes of roughly the same type.

The multiplicity of apparent reasons and rationalizations for reform and the apparent incapacity to determine clearly when sufficient change has been achieved reflect the rather inadequate state of theorizing about organizations and organizational performance in the public sector (Rainey 1997). Scholars and practitioners still find it difficult to ascertain whether one organizational format is likely to be more effective than others in particular circumstances in the public sector. They also find it difficult to determine whether one approach to reform will be able to produce desired outcomes when others will not.[19] In short, administrative science has a long way to go to become the predictive science that would make such useful advice about change within government possible. And although I have developed what appears to be an interesting catalog of the causes of continued efforts at reform, there is as yet no theoretical guidance for understanding the political and administrative processes involved in any of them, or any means for determining when reform is likely to be successful or not.

Reform of the public sector has been, and continues to be, an active concern of governments in Europe, North America, the Antipodes, and most other countries of the world. These reforms have been characterized by their advocates as providing a range of "solutions" and a variety of styles of intervention for political and administrative officials interested in improving government performance. Public administration certainly appears different from how it looked only a few decades ago, and a different language is used to describe the way in which government works. However, we must still ask whether the aphorism *plus ça change* applies here as well. That is, despite all the reforms—successful and otherwise—any number of problems remain in public administration in these countries, and some of these represent the products of previous reform activity. Governments have reformed and find that these processes have had their benefits, but they also have their costs, so that there remains a great deal of work (analytically and practically) to do in order to make government perform as most citizens and most politicians would like.

8

Administrative Reform in Developing and Transitional Governments

The ideas of the New Public Management and associated administrative reforms have spread around the world almost inexorably. Some of the dynamic of the propagation of managerialist concepts has been relatively natural, with academics as well as political and administrative leaders coming into contact with those ideas, accepting them, and then attempting to implement them in their own country. This natural spread of ideas has been most characteristic of administrative reform in the industrialized democracies (Peters 1998). Even this process may not be entirely autonomous, however, given that there are some subtle yet real pressures from international organizations to conform to the "best practices" available at the time, especially for countries within the European Union.[1] Simply labeling some type of reform as "best practice" may make an innovation desirable for administrators, politicians, or both.

Another component in the diffusion of these ideas has been substantially less autonomous, with international donor organizations and consulting firms responsible for the ideas being spread and adopted. This style of policy transfer has been more characteristic of the less developed countries and transitional regimes, which must trade compliance with what has come to be known as "good governance" for loans and grants from the major international donor organizations. The degree and type of coercion involved in having reform ideas adopted in these countries vary, but it is clear that there has been some external pressure involved in most cases. For the former socialist states in Europe, for example, the European Union is demanding adherence to basic administrative standards and the ability to administer the Union rules (*acquis communautaire*) as a condition of entry. This is not to deny that the ideas themselves have some appeal and some advocates, but there is some external pressure and an incentive to adopt the programs.

In this chapter I will address the political and administrative dynamics of change in two sets of countries that share some common features but that also have distinctive problems of their own. On the one hand, there are the less-developed countries of Latin America, Africa, and parts of Asia. On the other hand are numerous transitional regimes, the countries that until a decade ago were under control of the Communist Party. I will attempt not only to describe the changes that have been taking place but also to question the appropriateness of the types of reforms for improving governing within these countries. I have noted elsewhere (Peters 1998) that a question always arises concerning administrative reforms: does one size fit all, and should the same types of reform be implemented in all political systems? If that is a question for the developed countries (and it certainly is), then it is an even more important one for countries that have such different political and administrative histories and traditions.

I will focus on the implementation of the ideas and practices associated with New Public Management, but many of the ideas associated with Western-style management more generally may be inappropriate for use in other social and cultural settings. The implementation of these foreign management practices has been going on for some decades, harking back in some ways to colonialism and the imposition of the administrative model from the colonial master. The mechanisms used to impose Western ideas may be somewhat more subtle in the third millennium, but they still represent assumptions that one style of managing (whether in the public or the private sector) is best, and indeed is the only acceptable way. Though many more conventional Western administrative ideas may indeed help in ridding societies of corruption as an accepted way of doing public business, the ideology of NPM is not the universal panacea that its advocates appear to assume it is.

The NPM has had numerous failings in the developed world and almost certainly even more in the other groups of states where it is being implemented. My argument here is that governments in developing and transitional regimes need to build up their administrative capacities before they consider means of reform and dismantling the rather formalistic systems. Managing the transitions from centrally planned economies toward more marketized systems and helping to manage the creation of democratic systems of government will require a more rather than less effective system of public administration. In particular it will require an administrative system that comes as close to some of the traditional ideals of probity and equality as possible.

I will first present some ideas about the administrative system(s) in place before there were attempts at major reforms. These existing systems constitute the environment within which government functioned prior to the reforms and therefore establish some of the constraints under which reform will function. Next I will examine the implementation of planned changes in the developing and transitional governments. In this case there will be little need to develop the concepts of reform being adopted, given that they are in essence the same ones already discussed. What will differ is their meaning in different political and cultural contexts and the capacity of governments to implement the ideas.

THE TRADITIONAL MODEL OF ADMINISTRATION

No single traditional model of public administration can capture all the variations occurring in these two groups of countries, although there are some regularities among the cases. To some extent the traditional model found in these countries is little different from that of the industrialized democracies. Certainly countries that have derived their administrative systems directly from European countries have imported (voluntarily or not) many of the same conceptions of what constitutes proper public administration (see Braibanti 1966). Even after the colonial period had passed, the ideas about good administration inculcated in the systems persisted. In some cases the colonial power was extremely successful in inculcating its ideas, for example the British experience in India. In other cases, e.g., the Latin American countries, the connections with the former colonial power are more remote, and a particular administrative style, albeit with some distinctive Iberian ancestry, has been developed.[2] In the transitional regimes there may be a double process of reform in process, the first change being simply to rid themselves of the former Communist practices and perhaps to revert to some preexisting vision of proper administration. This change is being followed closely by the New Public Management reforms. The administrative styles to which the countries might revert are somewhat different. The German and Russian (imperial) styles were the most common alternatives, but the historical gaps were sufficient to mean that to a great extent public administration had to be reinvented from the ground up. For the period of the late 1930s until the 1990s, the countries of East and Central Europe had known one authoritarian system after another. Given that vacuum of indigenous ideas about more democratic styles of administration, the ideas of NPM can constitute something of a basis for the new systems. This pattern of change, however, may present severe problems in creating effective administration and especially in institutionalizing democratic accountability.

Although the traditional concepts of public administration in many regimes of these two groups of countries may appear somewhat similar to those found in the industrialized democracies, the reality may be rather different. As Fred Riggs (1964) pointed out decades ago, there may be marked differences between the stated values and the practices of public administration in many less developed systems, and certainly the same may be true for the transitional regimes. In most of these cases there is a clear understanding of what the nature of good—meaning both efficient and accountable—administration should be, but there are political and social conditions that frequently prevent achieving that desirable style of governing. This discrepancy between norms and practices should be an environment suitable for reform[3] but may have become so much a part of the existing system in many governments that it is hardly noticed. Therefore, in practice public administration may be far from the ideal, though there is still lip service to the ideals of good government.

Some of the chestnuts that have guided administration in the industrialized democracies are more undermined than are others through the administrative double-talk in these countries. For example, the idea of hierarchical management and reliance on formalized, impersonal rules when dealing with citizens appears to make less sense in many less developed societies that have strong family and social-group linkages. In such societies rules tend not be considered universal but as a place to begin bargaining about who gets what, with the criteria for allocation often being based on ascriptive rather than achievement criteria, and particularistic rather than universal in their application. The practices that result from the different social and ethical understandings characteristic of less developed countries may be considered corrupt in Western societies but would be considered appropriate, or merely necessary and desirable, in other societies (Quah 1999). Thus, the concept of corruption in administration that appears well understood in the industrialized democracies is far from accepted in much of the rest of the world.

In the transitional political systems there had been different sets of rules, rewards, and responsibilities, depending on the individual's connection with the dominant political party—the old nomenklatura system in the Soviet Union was the extreme case (see Obolonsky 1999). In short, the Weberian idea that rules should be applied *sine irae et studio* to all members of the society simply had not been central to the practice of government in these societies. The overt partiality and inequities manifested in these regimes tended to undermine any sense among the public that there was fairness and equity available through the administrative system. This loss of public trust, in turn, presents a difficult problem for the regimes that have followed to create a sense of fairness in the system and to create legitimacy. The evidence is, however, that public administration has been somewhat more successful in building that legitimacy than have other elements of the political system, perhaps because there is greater familiarity with the need for administration than with the need for representative institutions in these countries.

Following from that, the concept of a politically neutral civil service has been less central to governing in many of these countries—both less developed and transitional—than it has been in the industrialized democracies (but see Rouban 1998). This is very clear in many transitional regimes in which a hegemonic political party had been responsible for selecting members of the public service, and the scarcity of talent and the immediacy of demands for reform at present means that there is little room for competition and career structures. There was some discussion of "red vs. expert" as options for recruitment to the public service, but in reality the choice had been red *and* expert, with political reliability being a sine qua non for many positions. In many less developed countries the civil service is often committed to the developmental goals of the government, and it may also be linked by clientelistic practices and party loyalties to political leaders (Geddes 1994; Martz 1997). In these developing systems the state has played a major developmental role, and the civil service has been simply too important in the governing process to permit it to stand above the political fray and make decisions on purely technical criteria.

Further, the notion of a public service ethic that guides the actions of civil servants has not been ascribed the importance that is attached to those values in most of the industrialized democracies.[4] There was a formalized set of values that was considered important in regulating the behavior of the public service. In some cases the commitment to political party values, or to personal careers, dominated any commitment to independent public service values. And the relatively poor compensation offered to public employees in many of these administrative systems means that strong ethical commitments may be a luxury that these civil servants cannot afford economically. In short, for this dimension of public management and for others, the formal values of the public service diverge from practice, although that practice may diverge for many reasons beyond the control of the average civil servant.

The central problem for implementing public management reforms in these countries is that their success to some extent depends on the existence of public service values and practices that support accountability and effective management. For example, reforms associated with deregulating government assume that individual managers who are granted a good deal of autonomy in making decisions generally will make them with a concern for the public interest. That assumption may be accurate, given that traditional values of democratic administration have been common among the bureaucrats working within the public sector. When those values have not been fully institutionalized, however, any substantial latitude granted by deregulating government opens the door for nepotism, favoritism, and overt corruption—all in the name of more efficient management.[5] Even if the administration that results is indeed more efficient, it may be deficient on other grounds, obviously those of democracy and accountability.[6] Likewise, more participative forms of management assume that the empowered decision makers will use their new freedom to serve the public rather than to serve themselves alone, and that assumption also may be violated in practice.

IMPLEMENTING REFORMS

An all too brief survey of the implementation of reform programs in these two sets of countries follows. I will use the same categories to examine reforms in the industrialized democracies, emphasizing using the market and deregulation within the public sector. These two strategies have been the most prominent approaches to change and also perhaps the most necessary. Still, each represents dangers as well as opportunities in these countries. In particular, these societies have had little experience with markets and may still consider this approach as a suspect way in which to allocate resources. Further, deregulating the public service may not be viable before there is a set of values that will permit government to operate in an accountable and noncorrupt manner without the existence of formalized controls.

We should also remember here that administrative reform has been more frequent and ubiquitous in the less developed countries than in the more developed. Even before the industrialized democracies embarked on their orgy of reform in the 1980s and 1990s, many of the less-developed governments were already deeply involved in their second or third or fourth rounds of reform, largely at the instigation of international donors.

The most important fact about Latin America over the past four decades has been the stubbornness with which it has pursued administrative reform, despite so many failures and disappointments. Possibly nowhere else in the world have so many governments announced bold, imaginative reform plans to achieve so little in practice Latin America may have been in the reform business somewhat longer than other areas of the Third World—in part because these countries have been independent longer than those of Africa and Asia—but the continuing cycles of change have also been characteristic of the other countries' search for efficiency, effectiveness, democracy, and, perhaps most important, acceptance by national and international donors.

The transitional regimes have not been in the business of reforming themselves for very long, having only achieved the independence necessary to do so in the last decade. Still, they have been engaged in a continuing process of reform almost since they gained their independence. This has been to some extent a learning process in which the reforms adopted at the first stage of independence soon generated the need for more reform. Further, these countries have been faced with the need for implementing both economic and political reform at the same time. Reform therefore has been a constant of their political life, with the real possibility of reform fatigue and even backlash resulting as governments continue to impose change, change often driven by external rather than internal forces.

The Market

The idea of the market has been central to reforms in the industrialized democracies, and the same is true as reforming becomes a major activity in less developed and transitional regimes. In these two sets of countries, using the market may involve even more basic changes than in the industrial democracies, largely because the state has been a major economic actor in both types of regime. This has been partly a function of ideology, with the Communist regimes attempting to gain a virtual monopoly over economic activity. In the less developed countries there has been some commitment to socialist principles, but in many cases the state has been perceived as the only indigenous actor capable of mobilizing adequate capital for industrial development. In some cases that developmental role has been notable, and several of the "newly industrializing countries" have moved successfully to economic takeoffs (Evans 1995). In others, however, the role of the state has been less positive, with bureaucracy, in the pejorative sense of the term, standing in the way of the effective operation of the market.

The market-based reforms in these countries began with the basic steps of privatization and economic liberalization. These were commonly advocated steps toward making the economies more efficient and productive and were pressed by most of the donor organizations. This rather simple perspective on the role of markets, however, was a first step toward reforming the state. Numerous state-run industries have been privatized, and the regulation and protectionist policies characteristic of the state in many regimes have been reduced if not eliminated. Further, in general the state has been downsized and made a less pervasive part of the economic life in these societies, albeit not always to the benefit of the public. In addition to producing some measurable improvements in economic performance in at least some countries, privatization and reducing the role of the state also gained an ideological status in many reform efforts, with the point of diminishing returns for the use of the private sector being exceeded.

The simple rolling back of the state was an important step in its reform, but by no means was it the end of that process. After the initial rather direct and blunt attempts at producing change, the next round of market reforms began to adopt more subtle approaches to using this instrument for more effective management within the state sector. For example, after the first wave of almost total privatization of numerous productive organizations, the strategy in many cases has become similar to that characteristic of the industrialized democracies. These strategies include the creation of quangos, other quasi-public organizations, and organizations that bridge the state-society boundary as a means of providing public services in (presumably) a more efficient and effective manner (Bresser Pereira 1999).

Some of the generic management ideas that have become popular in the industrialized countries have also been introduced into the administrative systems of the less developed and transitional regimes. The traditional administrative style in these systems has been highly bureaucratic, although the seemingly rigid and inflexible practices have been reinforced by political invulnerability because of clientelistic connections with political parties and individual leaders.[7] Just as the managerialist models in the industrialized democracies have moved toward managing the public sector more in the style of the private sector, the same style of managing is being spread in the less developed and particularly in the transitional regimes (Kiggundu 1998). These reforms may have had some beneficial results for governments, but they often have been resisted by personnel who see the attempts to enhance efficiency as nothing more than the continuation of cutting the public sector (Therkildsen 2000).

Although market concepts are extremely popular in contemporary political discourse, their success depends on certain assumptions that may not be operable in the transitional and less developed countries. For example, Nunberg (1995, 41) has argued that using structural reforms based on the market, such as the Next Steps Agencies in Britain, would involve "technological and human resources skills beyond the present capacity of most reforming countries." The successful implementation of reforms, such as using generic management techniques and creating quasi-public organizations for providing public services, depends on the existence of needed managerial talent and the existence of private and quasi-public organizations that are capable of meeting the challenges implied in these reforms. This assumption does not appear to be met in many of these regimes, despite attempts to create them through training and the development of civil society (Robinson and White 1998). Likewise, attempting to contract out government services and develop quasi-contractual relationships within the public sector to some extent depends on the existence of willing participants in and out of government and on a market culture that can make those arrangements more than paper relationships.

Besides the absence of reality in the actual practice of these reforms, there is the danger that they may make things worse rather than better. Although the rigidities and inefficiencies of administration in many less developed systems are famous, in both the academic and literary worlds (Kafka, for example), these rigidities are produced by attention, sometimes slavish, to the probity and rectitude of decisions. Corruption and bribery have become the ways of circumventing that rigidity, but we must recognize the paradoxical notion that corruption may arise because of concerns about fairness and correctness. In the market model, however, the individual manager may be less bound by the ideas of bureaucratic probity so that discrepancies from the Weberian ideals of administration are less suspect and indeed may even be welcomed as reflecting the development of more of a market mentality within government. It is difficult to argue that performance and achieving goals are not important values for the public sector; the difficulty arises when these become the dominant goals and process and equity concerns are assigned a lower priority. This having been said, there are some instances in which market-based reforms have experienced some successes in these two sets of countries. For example, there are some accounts from Ghana of implementing the same type of purchaser-provider split found in the National Health Service in the United Kingdom (Larbi 1998). The problems encountered were far from insignificant, although different from those found in the United Kingdom, but there apparently have been some benefits created by the reform. Likewise, some of the less extreme forms of pay-for-performance also have been spread both to the less developed and to the transitional regimes, not without some successes, albeit also with some failures. And there have been some movements toward the agency model in some of the transitional regimes.

Therefore, the use of market-based organizations and practices may simply produce another version of the disparities between reality and norms that Riggs described decades ago. Managing the public sector's use of market principles is perhaps more difficult than the advocates of the market believe. There has been less than complete success in employing these ideas in the more affluent democracies, so there is no reason to expect any overwhelming successes in societies that lack both well-functioning private markets and, in most cases, a culture that lauds the market as the most desirable form of organization. There have been some notable successes for the market model, and these should be used to draw lessons about how to implement this style of reform in these societies.

Participation and Democracy

The second dimension of reform is enhanced participation, and with it an emphasis on greater democracy in the political and administrative systems. Just as these developing and transitional societies have had relatively little direct experience with the market, most also have had little with administering public programs in an open and democratic manner. This is certainly true for institutions designed for democratic political input, such as political parties and interest groups, but it may be even more true for the output institutions of government, i.e., the bureaucracy. Especially in transitional regimes, the bureaucracy had been authoritarian and permitted little if any options for the clients of the programs to express individual demands or complaints about the services being rendered. As Atilla Agh (1996) has expressed it, there is a continuing legacy in the former socialist states of treating the public as subjects rather than as citizens. Similarly, the internal management of public organizations had been hierarchical, with both political and administrative controls exercised over the decisions of the lower echelons.

A number of the less developed political systems have had substantial experience with participation, including that oriented directly toward the bureaucracy itself. In particular, India, for example, has developed a variety of mechanisms that allow the public to be involved in, and to express discontent with, the actions of the bureaucracy (Jain 1998). Many other political systems in less economically developed systems have had a less fortunate history and do not yet have the political infrastructure to support participation (Hentic and Bernier 1999). Further, just as the governments of the transitional regimes have had a negative image among the public, so too have the governments in many less developed systems, given their history of military domination and repression. Further, there may not be the reservoir of talent in public organizations that will permit large-scale involvement of lower-echelon workers in decisions. Therefore, attempting to transform these organizations into effective democratic public bureaucracies may not be a viable option, at least in the short run (Haque 1999).

The participatory style of reform thus appears to be not the most appropriate means of addressing the problems facing these systems, and in many ways that perception is indeed true. That having been said, however, there have been some attempts at creating greater opportunities for participation within organizations and between the public and the bureaucracy in those systems. For example, the concept of the citizens' charters is being imported into several transitional regimes, and similar ideas are being diffused to several less developed systems. Indeed, it appears that the more repressive the former regime had been, the greater are the subsequent attempts to institutionalize newer and more open forms of democracy. For example, the government of South Africa has begun to institutionalize several mechanisms that permit the public to influence government and to prevent it from being abusive, as it was in the past.

An even more fundamental option for creating additional participation in these systems may be to establish some rather basic conceptions of democracy rather than the somewhat more advanced ones involving the bureaucracy already discussed. Instead of thinking about internal democracy within public organizations and the empowerment of the public to exert direct control over public services such as education or housing, I am talking about building more basic forms of participation and democracy, that is, building the capacity for participation through political parties and interest groups. This can be seen in part in the increased emphasis of international donor organizations such as the World Bank in building "civil society" as a basis for good governance. The focus of a good deal of development work in the past has been that if institutions such as bureaucracies are built at the center, then effective government can be built. This has to some extent changed, with more concern now about building a popular political basis for governing.

The question is, however, whether those conventional ways of participating are indeed more fundamental than participation within the bureaucracy. It has been argued (de Vries 2000) that participation in government is in general becoming increasingly bureaucratic. The assertion is that the variety of mechanisms created to enable "consumers" to influence the way in which services are delivered has become at least as important in defining the relationship between citizens and the state as voting. These bureaucratic mechanisms do focus on the outputs of government rather than on choosing leaders, but they may imply a much shorter and more direct connection between the public and government. The opportunity for citizens to become involved in the delivery of services certainly constitutes a more direct linkage between participation and the nature of those services. Of course, citizens will not always be successful when they challenge the way in which their services are delivered, and there is the possibility of some disaffection and alienation resulting from depending on participation of this sort. Citizens may feel that participation in the delivery of the service is just a sham to co-opt them. This is especially true if participation has been presented as a panacea to a population that is as yet not politically sophisticated—but again there is perhaps more opportunity for redress here than through the political process in many political systems.

In summary, citizens in neither the countries that had been controlled by Communist regimes nor in the less developed systems have had much experience with democratic participation. The institutions of mass democracy are being built, and the question that faces public administration is whether institutions of participation in administrative decision making can be built at the same time. Building those participatory mechanisms in the bureaucracy ultimately may be as important as those of mass democracy. These institutions are closer to the actual delivery of service and therefore may make a more immediate difference in the lives of citizens than does voting or other means of choosing elites and policies.

Flexible Government

Just as the dominant conceptions of participation have less relevance for reform in these two sets of countries, the concept of enhancing the flexible reactions of governments to changing circumstances may not be the most important element. On the contrary, one dominant value that should be pursued through administrative reform is the creation of greater predictability. Many of these regimes have had a stated value of equality of treatment for all citizens, but in practice that commitment often has not been honored. In one set, membership in the hegemonic political party or faction has been the basis of preferential treatment while in the other, the criteria may have been political, but ethnic, religious, and linguistic criteria also played some role in determining the way citizens are treated.[8] Thus, in some ways these governments have been entirely too flexible in their responses to society.

However, part of the justification for pressing for greater flexibility in government is that public organizations become locked into certain ways of doing things, cannot adapt, and have difficulty in coordinating with other organizations that have their own deeply entrenched conceptions of appropriate public policy. That is no less a problem in these two sets of countries, although the breakdown of regimes has been a crucial punctuation in the "path dependence" of their policies (Steinmo, Longstreth, and Thelen 1992). In some cases, however, the natural rigidity of policies and institutions is exaggerated by their linkage with strong patron-client structures. Thus, it may be difficult politically to alter a pattern of policy delivery because it is linked with a stable political framework and provides a range of benefits for the participants in the clientelistic system (Geddes 1994). Even when this political reinforcement for existing policies and organizations is lacking, there is a relative absence of programmatic alternatives in the society so that programs have continued in their existing formats simply because of the inability to mobilize sufficient resources to move toward potentially more effective policies. Some programs, such as pensions, tend to be path dependent in almost all societies,[9] but in the less affluent countries innovation in programs such as education or health care may be excessively constrained by the absence of resources.

The task facing government in these countries is to locate paths for moving away from their clientelistic and/or rigid programs for coping with the demands coming from the public while at the same time preserving some predictability for clients about their treatment by public programs. One reaction to the unpredictability and arbitrary nature of government and its administrators in the past is to become obsessed with strict adherence to rules and regulations and therefore to replace arbitrariness with rigidity. Though undoubtedly the latter is the lesser of the two transgressions, they are still both administrative sins. This is a difficult demand to place on administrative systems undergoing large-scale change at the same time that the economic system and much of the rest of the political system are also being changed. Thus, as is so often the case, the solution to administrative problems may lie in finding balance rather than in pursuing one alternative in a more extreme manner.

Despite the arguments about the need for predictability, I could also argue that developing flexibility is at least as important for public administration in less developed and transitional regimes as it has been for the wealthy industrialized democracies. This argument would be that the socioeconomic settings within which these two sets of governments are functioning are themselves less predictable than are those of the wealthier states. Therefore, institutionalizing any policy in that setting may solve the problem being addressed at the time, but the nature and relative importance of problems, and even the problems themselves, may change rapidly. Thus governments need to be able to react to those changes and adjust policies rapidly. Further, if these countries also have relatively fewer resources available to the public sector, then it makes sense to ensure that they are used in the most effective manner possible and that they are coordinated. In this view, policies in many less developed and transitional countries may be entirely too predictable.

Choosing how much to emphasize flexibility versus predictability is an important design problem for reformers in these two sets of countries. As with most things in the public sector, both ends of the dimension are important and provide some value for government. On the one hand, governments need to be adaptable and to have the capacity for adjusting to environmental challenges. On the other hand, citizens and businesses want predictability and reliability from their government so that they can have reasonable expectations of fair and consistent treatment. The real trick in governing is to develop the means for producing policy flexibility while maintaining administrative consistency. Few governments, regardless of the level of economic or political development, have been able to bring about that happy combination, given the commitments of administrative organizations to their policies and the professional networks within which those organizations often are embedded.

Deregulating Government

Deregulating government has been proposed as part of the solution for governance in the less developed and transitional countries. In some ways deregulation appears even more appropriate for these regimes than for Western Europe and North America, given that they have been even more strictly regulated internally than the more economically and politically developed systems. The former Communist regimes imposed a large number of ex ante and ex post controls over the performance of their bureaucracies, with the consequence that they were rigid in the extreme. These controls were imposed both by the government and by the hegemonic political party, and much of that rigidity may be persisting after democratization, simply because much of the old elite remains in place and there are few if any options to replace them (Obolonsky 1999). Thus, the path-dependent style of governing would be one of a great deal of internal regulation.

In the less developed political systems, as Riggs would have argued, rigidity and formalism existed side by side with high levels of variability and personalism. On the one hand, the formal rules of bureaucracies have been well institutionalized and have been central to governing. On the other hand, those rules often were circumvented to benefit favored social and political groups. The rigidity in the system may be used as a defense against the demands being pressed by groups in the society. It is easy to employ formal rules to avoid having to make decisions and to preserve the power of the organization and the individual administrators. At the same time that formal rules can be invoked, there was also a well-developed capacity to ignore the rules and laws so that the favored elements of the society could be rewarded. The paradoxical mixture of rigidity and arbitrariness produced the worst of all worlds—arbitrary treatment of citizens and reduced efficiency and effectiveness of the public sector.

Given the rigidities that are often attributed to bureaucracies in many of the less developed and transitional countries, the strategy of deregulation might be considered a natural approach to reform. In some ways that is true. There are, however, also a number of significant problems embedded within that strategy when it is implemented in the context of these countries. The most important of these difficulties is that successful deregulation may require a set of values held by public servants and the existence of a tacit bargain between political leaders and the civil servants (Schaffer 1973). This strategy has been viable in locations such as the United States, Canada, and the Scandinavian countries because the civil servants who were being released from formal, ex ante controls had been socialized to accept the importance of democratic control, personal rectitude, and fair treatment of citizens. Further, they largely accepted that they could trade responsibility to their political masters in exchange for a stable career and a great deal of influence, albeit often thickly veiled influence, over policy.

This bargain between political and administrative leaders in government does not appear to exist in most of the less developed and transitional systems. Rather, the experience of most public servants has been that of observing the abuse of power, arbitrary decision making, and the use of public office for personal gain.[10] Therefore, if formalized rules of conduct are eliminated, there is little for the civil servant to rely on as guidance in making decisions. The most likely outcome might be to replicate the abuses of the past, albeit perhaps with different segments of society being favored. Of course, numbers of international organizations and donor countries have preached the virtues of good government and good administration, but that sermon may not be as effective as years of experience in the previous regimes.

Therefore, the transitional and less developed systems may require more rather than fewer rules if they are to meet the stated goals of good government. The very rigidities about the use of public money—budget laws and procurement laws, for example—that have been eliminated in many regimes may be crucial in these transitional regimes if the public is to gain any confidence that their tax money is being used properly. Likewise, rules for personnel management are important for limiting nepotism and the misuse of public office to favor friends and family. In short, these governments need to create properly functioning "old-fashioned administrative" systems before they can dismantle the formal rules in favor of greater flexibility and efficiency. Deregulation may be an appropriate long-term goal, but in the short run formal administrative rules and procedures appear crucial.

SUMMARY

Most governments in the world face pressures, either psychological or more tangible, to adopt the modern canon of administration in the form of New Public Management (Common 1998). For the two groups of countries just discussed, those pressures are likely to do more harm than good. Despite the appeal of ideas such as deregulation and flexibility, governments attempting to build both effective administration and democracy may require much greater emphasis on formality, rules, and strong ethical standards. The values of efficiency and effectiveness are important but in the short run not so crucial as creating probity and responsibility. Once a so-called Weberian administrative system is institutionalized, then it may make sense to consider how best to move from that system toward a more "modern" system of public administration.

At the same time that there is a concern about institutionalizing an effective Weberian system of administration, these systems must be cognizant of their historical tendency to have formalism without real adherence to the rules. Thus, the challenge is to create genuine adherence to the rules that exist, or rules that may be created to incorporate further the concepts of appropriate procedures of administration. This is in itself a more than adequate challenge, without having to adopt and implement ideas of the New Public Management that may or may not contribute to the effectiveness of the administration. The argument remains that it may be necessary to build a proper Weberian administration before there are any attempts to break that style down.

9

Can We Go Home Again?
Where Do We Go Then?

We now have examined four alternatives for moving government away from the traditional model of public administration. Recommendations from some of these models are already being implemented widely while others are only in their nascent stages, if that well developed. In each case, an implicit or explicit comparison is made with the traditional model of administration, with its clear separation of roles between administration and politics, a hierarchical management style and pyramidal structures (largely), permanent organizations and career civil servants, and accountability through political means.[1] In each instance some or all of the old system is found to be deficient, and the reforms being proposed are intended to create a governing system that will function better. The political and analytic problem is that there are very different definitions of what "better" might mean in this context.

For a capsule of the arguments advanced in the first section of the book, see Table 9.1. It is a means of recapping what has been said already and also of emphasizing the multiplicity of ideas of what is wrong in government and what needs to be done to correct the problems. One can see that most if not all of the "dependent variables" for the reformers are the same. Many of the reformers want to address the same perceived failings of government, e.g., the remoteness of command-and-control regulation and the inadequacies of program coordination. Although they do perceive many common problems in the public sector, their strategies for addressing them are quite different. Not only are the remedies different, but they are also often directly contradictory, so that selecting one option or the other should logically preclude simultaneous selection of other types of remedies.

It is also apparent that many of the problems that continued to arise in the application of one or another of these models are by no means novel for the public sector. For example, in almost all the cases coordination has been identified

Table 9.1. Answers to Basic Questions

	Market	Participation	Flexibility	Deregulation
Coordination	Invisible hand	Bottom up	Changing organizations	Managers' self-interest
Error detection/ correction	Market signals	Political signals	Do not institutionalize errors	Accept more error
Civil service systems	Replace with market mechanisms	Reduce hierarchy	Use temporary employment	Eliminate regulations
Accountability	Through market	Through consumer complaints	No clear recommendations	Through ex post controls

as a major problem. This is certainly true, but it has been a problem for government ever since differentiated bureaucratic structures began to be developed. Some of the reforms being undertaken, most notably the creation of "agencies" to deliver programs, may exacerbate the inevitable coordination problems, but they would still exist if governments were to return to an old-fashioned Weberian, ministerial bureaucracy.

These four models of reform raise new issues about accountability and the public interest, but that concept has been a dominant, if not the dominant, concern for the designers of democratic political systems from their inception (Day and Klein 1987). And these reforms have not yet come close to solving the problems of evaluating public programs or of measuring and evaluating the performance of public officials. Indeed, many of the reforms being implemented place an increasing demand on evaluative systems that are, at best, imperfect reflections of how the public sector is performing (Cave, Kogan, and Smith 1990). In short, the problems are not new, even if the solutions do at times appear to be innovative or at least are marketed politically as being so.

The reforms that have been proposed and adopted are in many ways not all that novel, either. Many of the same ideas for change have been around in government for decades, if not for centuries, and they keep reappearing, albeit with different names and with slightly different twists. Take, for example, the idea of greater worker participation in public organizations. This has been common in organizational and management theory since at least the 1940s. Likewise, the idea of empowering clients to participate more fully in making decisions about their own programs goes back at least to the days of urban programs such as Model Cities in the United States and the requirements for "maximum feasible participation" (Langton 1978; but see Moynihan 1969). The idea of enhanced organizational flexibility appears more feasible, given contemporary information technology, but there have been attempts since at least the era of the New Deal to facilitate the creation and dissolution of organizations and to move people in and out of government positions more readily than in traditional systems.

The fact that these ideas for change are not entirely new should not be seen as an excessively critical comment. There are relatively few entirely new ideas about organizations and management available for prospective organizational analysts.

Just as the problems appear ageless, so too do the solutions. As Simon (1947) pointed out almost a half century ago, the solutions for organizational problems tend to come in opposing pairs, and almost inevitably reformers will argue that organizations have gone too far in the direction of one end of the continuum and will propose the other end of that dimension as the solution (see also Peters and Wright 1998). When organizations become overly centralized, the obvious solution is to decentralize until the lack of control produced by that arrangement produces demands for a return to centralization, and then the circle starts again.

The standards by which success and failure of reforms would be judged are also not terribly innovative. Public-sector managers, with a few exceptions, have always wanted to produce policy outcomes efficiently and effectively, despite the denigration of traditional bureaucratic methods by these and other reform programs. Likewise, most reform efforts in democratic countries have valued the procedures by which policies are made as well as the substance of the policies adopted. Reformers also have wanted (while simultaneously enhancing procedural protections) to reduce the infamous red tape and bureaucratization of public programs (Kaufman 1977; Crozier 1964). What is perhaps most surprising in the midst of all this administrative change is how little systematic evaluation of reforms has been undertaken, especially of programs that allegedly are oriented toward improving the bottom line of the public sector (*FDA News* 1995). For the most part, analysts really do not know what has been happening as governments invest huge amounts of time and energy to change themselves (but see Carter and Greer 1993).

The other factor about these reform effects that is especially surprising is the collective faith of their advocates in manipulating formal structures and procedures.[2] This (apparently naive) structuralism and proceduralism are in marked contrast to other components of the management and organizational literature that stresses the need to transform the culture of organizations if there is to be successful long-term change in the functioning of an organization (Peters and Waterman 1982; Brooks and Bate 1994). An implicit target for many contemporary reforms is the traditional civil service culture or ethos, which is perceived (often incorrectly) to be excessively cautious, secretive, negative, or all three. One of the principal complaints about the traditional culture is that it focuses on procedures rather than on the outputs of government.

There appears, however, to have been little attempt to replace that old culture with another culture or ethos, except perhaps to laud the entrepreneurial ideal (see Dunsire 1995, 25–33). This absence of an alternative ethos for the public service may be a great mistake for government (Kernaghan 1994). An alternative ethos is necessary because many of the reforms may be successful or palatable only if there is a value framework that supports them and that protects the public from the potential excesses of unrestrained managerialism in government. In particular, there is a need to develop ethical standards that can supplement formal mechanisms for holding the public sector accountable.

Although numerous reforms were implemented during the 1980s and 1990s, that was not the end of the story. One of the most remarkable aspects of government reforms has been the extent to which they continue to be implemented. The expectation of most politicians and scholars has been that fatigue would have set in after the major reforms were adopted, following the ideas of the first four models. In reality, however, governments have continued to change, and more new ideas about management and policy have been implemented in the public sector. The impetus for continued reform has been in part from politicians and in part from the bureaucracy itself, but governments have continued to change.

Some of the very problems that were identified as targets for reform in the first round can be identified as central issues in the continuing reform efforts. For example, coordination and accountability have been two of the central concerns for the more recent rounds of change in government, and reregulation has been a logical reaction to the deregulation implemented during the first set of changes. Moreover, the successes of some of the initial rounds of reform have made governments sufficiently bold to consider thinking about quality and performance as goals in the reform process. Further, the ideas for change that have been common in the industrialized democracies are now being diffused to the developing countries, often to the detriment of governance in those systems.

THE IMPORTANCE OF CONTEXT

Before beginning a more thorough discussion of the similarities and differences found among the four models, I should first note the importance of other dimensions of comparing administration and administrative reform (Peters 1988). This book has been almost entirely about comparing the ideas informing contemporary reforms and the more tangible instruments through which they have been implemented. Context is also crucially important for understanding the ideas themselves and their relative success or failure in practice. I will now examine the impact of context on administrative change along two dimensions: time and national setting.

Time

The four basic ideas about reforming bureaucracy are products of their age. That should go without saying, but postmodernist analysts might tend to deprive the changes of this important contextualization. These reforms represent at least two of the more important, and still again contradictory, contemporary patterns of thinking about government and public affairs. First, the concept of the market has become a shibboleth for anyone attempting to change government. Market-based economies and their brand of open competition were said to have demonstrated their superiority through the fall of the former Soviet bloc.[3] This apparent or alleged victory of the market has meant that these solutions have gained increased legitimacy as a means of solving all manner of social and economic problems and are applied almost without question.

The other contemporary Zeitgeist that appears in these models is participation, in all its varied forms. Just as for some analysts the market is the solution for all the world's ills, for others "the people" would be capable of solving their own problems if large institutions—especially those of the public sector—would only get out of their way. Further, participation is seen to have value in and of itself, so that any mechanism that fosters participation in organizations or between the mass public and government is automatically thought to be beneficial. Just as the marketeers are somewhat overly ambitious in their claims about the successes of competition (Self 1993), so too are the participators excessively romantic about the capacity of the average person to understand and solve the complex and multi-faceted problems facing contemporary societies and their governments.

For both of these Zeitgeists, scarcity is a pervasive fact of life that conditions the behavior of actors. Scarcity has always been a central component in economic thought but has become more prominent in thinking about the political economy since the middle 1970s (Rose and Peters 1978). This is in part a function of real insecurities about economic performance and in part a function of increased popular resistance to taxation (Botella 1994). What this scarcity means is that any thinking about how to make government function better must have as one of its principal components mechanisms for saving money and reducing the size of the public sector. This is a central element of marketeers' thinking, but the participators' assumption is that the people should be allowed to decide what balance to adopt between taxation and public expenditure.[4]

Yet neither model advocates approaches to making government work better based on rationality and analysis (see Deleon 1994). Techniques such as program-budgeting and management by objectives that were popular during the 1960s depended on the application of highly rationalistic models of costs and benefits to the public sector, with the end of getting the most "bang for the buck" for each unit of resource expended.[5] The Zeitgeist of that time was rationality and the belief that government could be made to work better if only the right analytic techniques were applied and their "answers" adopted into law. The governing style for the 1980s and 1990s, however, is more ideological. The advocates of the reforms I have been discussing—especially for market reforms[6] and participation—push their brand of reform and do not talk about the application of analytic techniques to "prove" that their proposals will work. That proof is assumed to be self-evident, and, further, that the reforms are right simply because they are right.

The subsequent round of reforms also reflects the dominant political and administrative ideas of their age. In particular, the concepts of quality and performance represent a culmination of both the market and participation ideas. The idea of quality represents attempts to serve the consumer, a natural outcome of the earlier market reforms. The best way for government to serve that customer then is to provide services that are of high quality and to ensure that government performs its tasks as well as possible. This concept may de-emphasize the economy and efficiency inherent in the market approach, yet there is a clear market element.

The participatory element of quality is that one of the most important means of assessing it is for citizens themselves—as clients of the programs or just as citizens—to determine how well the tasks have been performed. There are some objective measures of performance that have been advanced, but many ideas are built around a concept of the public's responding to programs and making their views known. This concept of quality requires the identification of the appropriate clients or citizens. Using this form of quality assessment also may generate a decided class bias in the ability of different groups to make their views known effectively. When having to cope with professionals in education and other services, working-class citizens may be at a significant disadvantage.

Nation

The second important dimension of comparison is country. Most comparative politics use country as the unit of analysis, and in general this analytic focus produces interesting and useful results. In this case the principal focus of analysis has been ideas, and country has been secondary. There are, however, interesting and important differences among countries that merit some discussion. The ideas of reform have served as a relatively common stimulus to which the countries have responded, and those responses provide important insights into their administrative and political systems. Most of the examples of reforms provided are derived from the Anglo-American parts of the world, but similar changes are being implemented in other developed and less developed countries. This observation then leads to two relevant questions: why are the Anglo-Saxon countries the center of the reform universe? How do those reforms fare when they are taken out of that context and placed into different political and administrative environments?

Of the two questions it is somewhat easier to answer the first one. In the first place, this has been the home of much of the advocacy of free enterprise and the market while continental Europe has opted for a more restrained form of mixed-economy, welfare state, even when conservative political parties are in power. Moreover, government (at least in the United States and Canada) has been more subject to influence from private-management consultants and other purveyors of reform ideas (Gray and Jenkins 1995, 85; White and Wolf 1995). Many of the reform techniques, e.g., Total Quality Management and strategic planning, have been imported directly from the private sector into government (Walters 1992c). Even when government is more closed to outsiders, as in the United Kingdom, Conservative governments were willing to use talent from business, and the New Labour government installed in 1997 also has been perhaps even more willing to use outsiders.

It can be argued that governments in the Anglo-American democracies required more assistance from several of the types of reform being advocated than did some other countries. This need for change may be especially apparent for the reforms labeled deregulation. Because of the pervasive distrust of government and its lack of integration of bureaucracy into civil society, there has been a tendency for rules to be laid on top of rules as a means of ensuring control over the system. Some "legalistic" administrative systems, such as Germany, can survive with a relatively compact administrative code, but government in the United States (as perhaps the extreme example) developed thousands of pages of detailed personnel, budgeting, accounting, and procurement regulations. If government is to become more efficient, then perhaps there is a genuine need to clear away some of this underbrush of control and permit the managers to get on with the business of managing.

Further, and also because of the lack of a distinctive role assigned to the civil service constitutionally or in political theory (as would be found in most of continental Europe), the application of private-sector management techniques to the civil service is not a particularly radical action. To the extent that civil servants do hold an elite position in society in the Anglo-American systems, it is because they have almost seized it, rather than settling into it as a part of the state tradition. Public servants in these systems are meant to be serving the public and the political leadership, but treating them as mere employees, as one might in a bank or a shoe store, was not the insult that it might have been in Germany, France, or Scandinavia.

Nevertheless, these reforms have been spread to countries where they might not have been expected to be readily accepted. For example, the market-based idea of pay for performance has been implemented successfully in Norway and Sweden where, everything else being equal, it might have been thought to be an anathema (Sjölund 1994b; Laegreid 1994). Other changes such as decentralization are also proceeding without excessive opposition (Pierre 1995a) Likewise, some of the ideas of creating agencies and decentralizing government have been adopted in the Netherlands, which has had a highly centralized government for a number of years (Kickert 1994). Even France, with its long history of administrative centralization, has begun to decentralize and deconcentrate government significantly (de Montricher 1994), with the aim of increasing efficiency, participation, and "service to the customer" (Bezes 2001).

In many ways the countries in the Germanic tradition have been the least interested in reform. This is especially true if reform implies embarking on an announced program of change and placing a good deal of political and administrative emphasis on changing the manner in which government is conducted. Certainly public administration in Germany has changed over the past several decades, e.g., the emphasis on *Burgernähe,* or closeness to the citizen. However, there has been much less adherence to fad and fashion than in other countries. This is partly because the administrative system has worked, even with the additional load of assimilating former East Germany (Derlien 1993; Goetz 1993). Further, the cooperative federal nature of German administration requires extensive bargaining among central and *Land* governments and therefore tends toward incremental versus the comprehensive solutions advocated in most other countries.

COMMON PROBLEMS AND UNCOMMON SOLUTIONS

There are several problems that appear to arise with respect to each of the proposed models of reform. Some of these stem from the endless searches for the philosophers' stone of providing perfectly coordinated and error-free government, problems that also plague other large, complex organizations. That timeless characteristic, however, should not disqualify these models from serious consideration and from some analysis of the possible contributions of each. I will discuss three common problems: coordination, error detection and error correction, and the fate of the civil service.

Coordination

Given the importance of coordination as an administrative value, the most recent round of reforms has focused a good deal of attention on enhancing it. Although the issue has become even more prominent, the concepts guiding the first round of reforms also have something to say about it and, somewhat predictably, have rather different ideas about the importance of coordination and coherence and how to achieve these values in governing.

The four approaches to administrative reform address at least in part the three principal strands of social science thinking about coordination: markets, hierarchies, and networks (see Maidment and Thompson 1993). What unites the four, however, is the common perception of the importance of this administrative value and the extent to which it is becoming even more difficult to achieve. Many of the reforms that have already been implemented have helped create a greater need for coordinative structures and action while also to some extent reducing the capacity of governments to coordinate effectively. In an increasingly complex and interdependent world, government appears to be squandering its capacity to present an integrated and coherent set of policies just when it is most needed.

For the market model, the problem of coordination is not a separate managerial one, or at least it is not recognized as sufficiently significant to warrant deviation from the basic model of decentralization and entrepreneurship. The market is lauded by "true believers" because it *is* a coordination device. The virtue of the free market is its ability to coordinate the independent decisions of purchasers and sellers to produce prices that clear the market. The assumption therefore is that the same logic could apply to the public sector if only activities there were sufficiently marketized. Thus, the creation of agencies and quasi-governmental bodies to carry out public functions should in principle be sufficiently controllable (Modeen and Rosas 1988) to be sustainable, given the other virtues that use of the market is meant to create for government and society.

The implicit argument contained in the market approach to reform is that there should be enough efficiency gains from the application of market principles to justify any efficiency losses from reduced policy coordination. There is little evidence of the relative costs and benefits of those two possible outcomes, but market assumptions certainly would push in the direction of producing efficiency gains. For this reason, it appears that the application of the market model will still leave a definite role for central agencies as instruments for imposing some common goals and directions on government. The basic model of the free market, for example, assumes that sellers and buyers do have common interests—exchange and profit—while for agencies with competitive purposes that exchange is not so easy to foster. These central agencies will continue to have a role in deciding just how government is to be cut up into agencies and then in attempting to knit their policies back together again.

The participatory model tends to visualize coordination as being driven from the bottom up rather than from the top down. In this view the best way to consider coordination may be to think about its being centered in the clients of programs rather than in the organizations that deliver the services and their bureaucratic relationships with one another. This view requires a population of clients who can articulate their demands effectively, as well as a collection of organizations that is concerned with delivering more holistic services. The participatory approach to coordination may not entirely obviate the role of the central agencies, either. In some cases, central agencies, e.g., the Office of Prime Minister and Cabinet in Australia, have organized themselves around client groups as well as around the conventional functional policy areas in order to enhance coordination.

It is in its concern with coordination questions that the flexible state model comes into its own. One of the central foci of this approach to governing is providing means for putting organizations together on a short-term basis in order to solve problems of coordination and coherence. The creation of virtual organizations and the generation of short-term task force structures is one important way of integrating programs and generating comprehensive responses to the problems facing governments and their citizens. The flexible-state approach is to some degree the apotheosis of network coordination, although it lacks some of the long-term interactions that some scholars associate with networks.

There is some question, however, as to whether the flexible perspective on governing is adequately prepared to cope with the persistent and continuing coordination problems arising in the public sector. The question is not going to go away in a month or a year or ever, and therefore some coordination devices must remain in place for as long as there are programs to coordinate. That having been said, however, flexibility may be necessary simply because the coordination questions change frequently, depending on which political issues are at the top of the agenda. The organizations that need bringing together today may be very different from the ones that had to be coordinated yesterday, and making a coordinative device permanent may be as counterproductive as locking in any other organizational solution to policy problems.

The deregulatory argument about coordination is that rules requiring it will not do the job adequately. The problem is that there appears to be little coming from this approach as a substitute. If a major part of the ethos of the deregulatory model is to unleash individual managers to pursue their own organizational goals, then expecting them to invest in coordination with other equally aggressive and ambitious managers may be too much to ask. This approach to coordination, like that of the market approach, therefore must rely on an invisible hand, i.e., the managers would recognize that they could reach their own goals more cheaply and effectively in the aggregate if they invested more in coordination.

The recognition of the collective interest of managers in promoting coordination would create a classic collection-action problem. Though all managers could benefit, each individual manager and/or organization has little incentive to make the investment that would produce this collective benefit (Olson 1965). The requirement would be entrepreneurs who believe that they could gain enough from organizing the collective effort to justify the investment of time and other resources (Frohlich, Oppenheimer, and Young 1971). These might be entrepreneurs whose own agencies were particularly affected by coordination problems or who somehow believe that they could advance their careers by being the organizers of the collective effort.

Coordination is a central and increasingly important problem for government. In some cases structural reforms have tended to exacerbate the problems, and in no cases has there been a clear solution for this persistent difficulty. Much of the development of contemporary administrative structure and management appears to have progressed with little or no attention to how to put the system back together again. The civil service ethos of the traditional system, as well as command from above, generated more coordination than is sometimes realized, but these aspects now have been lost in the pursuit of other values.

Error Detection and Error Correction

Another of the common problems addressed by the four models, albeit sotto voce at times, is error detection and error correction. Organizations in government or in the private sector will inevitably make errors; there are simply too many decisions and too many people involved to get it right every time. Further, many contemporary ideas about public-sector management stress the importance of risk taking in environments that traditionally have been more conservative and risk averse. If the new entrepreneurial wind is to blow through the public sector, then there must be people willing to take some chances, and to fail.

The idea of risk taking in government runs counter to most political cultures as well as to bureaucratic traditions. The public sector is often expected to be error free, at least in the public mind (Savoie 1994b; 1995a). This is partly because the public sector spends taxpayers' money and is expected to be responsible with those funds. Further, the public sector is often concerned with the rights of citizens, not just with simple economic transactions. For whatever reasons, public-sector administrators and their elected representatives find the admission of mistakes unpalatable and attempt to find ways to minimize or deny them. Most of the traditional methods for ensuring accountability are organized to expose errors that have been committed but tend to be much less effective in finding ways to prevent them from reoccurring.

Some of these errors will be in the formulation of policy responses to problems, others will be in the allocation of resources within the organization, and still others will be in the implementation of programs. The public and many politicians tend to assume that problems arise in implementation and blame the bureaucracy, but many problems actually have their roots earlier in the process. Errors are inevitable, so the real question is how to detect, minimize, and then correct them. This is particularly important for public-sector organizations, given the rather low opinion in which they are held by much of the population and the pressures from politicians to publicize and punish errors.

Each of the four models provides its own distinctive perspective on the problem of detecting and eliminating errors in the public sector (see also Rose 1987). As with so many other issues, the answer provided by the market model is the clearest and simplest but also perhaps the least effective. The assumption of this approach is that the market will take care of the problem. This is a somewhat hyperbolic statement but not too much of an exaggeration. If a market functions effectively, it will let the leadership of any organization in that market know when an error has been made. That information will come through falling profits, loss of market share, or expressions of dissatisfaction by consumers. One of the presumed virtues of the market, in fact, is the numerous signals that it provides to its participants.

For organizations within the public sector operating within a market framework, or what passes for one in the public sector, the information flow does not appear to be nearly as good as that assumed by the conventional models of the firm in neoclassical economics. In the first place, most of these organizations still function with a virtual monopoly for their service. The Passport Agency in Britain may be called an agency and may be separated from the Home Office, but there is no other place that a citizen can go to get a permit to travel abroad.[7] In these settings, surrogate indicators—target service figures and benchmarks, for example—take the place of the usual market indicators. Targets do not appear as useful information for managers, in part because they often are manipulated by those very managers (Dopson 1993).

Even when there are markets, many of them within which public-sector organizations function are highly contrived, so that adequate signals could hardly be said to be generated from the convoluted interactions of purchasers and providers. For example, the quasi market developed within the National Health Service does not appear to be able to generate enough information about costs or quality to guide doctors or hospitals that may be making errors to correct them (Birchall, Pollitt, and Putnam 1995). Further, there may simply be no realistic alternative to the particular purchaser or provider with which a participant is currently paired, other than patients being trundled the length and breadth of the British Isles.

Consumerism in the market does provide some opportunities for error detection and correction, but even that device may have severe limitations. Most of the consumer standards used in government are generated by government itself and hence may be just those hurdles that organizations are confident they can jump. There may be less opportunity, albeit an increasing one, for citizens to define what they would like established as performance standards for each service. Further, many of the services that may be most prone to error may also be those for which consumer feedback is likely to be the most muted. Social services agencies, as the best example of this problem, have relatively powerless clients who typically are quite reluctant to complain about poor services or abuses of discretion for fear they will lose their benefits (but see Goodsell 1981a, 1981b).

The participatory model relies on the willingness of citizens to become active participants in the political and administrative processes. As a consequence, this model faces many of the same problems as those identified for the consumer in the market model. That is, the very people who may have the most to gain from participation may be the same people who are the least likely to participate in the policy process. Given the model's democratic ethos, however, its implementors may be more proactive and actually seek out participation rather than simply waiting for the ideas and complaints to come into public organizations. That initiative can be supplemented by politicians who may have something to gain, even while in power, from promoting citizens' involvement and even citizens' complaints.[8]

The participatory model does have the virtue that it seeks to involve the public at all stages of the policy process, not just in ex post complaints and feedback about the way a policy was executed. This active stance may enable errors to be corrected before they occur, although the decision makers will have to be open to innovative ideas that may be advanced, and that is often not the case. Administrators' range of vision about policies tends to be constrained by their professional and organizational allegiances so that only a limited number of proposals can be fit into the acceptable set. This range of acceptable ideas may be somewhat greater for instruments to be used to implement the program, but even then organizations tend to have commitments to tools as well as to policies (Linder and Peters 1989).

The flexible-state model depends on its very flexibility to generate the means for error correction. The argument from this approach would be that errors are inevitable, and the only significant problems occur when they become institutionalized as a part of a permanent solution to a policy problem. If the idea of impermanence can be made paramount in the minds of institutional designers, then there is a consequent ongoing opportunity for continual error correction and program improvement. Similarly, bringing people into government from outside organizations can be conceptualized as a part of the error correction process. If the employees of government have become excessively set in their ways, then bringing in outsiders to challenge assumptions may be crucial to forcing new ways of thinking and correcting well-institutionalized errors.

The deregulatory model has its own views on error correction. First, simply getting rid of large numbers of unnecessary and counterproductive regulations within the public sector is a step toward ameliorating errors in and of itself. This assumption would be contested, however, by more traditional administrators who would see deregulation as eliminating rules intended to prevent errors by constraining the latitude of civil servants. Thus, the deregulatory approach seems to need some other means of identifying and addressing errors, yet at the same time it appears more willing to accept error than other approaches to governing. It apparently is insufficient in a democracy to say simply that we are willing to trade more errors for greater ease of doing business and for a government that responds more quickly.

In addition to its presumed benefits, therefore, this approach would have to use some of the logic of the market and participatory approaches. It might not, however, be as willing to have decisions, and the definitions of error, determined primarily by citizen feedback. The operating assumption appears to be that if some of the ex ante controls are removed, then there will be more latitude for decision makers to make decisions. In that deregulated vision, the decision makers should be able to implement their decisions without having to look over their shoulders too much, either at the public or at politicians. The slogan of much of the managerial reform in government has been "let the managers manage," but there are few clear statements of the criteria for what restraints should be imposed on their actions.

This discussion of error correction may have been too negative in focusing on the inevitability of errors in the public sector and the means through which they may be corrected. I should also point out that another managerial task, one that is discussed less frequently, is the detection of outstanding performance. Most administrative effort is directed toward correcting the negative anomalies of government, and most analytic time is directed toward identifying regularities. If these reform efforts do indeed merit the time and trouble invested, then there should be some exceptional outcomes to report and to emulate (Miller 1984). Government reform need not just be about preventing problems; it should also recognize when the experiments (and reforms are always experiments [Campbell 1988]) do indeed bear fruit.

The increasing concern with applying performance measures in public administration, comprising a major dimension of reform in the later period under investigation, is one means of addressing the search for exceptional performance. Although I have phrased this discussion in terms of error detection, an emphasis on performance and quality will detect both the best and the worst. This is also true of the manner in which a good part of the reregulation of government has been implemented, with inspectorates identifying successes and failures.

Although the emphasis on exceptional performance in government should in many ways be a welcome change in public management, it is not without its problems. Primarily, there is some sense that these measures are more oriented toward the negative than the positive and are perhaps used more to punish than to reward. This may be entirely perceptual, but given that they are being applied at a time in which the public sector is reducing employment by a significant amount, it is not surprising that some people feel threatened by them.

The Civil Service

Each of these approaches to reform must cope with the "problem" of the civil service. The system was developed over decades to solve some important political and managerial problems. These weaknesses included political favoritism in recruitment, inadequately trained professional staff, and no regular career paths for capable personnel. For the most part, civil service laws and systems were extremely successful in meeting these objectives. In fact, to their critics, these personnel systems were far too successful and have become overly institutionalized to the point that public managers could not adequately control their own staffs. Each of the four models sees the civil service from a somewhat different perspective, as presenting somewhat different problems, and as requiring somewhat different solutions. For each of the models, however, the civil service as we have known it represents a problem to be overcome and reformed.

For proponents of the market model the civil service is not conceived of as a service but rather as a group of self-aggrandizing individuals using public office and public money for their own purposes. The principal problem here is that bureaucratic agencies and their permanent employees have established monopoly powers over particular domains within the public sector. Those monopolies have enabled each agency to extract excess money from the budget for its own purposes rather than using those available funds to provide genuine public services. Thus, to these critics the civil service is a principal villain, if not the principal villain, in the story of how government grew too big (at least too big according to their own standards).

To rectify those problems, the civil service needs to be changed fundamentally, according to the market advocates. Primarily, the sense is that the civil service needs to be disaggregated so that the traditional model of a career, integrated personnel system would be eliminated. Similarly, the reward system of the civil service, with all individuals in the same rank being paid the same, would be eliminated in favor of a more personalized regimen. Then the closed personnel system would be opened up to encourage or even to require more movement between the public and private sectors. These changes would ensure that the values and experiences of the public service would not be significantly different from the private sector.

For the participatory model, the civil service also presents a problem, although not nearly so much as it does for the market model. The traditional civil service is a hierarchical system of ranks and grades, and the participatory model is attempting to create greater equality within organizations. Moreover, the civil service tends to be closed to outside applicants. The participatory model is more concerned with the injection of the values of nonofficial groups into society, perhaps most important the clients of public programs. However, the civil service, by granting tenure and permanence to its members, may in fact liberate them for greater participation and frankness than would be true if they were all political appointees dependent on the whims of their political masters.

For advocates of greater flexibility in governing, the civil service is visualized as a significant impediment to good governance. Almost by definition the civil service confers permanent employment on its members. Thus, a personnel system organized around a civil service system will make managing personnel in a more flexible manner, using more temporary employees, more difficult. Personnel management of that sort would not be impossible, and indeed most public personnel systems already are increasingly dependent on temporary and part-time employees. Still, there are impediments to creating the type of flexibility envisioned by some more extreme versions of flexible government. Yet the career protection afforded by civil service systems may facilitate institutionalizing greater change in public organizations themselves. In most instances career civil servants will not have to worry about their jobs and therefore should be more willing to envision the rapid creations and terminations of organizations advocated by flexible government.

The deregulatory approach to reform appears to have some implications for the civil service similar to those from the market approach. These are derived, however, from rather different first principles. Both approaches seemingly would dismantle much of the legal and regulatory structure for personnel management in the public sector. The logic of this dismantling for the market advocates is to be able to impose greater discipline on public employees and to make them be more efficient and conform to market logic. For the deregulators, however, the principal purpose of removing the personnel regulations is to release the creativity and energy of public employees so that government can be effective.

The similarity of the market and deregulatory approaches, however, may be more apparent than real. The marketeers generally want to dismantle the civil service and the ethos that has supported it. They tend to regard the civil service as part of the isolation of public employees from the real world, e.g., the market.

The deregulators, though, in some way require a career, professional civil service for their reforms to be manageable. In order to be able to remove the ex ante controls over personnel, purchasing, and budgeting, there must be an ingrained commitment to public service values and personal probity. That type of civil service is unlikely to be found in a public sector dominated by market principles.

The civil service system as it has been developed over numerous decades is unlikely to disappear easily. The reforms that have been proposed would modify the existing system more or less extensively, but probably only the extreme version of the market approach would fully dismantle it. There will probably always be a need for a core of public employees who have gained substantial experience in making and administering policy. They must serve as the repository of values and organizational memory for the governing system. Indeed, if the plans for introducing greater flexibility into government are implemented, and increasing numbers of managers are recruited from outside the career system, then the career employees who remain in office will become even more important.

The principal importance of the civil service will be in ensuring the accountability of the public sector. I have argued that many of the reforms implemented as components of the market and deregulatory models in particular have had the effect of reducing some of the traditional accountability of the public bureaucracy. Given those structural changes, preserving the values of the civil service may be crucial for maintaining its ethical stance as the servant of the public rather than as a corps of value-free managers.

Matching Problems and Solutions

These four approaches to reform are united in providing almost ideological conceptions of government and governing. In at least two of the models—the market and participation—these prescriptions for reform are indeed linked closely with broader intellectual and ideological conceptions of government (Self 1993; Dryzek 1990; Wilson 1989). Even for the other two models, however, there is a tendency to advocate one perspective or the other as an overall solution to governing problems rather than as a particular solution to a particular problem. The true believers in each camp appear to think that their particular remedy is just the answer to the ills of the public sector and to see the specific deficiency they recognize in government as pervasive.

I am arguing, however, for the need for a more highly differentiated and contingent view of the problems and prospects for governing. There is some validity to all the positions advanced about the public sector, including the traditional notions that serve as the backdrop for the attempts at reform. The question then is when and where is each reform perspective of greatest utility and how can we choose in advance. The history of contingency theories in the public sector has not been a happy one, with most of the attempts to develop such approaches to problems and solutions failing (Greenwood, Hinings, and Ranson 1975a, 1975b;

but see Dunsire and Hood 1989). That having been said, however, these contending approaches to reform call out for analytic attempts to relate them more closely to specific problems and situations (Pollitt 1995).

For example, matching the market model with particular situations would be perhaps the easiest part of the analysis. The public sector already provides a number of services that are, in principle, marketable (Rose et al. 1985). It is certainly true that there are a number of public corporations making products— steel, airplanes, gasoline—or providing services—transportation, banking—that are marketed in many countries. Other services that are often thought of as appropriately being in the public sector—education, pensions, health care—are in principle marketable, and some countries do provide them, in whole or in part, through the private sector. It seems logical, therefore, to think that there are a number of policy areas here for which the market model might provide a reasonable form of structuring public services.

The marketization of services, however, may be limited by a conception of entitlement to the service. For example, although pensions may be in principle readily marketable, they may not be if government has begun to provide them through social insurance. Once citizens perceive that they have paid their "premiums" for the insurance (their payroll taxes), they believe that they have the right to collect that pension under the terms that have been operative now for decades. Other programs, such as housing, that lack this contributory and entitlement characteristic may be converted into market programs much more readily.

The market model is also limited by being inappropriate for policy areas where efficiency is not really an immediate concern. Take, for example, preparing for unusual events and natural disasters. Organizations such as the Federal Emergency Management Agency (FEMA) in the United States prepare for eventualities such as earthquakes and hurricanes that are unpredictable and that may not occur for years. Some areas where planning of this sort goes on may never suffer a significant disaster. A market approach to governance might contend that all this preparation and stockpiling of resources is really inefficient. Government might be better off in the long run (in economic terms) not to plan at all for these events but simply to cope with them when and if they do occur. And given organizations such as the Red Cross, the private sector may be able to handle the problems. Although FEMA clearly could be more efficient than it sometimes is, the answer of neglecting preparation is clearly unacceptable.

Similarly, certain types of programs and policies appear to require a more participatory mode of service delivery than do others. There has been some change in this direction in all policy areas across time, as most contemporary societies become more participatory (Berman 1995). Still, there are differences in the extent of participation being demanded. For example, education has almost always been a policy that citizens, and especially parents, have believed to be in need of being more open to their inputs. More recently, land-use planning and environmental issues, through the NIMBY and NOTE phenomena, have generated a great deal of public involvement in policies.[9] These issues have also demonstrated some of the potential difficulties with encouraging participation, given the tendency for mobilized citizens to block any proposed solution, no matter how pressing the problem, e.g., in the disposal of nuclear wastes.

The match between flexible organizational solutions and particular policies is somewhat less clear, but some points can still be made. Although it may be difficult to determine this in advance, some problems and policies will require greater linkage with other policies. Although on average the needs for coordination appear to be increasing across all policy areas, still, policies such as drug enforcement and programs dealing with specific target populations—the elderly, youth, women, aboriginal peoples, immigrants, and so on—require greater coordinative activity and greater flexibility. And it is relatively easy to identify programs that have a need for seasonal employment, but it may be less clear which programs may be well run with seasonal employees (recreation, road repairs) and which may suffer if there is excessive seasonal and temporary employment (tax policy).

In some ways the deregulatory model applies across the entire range of the public sector. The argument is a general one: if there are fewer internal rules, government will function better.[10] Still, it is also clear that governments in the countries being discussed will almost certainly require some internal rules for purposes of accountability and democratic control, if not also to address some basic management requirements. The question then becomes which rules are appropriate or inappropriate and for which organizations. One of the clearest targets for deregulatory reforms has been central agencies and their tendency to second-guess the line departments that actually deliver public services. However, the central agencies are the actors charged with coordinating the program of the government of the day and with pursuing other goals (cost reduction, affirmative action) through their central positions in the policy process. How can those tasks be performed without using some internal regulatory devices?

The best way to think about imposing the deregulatory model may be not to think so much of differences among organizations but to think about differences among the rules themselves. In the first place, we know that a number of rules in government are redundant. These are rules sometimes being imposed on outside organizations and individuals but sometimes internally as well. Clearly, a deregulatory strategy should attempt to reduce redundant and contradictory rules. Second, the deregulators might want to attack primarily rules that established strict prohibitions or confining mandates and leave in place rules that tended to set standards and goals for behavior. Similarly, they appear much more concerned about ex ante prohibitions than they do about ex post evaluations and even punishments.

Indeed, are there policy areas that are more suitable to deregulation than others? The question is actually easier to answer the other way round: which policy areas are less suitable to deregulation? I would argue that those concerned with basic rights of citizens—criminal justice, civil rights, and so on—should be poorer candidates for deregulation than those issues concerned with simple economic benefits (or costs) of citizenship. The distinction between rights and economics is not always easy to maintain. This is very clear for many social and economic programs that have come to be defined as "entitlements" or "the new property" (Reich 1973; but see Epstein 1990) and the crucial role that some programs play in maintaining the lives of some citizens. Still, there are marked differences between being denied free access to a park and being faced with capital punishment.

Weakness of the Approaches

The relative weaknesses of the four models should also be considered. Success may be created by the careful matching of approaches to problems. However, it may be easier to prevent disasters by understanding what can go wrong, or is likely to go wrong, and where the sources of failures reside for each model. For all the models the principal danger arises from overstepping the bounds and assuming that something that will work well for some policies and some issues will work for all. Beyond that general problem there are some specific difficulties that arise from each. The fundamental weakness of the market model, for example, is that it assumes patterns of behavior that simply may not be present in the real world. There may be some policy areas in which actors are not concerned with maximization so much as they are with pursuing collective values.

Empirical Implications

I have been discussing the contingencies for selecting one or another of the models of reform primarily from a normative perspective—what should government do. These contingencies can also be considered as empirical predictions of success and failure, and perhaps even empirical predictions about the adoption of one form of administrative change or another. It appears that policy areas have been differentially affected by reforms, with some—health care in the United Kingdom and land use in Canada as but two examples—being especially prone to them, albeit of different types. What is it about these policies that has tended to place them at the center of controversies about how to manage government, and what goals should be pursued through collective activity?

EXPLORING CONTRADICTIONS

One feature of the emerging patterns of governance that led to my writing this book was the sense that academics and practitioners alike were advocating a series of ideas about reform and that they were being adopted willy-nilly. Further, they were being adopted without careful examination of the contradictions inherent in the disparate approaches. The problem was not a shortage of ideas about how to make government work better; it was too many ideas and not enough systematic thinking about which ideas were applicable to particular situations and how the ideas were compatible with one another. Government reformers were like candidates in a New York City election who go through the city eating pizza in an Italian neighborhood, pierogies in a Polish neighborhood, blintzes in a Jewish neighborhood, enchiladas in a Hispanic neighborhood, and so forth. Each of these is itself a tasty dish but at the end of the day the politician is quite dyspeptic.

Some of the apparent problems with sorting out contradictions arise from different schools of reformers meaning quite different things while using the same terms. People have a right to use the terminology they choose, but when the same term is used to imply different ways of solving a problem, then confusion results. Take, for example, the terms "consumerism" and "choice." These are central concepts in both the market models of change and in the participatory approach. In both cases they imply something about an enhanced role for the citizen in the policy process, but they would achieve that goal through very different means (see Ranson and Stewart 1994, 74–76). Choice, for example, can mean either the right to make an individual choice in a quasi market providing a service or the right to participate in a political process that will make collective choices.

Many of the contradictions go well beyond mere semantics and involve fundamental differences about what is "wrong" with government and what should be done to fix it. When the discussion is carried on at the level of identifying problems and broad categories of interventions, the incompatibility of different ideas is obvious. Market advocates and participation advocates tend to begin with very different perceptions of the world and its problems, and their mutual lack of confidence can become apparent rapidly. These contradictions are also probably irrelevant because the theoretical discussions have little real impact on government until the ideas are converted into programs and mechanisms for making things work better.

When these more philosophical ideas are converted into specific proposals for action, however, their roots are sometimes forgotten and the contradictions are less obvious. Take, for example, a case in which a reformer may decide that the fundamental solution to the problem is empowerment of workers. That may well be the case, and involving employees in their jobs and in their organizations often produces real benefits for the workers and for their organizations. Yet such a reform would be incompatible with some of the ideas about flexibility on the job and the creation of virtual organizations and virtual employees. Those employees would not be prepared to invest the time and energy required to participate effectively, not knowing just how long they would be a part of the organization. Further, treating employees as interchangeable parts of a machine is in fundamental opposition to the organizational humanism of the participative model (Donkin 1995). This example is not totally hypothetical; the human resource management report to the Gore Commission (National Performance Review 1993b) appears to contain all these ideas and more.

The more recent rounds of reform have had less incompatible assumptions about the problems and the solutions of public management. This relative agreement reflects to some extent that the first major reforms—those using the market, participation, and other approaches to change—were successful and have addressed some of the most obvious problems. The second round therefore can build on those earlier successes and consolidate the gains that have been made. The second round also to some extent compensates for problems created by the initial reforms, but this compensation can be seen in some degree as fine-tuning rather than as more fundamental change. That is particularly true for the emphasis on quality and on reregulation of government.

HOW CAN WE INTERVENE?

Each of the four models discussed in the first portion of the book has offered a diagnosis of the problem, and each has had a solution. What each appears to lack, however, is a clear strategy for guiding public-sector intervention. Much the same is true for the reforms adopted during the more recent period. Changing an institutional structure as large as the public bureaucracy is a difficult chore; even changing one organization within it has been enough to defeat some experienced and skilled practitioners (Szanton 1981). Therefore, the success of any (or potentially all) of these models requires careful attention to the strategy and tactics of change.

Interestingly, to the extent that these models do have prescriptions about how to intervene, they tend to favor (or actually assume) the use of political power to force, or to "encourage," the transformation. This strategy might be expected in the market model, given its close connections with political leaders who had few compunctions about using political power, but it is surprising in the other three. Indeed, it appears to run exactly counter to the philosophy of the participative and the deregulatory models. The assumption appears to be that organizations must be forced to be participative and flexible, even if impelled by other organizations, e.g., central agencies, that themselves are not noted for their flexibility.

Another aspect of the strategies for intervention that is somewhat surprising is the emphasis placed on formal structure and procedure. In each of the four models it seemed easier to uncover the recommendations about structure and formal rules within the organization than about any other aspect of the proposed changes. Apparently lacking in this discussion and implementation of change was an emphasis on organizational culture and changing the way in which employees, managers, and clients thought about the organization. Although the strategy of changing organizational culture appears loose and inchoate, doing so may be at once extremely difficult and rewarding, as has been asserted in some of the private-sector literature on organizational change (Peters and Waterman 1982).

The concept of "institutional negotiation" provides another way of looking at strategies for generating change in organizations (Zifcak 1994, 186–88). This is a view not dissimilar to the concept of bureaucratic politics (Allison 1971), although it would occur more within government instead of being directed toward some external policy goal. The fundamental idea is that any attempt to produce organizational change, especially when conducted systemwide, as many of these programs are, will upset long-standing institutional arrangements and power configurations. Somebody is going to win and somebody is going to lose in that process, and the probable losers will attempt to forestall the changes, using any legal mechanisms at their disposal (and perhaps a few more).

In reality, most major administrative changes produce the political battles described so politely as "institutional negotiations." A more appropriate strategy for producing enduring change, however, might not be imposition, especially not by a political or central agency actor who is unlikely to lose out in the process, but through more genuine bargaining and negotiation among the members of the organization. This approach would appear to be a natural outflow from thinking about enhancing participation in organizations. Creating a bargaining arena of that type is difficult, especially given that many of the participants will be distrustful of at least some other participants—usually the central financial and management agencies. Still, if such a bargaining arrangement can be reached, then any outcomes are likely to be more enduring than those imposed on unwilling victims.[11]

It might be argued, however, that building enduring change may not be the most appropriate goal for reformers in the public sector. The experiences of the past several decades have been that change is not enduring, and that as the "technology" for managing the public-sector changes, there will be continuing needs to adapt and to adjust. Reforming effectively appears to be more than ever a process of continual learning, both from the experiences of the past and from those of other countries; therefore maintaining flexibility could be preferable to institutionalizing formal structures.

Zifcak discusses changing the "appreciative system" of an organization, or of the organizational environment of government, as a means of generating change. This approach is very much like producing cultural change, but it may go even further. The fundamental point is that organizations often operate the way they do because of their own images of themselves (Morgan 1986). Therefore, to produce meaningful change may require changing that self-image and with it the pattern of behavior. This view is similar to Schon and Rein's ideas (1994) of altering perceptual "frames" in order to produce meaningful policy change. They argue that individuals and organizations tend to become locked into one frame or another and therefore cannot visualize alternative ways to do things, much less to implement them.

To generate this type of fundamental appreciative change, however, may require significant challenges to the existing ways of doing business in the public sector. Most administrative systems are locked into long-standing traditions and modes of thought that prevent consideration of alternative conceptualizations. Developments in the environment of the public sector over the past several decades, however, have constituted sufficient shocks for many people in administrative systems to make them at least consider change. The loss of secure and seemingly endless tax funding for programs and political assaults from leaders such as Reagan and Thatcher, and to some extent even from politicians on the political left such as Clinton and Blair, have made the lives of public administrators much less comfortable than they had been. For other countries such as Germany, however, the stimuli for reform have been much less overt, and there may be fewer pressing reasons to consider significant reform. In fact, the major change in German government and administration, reunification with the Eastern *Länder,* has to some extent strengthened the dominant model of administration, not weakened it (Konig 1993). To the degree that changes have been implemented, they have been incremental as opposed to the more radical shifts seen in many other countries.

Where reform initiatives are occurring through altering the appreciative system of public organizations, conflict within them almost certainly is being created. Conflict during times of organizational change is to be expected, but what may differentiate change within the context of altering appreciative systems is the extent to which the issues raised will be based on first principles. Different segments of an administrative structure within the public sector may have extremely different fundamental beliefs about the role of government, the most effective ways in which to manage organizations, and the role of the civil service in providing governance. Attempting to reconcile these disparate internal views and still make an organization function will be a continuing challenge for public managers in the foreseeable future, and probably forever.

SUMMARY

Even if the participants in government wanted to, could they ever return to the comfortable system of running the state that is now largely lost? To some degree the emphasis on management, on the greater political reliability of civil servants, on the empowerment of staff and clients, and on flexibility drives the political system toward an alteration of the tacit social contract that had existed among the participants in governance. No longer are politicians willing to cede some control over policy to their civil servants in exchange for the expertise and skills of the permanent staff. Nor do civil servants appear to be willing to accept job security in exchange for relatively low pay, loss of real influence over policy, and a diminution of their professional standing (whether real or only perceived by them).

Both sides of this contract can gain some advantages from the changes in their relationship, although the advantages seem to go primarily in the direction of politicians and secondarily to previously disadvantaged tiers within public organizations. Similarly, the principal disadvantages of reform appear to accrue to the senior civil service. Politically, then, returning to the status quo ante may be virtually impossible. The one group most disadvantaged by the changes also may have the least legitimacy with relevant groups other than itself. It lacks connections with the public either electorally or as the direct provider of services, so that generating any movement to restore the (self-perceived) rightful place of the senior bureaucrat is unlikely to stir many hearts among the public. That having been said, however, governance may be better served by some attention to the experience and expertise that these senior career leaders in the public sector can provide.

If there is to be a return to the bureaucratic Garden of Eden, then a strong restatement of the desirability of that move will be required. Given that the public service is not the most popular element of government in most political systems, there is probably not a natural constituency for such a move. Therefore, political activity is required to produce the movement. This can be justified in part through the traditional values of neutrality and competence in the civil service and the need to stress values such as public service rather than thinking of government as providing services as would any other "business." The waning of market ideology in a number of other Western countries[12] may initiate public discourse on ideas of public service in a way not possible until recently.

The governance role of public administration is perhaps the most significant aspect of a reassertion of the role of the public service. Yet one must contrast the role of the civil service as expressed through the "ideology" of the traditional model of governance to the reality of the role in the model in practice. The existence of a powerful and entrenched civil service created in essence the conditions for a strong policy role for that bureaucracy in governance. Although the market model in particular would appear to give somewhat enhanced power to the civil service, any redistribution of power would be in its role of manager rather than of policy maker and adviser. Indeed, the practice of the market model has been to attempt to centralize power in the political leadership and to limit the autonomy of the presumably entrepreneurial actors created by the reforms.

The traditional model of the public service and its role in government is, however, more than merely a rationalization for civil servants to make policy. It is also a statement of basic values on matters such as probity, accountability, and responsibility about which the present alternatives, and the market model in particular, have little to say. The concept of a permanent and professional civil service providing policy advice and management is seen by advocates of the traditional model as almost a sine qua non for good government. It is seen by traditionalists as embodying the mechanisms of providing citizens (and politicians) both the best advice and the best service. Though to critics the permanence of the bureaucracy is a severe problem, to its advocates it is the source of stability, reliability, and predictability. That organizational permanence is also seen as the best means of ensuring that government can be held accountable for its actions.

I have been discussing these four models as distinct alternatives for organizing the entire public sector. Another way to consider this set of options is to think of the possible desirable matches between particular governmental tasks and the alternative forms of organizing and managing (Wilson 1989). It may well be that for the provision of certain marketable services the market model is adequate and desirable, yet that same model would be totally inappropriate for many social services, education being one commonly discussed exception. Likewise, the participatory model would be well suited to urban planning or environmental issues but would produce difficulties for many criminal justice programs. The flexible model probably would suit complex issues such as drugs and transient concerns, like disaster relief. Though attempts at complex contingency theories for public administration appear to have generated relatively little benefit, we should still think about ways of making the punishment fit the crime.

My purpose in this book is not so much to force choices among the alternative visions of governance but to make the implications of the choices that now face governments more evident. To the extent that these models have been implemented in the real world (particularly the market model), they have been put forward for ideological reasons as much as from any thorough and impartial consideration of their relative merits. Each of the four alternatives does have its merits, but each also will impose some costs on society and on actors involved in government. Any choice of paradigms for government and administration is unlikely to be Pareto optimal, but we should be clear about what we receive and what we sacrifice when called upon to make these judgments about governance.

Perhaps fundamentally, analysts and citizens alike should ask what components are worth saving of the old system that is abandoned. Clearly, some critics would say absolutely nothing should be salvaged and would be quite willing to throw it all out and start anew. It should be clear by now that I am less confident of the vices of the old system or of the virtues of the alternative replacements. If nothing else, the old system did place a high value on accountability and on service to the public as a whole, if not always to each individual client or "customer." Those are crucial values for any public organization and are not ones that should be dismissed without adequate reflection. Through this book I am attempting to stimulate more of that necessary reflection.

As citizens and as analysts we also need to understand that the changes observed in these two time periods are not the end of the evolution of public management. The New Public Management in all its manifestations has initiated a process of change that does proceed, if perhaps at a somewhat diminished pace. The pattern of evolution seems to be in general toward one of greater democracy, both within organizations and between organizations and the public. It is also one in which the public has ever greater capacity to exert demands on government, instead of accepting what is given them. The emerging pattern is one in which delivering public services will continue to involve the private sector, seemingly at ever-increasing levels. Yet many of the fundamental issues—accountability, fairness, effectiveness—remain as important as before. Indeed, only the ways in which they are achieved change.

Notes

1. CHANGING STATES, GOVERNANCE, AND THE PUBLIC SERVICE

1. That claim has, however, been overstated in much of the literature. See Hirst and Thompson (1999).

2. This claim may also may be exaggerated, at least when governments decide to use the power and authority at their disposal, as in the Microsoft cases in both the United States and the European Union.

3. We should separate imperialism within government, in which organizations fight for control of problems and budgets, from imperialism, in which government goes searching for problems to solve. The former is much more common than the latter.

4. To the extent that there was a model for the traditional system, it was based on Max Weber's writings for continental Europe and perhaps on Woodrow Wilson's for the United States.

5. There may now be a substitute consensus developing around the market (Grice 1995).

6. Nixon did, of course, attempt to curb some of the power of the existing bureaucracy and can hardly be considered a benign figure in American politics, but it is also too easy to ignore some of his domestic policy achievements.

7. For an excellent discussion of the (no longer?) conventional wisdom, see Walsh and Stewart (1992) for the United Kingdom and Stillman (1991) for the United States.

8. The implementation of merit ideals has been far from perfect in many of these settings, but the principles do tend to be enshrined in law.

9. It should be remembered, however, that at least for Wilson and the other Progressives public administration was superior to politics because administration could be studied and reformed scientifically, but politics was more an art. See Doig (1983).

10. The Republican Contract with America was pledged to reduce the volume and intrusiveness of rule-making activity, but that may be difficult to do in any modern government.

11. Indeed, the most radical use of the variety of market-based reforms available to

government was implemented by the Labour government of New Zealand (Scott, Bushnell, and Sallee 1990). More recently, the Social Democratic Government in Sweden has undertaken a number of market-oriented changes in governance, and Tony Blair as leader of the Labour Party in Britain now accepts many of the administrative changes imposed during the Thatcher years.

12. Even some Conservatives now argue that the same has occurred during the privatization of public utilities in the United Kingdom, with directors awarding themselves massive salary increments with little or no control (Riddell 1995). The tales of scandals in privatized firms in Italy also have become legion.

13. This autonomous role is not unfamiliar in the United States but is extremely unusual and threatening in Westminster systems. The Ponting affair in Britain and the Al-Mashat case in Canada are important examples of the significance of this change in the norms of governing in Westminster governments (Chapman 1993; Sutherland 1991).

14. This pattern is already used rather widely in several European systems. See, for example, Fournier (1987) and his discussion of coordination within French government. In other settings such as task forces, *projets de mission, Projektgruppen,* and a variety of other organizations, devices are used to coordinate and manage crosscutting issues (Timsit 1988).

15. When there have been such attempts, the record appears to indicate that they have closed down more or less as intended. Even if they did not, the real culprit seems to be the legislatures that continued to fund them.

16. This is similar to the "Tiebout model" of local taxation and expenditure in public finance. See Tiebout (1956).

17. This has been true even in Britain and Canada, which have histories of more deferential political cultures. See Taggart (1995).

18. This is to a great extent a function of the shifts of employment in Western countries from manufacturing to service, a shift linked with the globalization driving other parts of these changes.

2. MARKET MODELS FOR REFORMING GOVERNMENT

1. For good reviews, see Wright (1994).

2. In these cases the market model is generally not adopted autonomously but is imposed by granting agencies such as the World Bank and the International Monetary Fund, which are seeking to ensure that their money is used effectively (see chapter 8).

3. This is not to say that some members of the administration such as David Stockman were unwilling to press those ideas, but only that at the top there was more of a vague ideology instead of a real set of intellectual principles (Stockman 1986, 9). Reagan appeared to practice the "politics of impulse" rather than the politics of ideas.

4. Some of these critiques pertain specifically to its application to the public sector; others concern its applicability even for private-sector organizations.

5. This includes some analysts who would not normally be associated with the political right.

6. This characteristic of bureaucrats does not differentiate them from other individuals. The problem is the assumption, inherent in the traditional model, that members of the public service will necessarily act in the public interest.

7. This discussion runs counter to Simon's famous argument (1947) that administrators will be satisfiers instead of maximizers. That is, they will seek solutions that are "good enough" rather than those that are optimal.

8. Firms may compete over quality rather than just price, however. No two products or services are exactly identical, so that the customer may choose according to price, quality, or other attributes.

9. In practice, governments have established redundant organizations and allowed them to compete. For example, Franklin Roosevelt's New Deal in the United States had a number of organizations performing about the same duties.

10. For the regulated, redundancy may enable them to play one agency off the other. For example, both the Federal Trade Commission and the Antitrust Division of the Department of Justice enforce antitrust laws in the United States, with some capacity for firms to "choose" one over the other.

11. Britain has attempted to create some competition among its water and electricity companies, but even these are segmented regionally so that there is no effective competition.

12. This artificial creation, in the view of the New Public Management, could be used to enable civil servants to enhance their own position. Thus, this approach to the role of the market in public affairs is not entirely distinct from the first one discussed.

13. They usually want to export these techniques at a profit.

14. The United States also has a tradition of autonomous agencies within the cabinet departments, although that autonomy is derived as much from political realities as from institutional design (Seidman and Gilmour 1986).

15. Devolving services to lower levels of government is sometimes seen as a solution to many problems of government but often may be just substituting one hierarchy and one bureaucracy for another.

16. It appears that large corporations in the private sector had an equal, or greater, propensity to reward middle managers with corporate welfare and, like the public sector, are being forced to change. See Sampson 1995.

17. Pay in the public sector has tended to be somewhat more egalitarian than in the market, with lower echelons paid better than the going market rates and the senior managers being paid substantially less than people with equal responsibilities in the private sector (Smith 1977; Sjölund 1989).

18. Actually, in the private sector there appears to be an inverse relationship between performance of businesses and the rewards of their top managers, as noted in the *Economist,* "Failure-Related Pay," September 2, 1994.

19. In some cases, e.g., the Department of Social Services in the United Kingdom, overhead services such as information technology are devolved to a separate organization, which then charges other agencies for its services.

20. The United States has been a visible laggard in this regard but is considering modernization of its budgetary processes. See Paul L. Posner, Budget Structure: Providing an Investment Focus in the Federal Budget, Testimony to House Committee on Government Reform and Oversight, June 29, 1995.

21. In Canada, the same types of reviews are being undertaken by the Chretien government, more at the initiation of the government itself than through the Treasury, as in Britain. In the United States, the Department of Defense has been engaging in a bottom-up review of its spending.

22. Private-sector contractors appear to do well when bidding for routine functions such as janitorial services, managing food services, and so forth, but to do much less well for more policy-focused activities or for delivering more complex services.

23. That entrepreneurship would probably be frowned upon if the creativity cost more money. Further, this is risky behavior that may in the end cost money, even when attempts are made to "make" or save money. The risk element of the market model is sometimes ignored when advocating moving to marketlike provision of services.

24. Those of us who deal regularly with airlines and Blue Cross–Blue Shield may consider being treated like the customer of a private concern to be a threat.

25. It is interesting, however, that some of the countries most satisfied with their educational system are virtual state monopolies, e.g., France and Japan. Perhaps some other variable is to blame for the perceived poor performance of American and British education.

3. THE PARTICIPATORY STATE

1. Perhaps the most important alternative description would be communitarianism, although that model appears to lack some of the direct participatory ethos that motivates this particular conceptualization.

2. This view is then in sharp contrast to the conception of the public primarily as the consumers of public services, as in the market approach.

3. Jack Kemp as Secretary of Housing and Urban Development in the United States is one prime example. He pioneered efforts to debureaucratize housing projects and permit tenant self-management. For a discussion of debureaucratization of housing projects in the United States, see Hula (1991).

4. As with those involved in the market approach, these scholars tend to assume that public and private organizations are the same. It should be pointed out that this group is basing their assumptions on human behavior in organizations rather than on a set of techniques.

5. It is market-oriented in the sense that it is designed to increase productivity and improve products, but the logic for achieving those goals is not that of monetary incentives.

6. Most Americans regard the title of this organization as an oxymoron.

7. Performance and quality have a renewed life in Washington with the Government Performance and Results Act, but the thrust of this legislation is more top down.

8. The limited evidence available indicates that things are not so good in the less developed systems. See Goodsell 1976.

9. The various horror stories notwithstanding, most encounters with the Internal Revenue Service in the United States are rated favorably by clients. Indeed, enhancing the relationships between examiners—the street level of this organization—and their clients is considered crucial for taxpayer compliance.

10. Although somewhat beyond the scope of this book, the same paradox holds true for elected officials, at least in the United States. Voters hate Congress but love their individual senator or representative.

11. The term "contravention" actually comes from Simmel (see Gillin and Gillin 1948).

12. The Food and Drug Administration is required to use a formal rule-making procedure, a public hearing in which evidence is taken from interested parties and then a formal ruling on a drug license is issued. The errors that are made tend to be in refusing to license potentially useful drugs rather than in licensing harmful drugs.

13. As the street-level bureaucracy people would argue, however, determining how to do something is often determining what that something really is.

14. The United States allows more participation than do most other Anglo-American countries, including allowing broad participation even in court decisions through amici briefs (Caldiera and Wright 1990). Further, even the former East German regime used consultation as a means of legitimation, although certainly not of real policy formulation (Boyle 1994).

15. The leader of the Labour Party in Britain went so far as to praise, albeit in guarded terms, the actions of the British Conservative Party in creating organizations of this type.

16. See chapter 6.

17. Of course, within Europe there are also marked differences in levels of involvement in public life. The Scandinavian countries are accustomed to opportunities to express grievances about government while German and British citizens may be more reluctant to do so.

18. The Citizens' Charters in the United Kingdom are the most widely known example, but charters have been developed in a large number of countries.

19. This language is usually reserved for the implementation process but can also be applied to the process more generally.

20. Market advocates argue that the market does provide the strongest control, the capacity for customers to take their business elsewhere. Monopolies in the public sector eliminate that restraint.

21. The quotation comes from the Administrative Procedures Act of 1946 in the United States.

22. Co-optation is not meant to be a pejorative here but only a statement of the manner in which groups and individuals are made parts of a larger program. In these cases there is really a form of mutual co-optation.

23. This study was performed before the current spate of interest in "empowering" individuals and organizations. It is difficult to ascertain just what the differences might be after that cultural change.

24. In fairness, other scholars of coordination of organizations such as Mary Parker Follett (1940) and Russell Hardin (1982) have also noted the extent to which zero-sum games emerge in interactions among organizations.

25. The fear of technocracy is a long-standing concern of scholars committed to participatory and democratic values in public policy. See, for example, Ellul (1980) and Meynaud (1969).

4. FLEXIBLE GOVERNMENT

1. Aberbach, Putnam, and Rockman (1981, 67–71) found that the large majority of public employees in the developed democracies they studied had spent almost none of

their working lifetimes outside central government. This varied substantially by country, with almost no British civil servants working elsewhere but half of German civil servants having such experiences. In other countries, e.g., France and Japan, public managers frequently leave government for lucrative positions in the private sector, but there is little flow in the other direction.

2. One interesting manifestation of this is the demand for term limits for public officials in the United States. This idea appealed more to politicians when they were on the outside than it did after they were elected, and the initial proposals were defeated in the House of Representatives in March 1995. Several politicians who campaigned saying that they would leave office after a set period have chosen to remain.

3. Interestingly, some of the public-choice literature has been seeking means of designing organizations that will be conservative and will preserve the same policies over time (McCubbins, Noll, and Weingast 1989).

4. This self-delusory activity is not confined to public-sector organizations. Some private-sector firms have persisted in keeping to their own losing paths even in the face of overwhelming evidence. These instances are often the result of organizations performing well at one time but then being incapable of responding to change.

5. For Niskanen and his allies, permanence appears to have been assumed as a part of the argument, but the important dynamic forces were monopoly and the ability to mask the true costs of production from the sponsor.

6. One argument is that public spending will go up more rapidly than private-sector spending because of the lower returns to capital investment (Baumol 1967). The revolution in information technology, however, may have made that argument outmoded.

7. It is probably more fallacious, given that any policy that has survived for some period of time must be doing something right. There are anecdotal examples to the contrary, but on average the evaluative mechanisms of government are not totally inadequate.

8. The possibility that private-sector employees and their organizations might understand government better does not appear to be a part of the thinking, although it is certainly an equal possibility.

9. This has been most obvious at managerial levels (Mackenzie 1987) but is also true for other positions at all levels of government.

10. The usual models of "bounded rationality" may not be applicable since we are asking decision makers to think about fundamental shifts from the status quo rather than from marginal adjustments.

11. State and local governments in the United States have already made more moves in this direction with sunset laws and other devices that force relatively frequent reconsideration of the existence of their organizations. The assumption is that unless an organization is reauthorized, it will go out of existence automatically. This reverses the usual presumption that unless an organization is actively terminated, it will remain in existence.

12. For example, it has been argued that budgetary reforms such as PPBS failed because they threatened organizations (Wildavsky 1978). The perhaps excessive focus on organizations tended to undermine what could have been an important change in the budgetary system.

13. An increasing number of accountability issues in the public sector have to do with private-sector firms and individuals, rather than with members of the public sector itself, using public money inappropriately.

14. It is not clear when governments ever can be really sure of an outcome, but certainly the outcomes of some programs are more predictable than others.

15. Dror (1986) has discussed policymaking as "fuzzy gambling," derived from the ideas of fuzzy sets in mathematics. In this view decision makers do not know the parameters of the risks they are assuming. Given the lack of knowledge about probabilities in some important policy areas, e.g., nuclear regulation, this term is not inappropriate.

16. "Minimax" is a term drawn from game theory meaning that one optimal strategy for a player may be to "minimize maximum losses."

17. As something of a record, the Defense Public Works Division of the Federal Works Agency remained in existence only sixteen days before being absorbed into a larger organization. See Peters and Hogwood (1988).

18. This phrase is usually attributed to Justice Louis Brandeis. The exact quote is, "It is one of the happiest incidents of the federal system that a single courageous state may, if its citizens choose, serve as a laboratory, and try novel experiments without risk to the rest of the country" (*New State Ice Co. v. Liebmann,* 285 U.S. 262, 311 [1932]).

19. A classic example is the Renegotiation Board, established to review defense contracts (see Kaufman 1976, 1991).

20. Arguably, after some period of existence, organizational motivations become less about serving their clients and more about simple self-preservation, regardless of the needs and wishes of these clients.

21. This is, of course, the exact opposite principle of Rawls's (1972) "justice principle," in which the interests of the least advantaged should be considered paramount in determining policy.

22. The reverse problem is a program that has positive benefits in the short term, but with those benefits decaying over time to the point that the beneficiaries become no different from members of the population who had not been beneficiaries.

5. DEREGULATED GOVERNMENT

1. On the concept of red tape in the public sector, see Kaufman (1977).

2. The abuses of military purchasing rules have been most notorious, e.g., eight hundred dollar toilet seats. But some of the same restraints (and apparent silliness) also have applied in domestic-policy sectors. The ashtray example that Vice President Gore developed as a part of "reinventing government" in the United States pointed clearly to some of the dysfunctions of purchasing controls.

3. The budget "game" tends to be that no managers want to underspend lest they be seen not to need the same amount of money (or more) in the next budget year. Therefore, the last weeks of the budget year often find somewhat ill-considered decisions being made just to get rid of the money.

4. Of course, citizens in any country will complain, but perhaps not with the intensity recently encountered in Anglo-American systems. See Peters and Pierre (2001).

5. In many cases the rules in these systems are procedural rather than substantive, e.g., requiring referral of prospective regulations to the Conseil d'Etat.

6. See the discussion of "reregulation."

7. The Quality Assurance process in the United States had these assumptions about the appropriate direction of error.

8. We may question whether any such powerful indicators exist for public programs.

9. There was also a financial reason for cutting back on evaluators. If the goal was to reduce the size of government, employment cutting evaluators could achieve that end without directly affecting service delivery.

10. One possible counterargument would be that the new rules are conceptualized as aids to managerial decision-making rather than as ex ante controls.

11. PPBS stands for Planning, Programming Budgeting Systems; RCB for Rationalization des Choixs budgetaires.

12. This is the classic "displacement of goals" problem in public organizations, or indeed in any highly structured organization.

13. This is in many ways a reworking of the old "Theory X" and "Theory Y" arguments about human nature within organizations. Deregulating does not necessarily have a pessimistic view of human nature, but it does not assume that public employees are clamoring to be made more personally liable for their actions.

14. By negative redistribution I do not mean any normative claim but only that the more affluent will become even more so and the less affluent even less so.

15. This statement assumes that these goals are relatively unpopular. For some politicians, e.g., those with strong ties to minorities and women, the goals may be very popular and they may want to push to deliver these programs more visibly. The politician, however, will have a higher probability of having the programs implemented through the less obtrusive means.

6. FROM CHANGE TO CHANGE: PATTERNS OF CONTINUING ADMINISTRATIVE REFORM

1. See Pollitt and Bouckaert (2000) for a detailed assessment of reform in the developed democracies. Much of the same pattern of administrative reform is now being replicated in the less developed countries (see chapter 7).

2. The obvious example is the combination of the Fulton and Plowden Reports in the United Kingdom and the succession of Glassco and Lambert in Canada. Earlier the two Hoover Commissions in the United States were implemented in rapid succession.

3. In this analysis I will not discuss changes in fundamental state responsibilities, e.g., privatization, but will focus on reforms more concerned with administration per se. The same general finding of one change begetting another would be found here as well, as privatization produced regulation of the same economic activities, with subsequent attempts to deregulate.

4. Given the indefinite nature of managerialism, and its multiple meanings, that is not a particularly narrow band of possible approaches to reform. Still, much of the change is justified as continuing managerialism forward in the public sector.

5. Actions taken in respect of individuals may be more transparent, with the requirement to explain the decisions and to identify the individual making the decision.

Yet the use of corporate models of procurement and personnel actions may make those major decisions less visible.

6. This is simply another statement of the familiar Friedrich-Finer debate over control of bureaucracies. The question is whether any amount of formal institutional control will be sufficient to deter a public official who does not have the normative basis of appropriate behavior.

7. The good news is that most of the evidence available is that citizens tend to rate the services they receive from government about as highly as those they receive from the private sector.

8. The possible exception to that generalization is quality management, which is developing an extensive literature. Likewise, accountability has a huge literature, but the present concern with it adds relatively little conceptually (but see Day and Klein 1987).

9. This idea showed up, for example, rather strongly in the execrable Osborne and Gaebler book (1992) as well as in other early testaments about the need to change the public sector. Further, there were some efforts to institutionalize the concept, e.g., the Federal Quality Management Institute begun by former President Bush in 1990.

10. Concerning accountability, however, in a democratic government there must still be substantial concern about due process and some aspects of process within the public sector.

11. For example, who should be consulted about good performance in the prison system or in tax collection agencies? In the former case the public at large will want prisons to be humane but probably not terribly comfortable and above all secure. The most immediate "clients" of the facilities may have rather different desires.

12. This is to some extent analogous to problems of interpersonal comparisons of utility in welfare economics. That is, how do we compare the levels of perceived benefit for different individuals?

13. One is reminded of Richard Nelson's book, *The Moon and the Ghetto* (1968), in which the difficulty of transforming complex social situations is contrasted to the relative simplicity of rocket science.

14. Personal interview, Colin Sankey, responsible for the quality program, government of Hong Kong.

15. Parrado-Diaz (1999) notes this effect with respect to personnel policy in Spain. He demonstrates that although government, in principle, had deregulated personnel policy, the Ministry of Finance indeed increased its discretion over which agencies could actually use contracts and other flexible instruments.

16. These inspectorates have indeed been successful in capturing public attention in the United Kingdom. See, for example, Timmins (2000) and the *Guardian* (2000).

17. The length of that arm, however, may be sometimes exaggerated. Agencies may well attempt politically to construct their relationships with ministries and central agencies in ways that make them appear more autonomous.

18. Increasingly, this function is being given a separate institutional existence in government.

19. This was especially true, given that there was an increasing number of managers recruited from outside government who did not necessarily understand the limits of appropriate action within the public sector.

7. THE LOGIC OF CONTINUING CHANGE

1. To some extent the National Performance Review (now the National Partnership for Reinventing Government) used the opposite strategy and to some extent was a stealth program that has been relying more on slow, noncontroversial implementation rather than on hype.

2. Although counted by most analysts as a failure, this program did lay the groundwork for subsequent rounds of reform and did serve as a model for rather similar programs in (among other places) Australia and France.

3. Using the word "completing" is perhaps inadvisable, given the succession of reforms in the United Kingdom and the majority of other industrialized democracies.

4. Perhaps more than any of the other Nordic countries, Finland has been engaged in almost continual reform of the public sector for the past several decades (Tiihonen 2000).

5. For a more complete analysis of these types of outcomes in the reform process, see the studies contained in Hesse, Hood, and Peters (2000).

6. In fairness, much the same could be said of the literature on organizational design in the private sector.

7. These dualisms were identified by Herbert Simon (1947) as "the proverbs of administration."

8. Dimaggio and Powell (1991) discuss learning as one of the processes by which institutions become isomorphic, and that certainly does appear to be the case here.

9. It is also interesting that at least in Finland, as the evaluation system was institutionalized, it, too, was evaluated and refined as more was learned about the nature of administrative reform and the ways in which it could be assessed (Tiihonen 2000, 44–45).

10. The Swedish government has referred to this program as "the cheese slicer," meaning that, as with an *osthovel*, a thin slice can be pared off; in this case it is a thin slice of the budget being pared off each year. The organizations being subjected to these reductions in operating funds are expected to make up the difference in efficiency gains, but for how long can they do so?

11. Labour in Britain was rather successful in doing this during the dismissal imbroglio around the head of the Prison Service.

12. These reforms are not dissimilar to some of those in the Financial Management Initiative in the United Kingdom, and the FMI is generally considered to have been a major failure.

13. One obvious exception has occurred in the United Kingdom, where the Blair government has continued and even expanded the types of administrative reforms begun by the Thatcher and Major governments.

14. The decentralization may be either to lower levels of government or to lower levels within the organizational structure of the public sector.

15. Some countries—three in a recent review of developed democracies—have maintained a separate budget ministry. There is also an increasing tendency to separate the foreign-trade component of economic policy from its other aspects, given the importance of trade issues for economic management in a more globalized economy. In governance terms, this reorganization of portfolios reflects the capacity of governments to adjust to the changing demands of their environment.

16. A major exception is the United Kingdom, where the Treasury had performed

the personnel function as well as economic management, except for a relatively short period of time.

17. These patterns of change in organizations in the public sector are documented fully in Bouckaert, Ormond, and Peters (2000). For example, Dutch administration has undergone a major transformation from extremely autonomous organizations to those with closer connections with ministerial authority.

18. This finding is to some degree analogous to the familiar capture arguments concerning independent regulatory agencies. That is, as organizations become dependent on the private sector for political support and other resources, then they may, by conscious choice or not, begin to favor their private-sector partners.

19. There have been some attempts to develop contingency theories for organizations in the public sector, but in general these have been less than fully successful. See Pitt and Smith (1984).

8. ADMINISTRATIVE REFORM IN DEVELOPING AND TRANSITIONAL GOVERNMENTS

1. The countries of the European Union had a conference on "best practices" in public management in Lisbon in early 2000.

2. The United States has had a major influence on the structure of political systems in Latin America, e.g., the dominance of presidential systems, but the administrative style appears more Iberian or in the case of Uruguay more shaped by French administrative practice.

3. This is very much the situation that Brunsson (1989) describes as "organizational hypocrisy," with talk and action being markedly divergent.

4. The exact nature of the values deemed important does vary among the industrialized countries, although this is a matter of degree rather than of type. See OECD (2000).

5. This is not just an indictment of public administration in less developed and transitional countries. The same behaviors have been noted for administrators in the industrialized democracies who are brought in from outside and who do not necessarily carry public-interest values as a part of their intellectual baggage.

6. For examples of successful entrepreneurship in developing political systems, see Ramamurti (1986).

7. Again, we must remember that there was this formal rigidity at the same time that there was the informalism and "canteen" behavior that undermined the formal equality of the treatment of citizens (Riggs 1964).

8. In the terms used by Talcott Parsons to describe development in these systems, particularistic criteria have been dominant, in contrast to the universalistic criteria that are argued to be dominant in more developed societies.

9. These are "stock" programs, meaning that they require accumulating a stock of resources, and meaning also that after initial decisions, the individuals in question do not have the opportunity to make alternative choices—they cannot relive their working lifetime. Other programs, e.g., health, are in essence flows so that (with the exception of resources such as hospitals) programs can be altered more readily. For these distinctions, see Hogwood and Peters (1983).

10. Or if not personal gain, then they certainly expect gain by family, friends, and/or political allies.

9. CAN WE GO HOME AGAIN? WHERE DO WE GO THEN?

1. These attributes are more characteristics of administrations in the Anglo-American democracies than in other countries, but these features do have some applicability in all industrialized democracies.

2. In contrast, a recent reform effort by the government of Finland emphasized the need to do something other than "move boxes" if real results are to be achieved. See Bouckaert, Ormond, and Peters 2000.

3. Henry Mintzberg, however, makes the point that it was not the market that triumphed but balance between the market and political forms of allocation. Not even the United States could have been said to have been a truly free market.

4. That exercise is doomed to be disappointing to the advocates of participation, given that the public tends always to choose lower taxes and higher expenditures.

5. In France, is it "frappe for the franc"?

6. Terms such as "Thatcherism" and "Reaganism" came to be applied to the reforms implemented during the 1980s while some of the market reforms advocated by Republicans after the 1994 elections have a pervasive ideological, extrarational element.

7. In fact, before the creation of the Passport Agency, British citizens could obtain short-term passes from their local post office to travel to the Continent. That practice was eliminated as "inefficient" by the Passport Agency.

8. Politicians elected from single-member districts or by transferable vote systems, e.g., those in the United States, the United Kingdom, and Ireland, have more incentive, and more opportunity, to use constituency service to promote their own careers.

9. NIMBY = Not In My Backyard; NOTE = Not Over There Either.

10. This is, of course, an overstatement; but like all hyperbole it is intended to make a point.

11. The idea of "envelope budgeting" in Canada has some similarities to this idea. This system made an initial allocation of funds to a number of large "envelopes" and then made the ministers within that broad policy area negotiate among themselves over the allocation to the various programs.

12. The Major government was substantially less ideological than the Thatcher government before it and was then replaced by the Blair government; the Tories lost power in Canada after implementing part of the NPM agenda; the right-leaning Schluter government lost office in Denmark, and so forth.

References

Aberbach, J. D., R. D. Putnam, and B. A. Rockman (1981). *Politicians and Bureaucrats in Western Democracies*. Cambridge: Harvard University Press.

Aberbach, J. D., and B. A. Rockman (1976). Clashing Beliefs Within the Executive Branch: The Nixon Administration Bureaucracy. *American Political Science Review* 70: 456–68.

—— (1988). Mandates or Mandarins? Control and Discretion in the Modern Administrative State. *Public Administration Review* 48: 607–12.

—— (1989). On the Rise, Transformation, and Decline of Analysis in U.S. Government. *Governance* 2: 293–314.

Adler, M., and S. Asquith (1981). *Discretion and Power*. London: Heinemann.

Adley, M., A. Patch, and J. Tweedie (1990). *Parental Choice and Educational Policy*. Edinburgh: University of Edinburgh Press.

Agh, A. (1996). The Actors of Systemic Change: The Political Context of Public Sector Reform in Central Europe. *Budapest Papers on Democratic Transition*. Budapest: University of Economics.

Agresta, R. J. (1994). OPM Needs a Mission—Not a Funeral. *Government Executive* 26 (9): 70.

Alexander, E. R. (1992). A Transaction Cost Theory of Planning. *Journal of the American Planning Association* 58: 190–200.

Allard, C. K. (1990). *Command, Control and the Common Defense*. New Haven: Yale University Press.

Allison, G. T. (1971). *The Essence of Decision*. Boston: Little, Brown.

—— (1987). Public and Private Management: Are They Fundamentally Alike in All Unimportant Respects? In J. M. Shafritz and A. C. Hyde, eds., *Classics of Public Administration*. Homewood, IL: Dorsey.

Almond, G. A., and H. D. Lasswell (1934). Aggressive Behavior by Clients Toward Public Relief Administrators. *American Political Science Review* 28: 643–55.

Altfeld, M. F., and G. J. Miller (1984). Sources of Bureaucratic Influence: Expertise and Agenda Control. *Journal of Conflict Resolution* 28: 701–30.

Andersen, N. A. (1994). Danmark: Forvaltningspolitikkens utvikling. In P. Laegreid and O. K. Pedersen, eds., *Forvaltningspolitik i Norden*. Copenhagen: Jurist-og Økonomforbundets Forlag.

Anheier, H. K., and W. Seibel (1990). *The Third Sector: Comparative Studies of Non-Profit Organizations*. Berlin: De Gruyter.

Argyris, C. (1964). *Integrating the Individual and the Organization*. New York: Wiley.

Ascher, K. (1987). *The Politics of Privatization: Contracting Out Public Services*. London: Macmillan.

Ashton, C. (1993). A Focus on Information Overload. *Managing Service Quality* (July): 33–36.

Atkinson, A. B., and J. E. Stiglitz (1980). *Lectures on Public Economics*. New York: McGraw-Hill.

Aucoin, P. (1990). Administrative Reform in Public Management: Paradigms, Principles, Paradoxes and Pendulums. *Governance* 3: 115–37.

Aucoin, P., and R. Heintzman (2000). The Changing Nature of Political Accountability. In B. G. Peters and D. J. Savoie, eds., *Revitalizing the Public Service*. Montreal: McGill/Queens University Press.

Australia (1992). *Performance Assessment of Policy Work, Report of the Working Group*. Canberra: Australian Government.

Bachrach, P., and M. S. Baratz (1962). The Two Faces of Power. *American Political Science Review* 56: 947–52.

Bachrach, P., and A. Botwinick (1992). *Power and Empowerment: A Radical Theory of Participatory Democracy*. Philadelphia: Temple University Press.

Baggott, R. (1995). From Confrontation to Consultation Under John Major? *Parliamentary Affairs* 48: 234–49.

Baldersheim, H. (1993). Kommunal organisering: Motar sel, men ressursar avgjer? In P. Laegreid and J. P. Olsen, eds., *Organisering av Offentlig Sektor*. Bergen: TANO.

Baldwin, R. (1995). *Rules and Government*. Oxford: Oxford University Press.

Ban, C., and P. W. Ingraham (1984). *Legislating Bureaucratic Change: The Civil Service Reform Act of 1978*. Albany: State University of New York Press.

Banks, J. S., and B. R. Weingast (1992). The Political Control of Bureaucracies Under Asymmetric Information. *American Journal of Political Science* 36: 509–24.

Barber, B. (1984). *Strong Democracy: Participatory Politics for a New Age*. Berkeley: University of California Press.

Bardach, E. (1998). Getting Agencies to Work Together. Washington, DC: Brookings Institution.

Barker, A. (1994). Enriching Democracy: Public Inquiry and the Policy Process. In I. Budge and D. McKay, eds., *Developing Democracy: Comparative Research in Honour of J. F. P. Blondel*. London: Sage.

Barker, A., and B. G. Peters (1993). *Advising West European Governments*. Edinburgh: Edinburgh University Press.

Barnes, M., and D. Prior (1995). Spoilt for Choice? How Consumerism Can Disempower Public Service Users. *Public Money and Management* 15 (3): 53–58.

Barzelay, M. (1992). *Breaking Through Bureaucracy*. Berkeley: University of California Press.

Baumol, W. J. (1967). The Macroeconomics of Unbalanced Growth. *American Economic Review* 57: 415–26.

Behn, R. D. (1991). *Leadership Counts: Lessons for Public Managers from the Massachusetts Welfare, Training and Employment Program*. Cambridge: Harvard University Press.

—— (1993a). Customer Service: Changing an Agency's Culture. *Governing* 6 (12): 76.

—— (1993b). Performance Measures: To Reward or to Motivate? *Governing* 6 (10): 84.

Bendor, J. S. (1985). *Parallel Systems: Redundancy in Government*. Berkeley: University of California Press.

—— (1990). Formal Models of Bureaucracy: A Review. In N. Lynn and A. Wildavsky, eds., *Public Administration: The State of the Discipline*. Chatham, NJ: Chatham House.

Bendor, J., S. Taylor, and R. Van Gaalen (1985). Bureaucratic Expertise and Legislative Authority: A Model of Deception and Monitoring in Budgeting. *American Political Science Review* 79: 1041–60.

Benson, J. K. (1982). A Framework for Policy Analysis. In D. L. Rogers and D. A. Whetten, eds., *Interorganizational Coordination*. Ames: Iowa State University Press.

Berman, E. M. (1995). Empowering Employees in State Agencies. *International Journal of Public Administration* 18: 833–50.

Beyme, K. von (1993). Regime Transition and Recruitment of Elites in Eastern Europe. *Governance* 6: 409–25.

Bezes, P. (2001). Reforming French Public Administration. In B. G. Peters and J. Pierre, eds., *Politicians and Bureaucrats in Administrative Reform*. London: Routledge.

Bipartisan Commission of Entitlement and Tax Reform (August 1994). *Interim Report to the President*. Washington, DC: Government Printing Office.

Birchall, J., C. Pollitt, and K. Putman (1995). Freedom to Manage: The Experience of the NHS Trusts, Grant-Maintained Schools and Voluntary Transfers of Public Housing. Paper presented at UK Political Studies Association, York, April 18–20.

Black, J. (1993). The Prison Service and Executive Agency Status—HM Prisons PLC? *International Journal of Public Sector Management* 6: 27–41.

Blau, P. M. (1960). Orientation Toward Clients in a Public Welfare Agency. *Administrative Science Quarterly* 5: 341–61.

Bleecker, S. E. (1994). The Virtual Organization. *Futurist* 28: 9–12.

Blondel, J. (1988). Ministerial Careers and the Nature of Parliamentary Government: The Cases of Austria and Belgium. *European Journal of Political Research* 16: 51–71.

Blumann, C., and A. van Soligne (1989). La commission, agent d'exécution du droit communitaire: La Comitologie. In J.-V. Louis and D. Waelbroeck, *La commission au couer du système institutionel des Communautés Européennes*. Brussels: Université de Bruxelles, Institut d'etudes Européennes.

Bodiguel, J.-L., and L. Rouban (1991). *Le fonctionnaire detrone?* Paris: Presses de la Fondation Nationale des Science Politiques.

Booker, C., and R. North (1994). *The Mad Officials: How Bureaucrats Are Strangling Britain*. London: Constable.

Borins, S. J. (1995a). Public Sector Innovation: The Implications of New Forms of Organization and Work. In B. Guy Peters and Donald J. Savoie, eds., *Governance in a Changing Environment*. Montreal: McGill/Queens University Press.

—— (1995b). The New Public Management Is Here to Stay. *Canadian Public Administration* 38: 122–32.

Borjas, G. J. (1995). The Internationalization of the U.S. Labor Market and the Wage Structure. *Economic Policy Review* 1: 3–8.

Boston, J. (1991). The Theoretical Underpinnings of State Restructuring in New Zealand. In J. Boston et al., eds., *Reshaping the State*. Auckland: Oxford University Press.

—— (1992a). Assessing the Performance of Departmental Chief Executives: Perspectives from New Zealand. *Public Administration* 70: 405–28.

—— (1992b). The Problems of Policy Coordination: The New Zealand Experience. *Governance* 5: 88–103.

—— (1993). Financial Management Reform: Principles and Practice in New Zealand. *Public Policy and Administration* 8: 14–29.

Botella, J. (1994). How Much Is Too Much? An Overview of Fiscal Attitudes in Western Europe. *Working Paper* 1194/54. Instituto Juan March, Madrid, Spain.

Bothun, D., and J. C. Comer (1979). The Politics of Termination: Concepts and Processes. *Policy Studies Journal* 7: 540–53.

Bouckaert, G. (1995). Improving Performance Measurement. In A. Halachmi and G. Bouckaert, eds. *The Enduring Challenges of Public Management*. San Francisco: Jossey-Bass.

Bouckaert, G., D. Ormond, and B. G. Peters (2000). *A Potential Governance Agenda for Finland*. Helsinki: Ministry of Finance.

Bovens, M. A. P., and P. Plug (1999). Accountability at a Distance: Reconciling Public Accountability and Administrative Autonomy. Paper presented at International Institute of Administrative Sciences Conference. Sunningdale, UK, July 12–15.

Bowen, D. E., and B. Schneider (1988). Services, Marketing, and Management: Implications for Organizational Behavior. In *Research in Organizational Behavior* 10: 43–80.

Bowler, M. K. (1974). *The Nixon Guaranteed Income Proposal: Substance and Process in Policy Change*. Cambridge, MA: Ballinger.

Boyle, M. (1994). Building a Communicative Democracy: The Birth and Death of Citizen Politics in East Germany. *Media, Culture and Society* 16: 183–215.

Boyne, G., J. Gould-Williams, J. Law, and R. Walker (1999). Competitive Tendering and Best Value in Local Government. *Public Money and Management* 19 (4): 23–30.

Boyte, H. C., and F. Riessman (1986). *The New Populism: The Politics of Empowerment*. Philadelphia: Temple University Press.

Braibanti, R. J. D. (1966). *Asian Bureaucratic Systems Emergent from the British Imperial Tradition*. Durham, NC: Duke University Press.

Bresser Pereira, L. C. (1999). *Reforming the State: Managerial Public Administration in Latin America*. Boulder, CO: Lynne Reiner.

Breton, A. (1974). *The Economic Theory of Representative Government*. Chicago: Aldine.

Brockman, J. (1992). Total Quality Management. *Public Money and Management* 12: 6–9.

Brooks, J., and P. Bate (1994). The Problems of Effecting Change Within the British Civil Service: A Cultural Perspective. *British Journal of Management* 5: 177–90.

Brunsson, N. (1989). *The Organization of Hypocrisy*. New York: Wiley.

Budge, I. (1996). *The Challenge of Direct Democracy*. Oxford, UK: Polity.

Burkitt, B., and P. Whyman (1994). Public Sector Reform in Sweden: Competition or Participation? *Political Quarterly* 65: 275–84.

Burstein, C. (1995). Introducing Reengineering to Government. *Public Manager* 24: 52–54.

Butler, D., and A. Ranney (1994). *Referendums Around the World: The Growing Use of Direct Democracy*. Washington, DC: AEI Press.

Byrne, P. (1976). Parliamentary Control of Delegated Legislation. *Parliamentary Affairs* 29: 366–77.

Cabinet Office (2000). *Annual Report: Modernising Government*. London: Cabinet Office.

Caiden, G. (1990). *Administrative Reform Comes of Age*. Berlin: Aldine de Gruyter.

Caldeira, G. A., and J. R. Wright (1990). *Amici Curiae* Before the Supreme Court: Who Participates When and How Much? *Journal of Politics* 52: 782–806.

Calista, D. J. (1989). A Transaction-Cost Analysis of Implementation. In D. Palumbo and D. J. Calista, eds., *Implementation Theory*. Lexington, MA: Lexington Books.

Campbell, C. (1983). The Search for Coordination and Control: When and How Are Central Agencies the Answer? In C. Campbell and B. G. Peters, *Organizing Government, Government Organizations*. Pittsburgh: University of Pittsburgh Press.

—— (1993). Public Service and Democratic Accountability. In R. A. Chapman, ed., *Ethics in Public Service*. Edinburgh: University of Edinburgh Press.

Campbell, C., and J. Halligan (1992). *Political Leadership in an Age of Constraint: The Australian Experience*. Pittsburgh: University of Pittsburgh Press.

Campbell, C., and B. G. Peters (1988). The Politics/Administration Dichotomy: Death or Merely Change? *Governance* 1: 79–99.

Campbell, C., and G. Szablowski (1979). *The Superbureaucrats: Structure and Behaviour in Central Agencies*. Toronto: Macmillan of Canada.

Campbell, D. T. (1982). Experiments as Arguments. *Knowledge: Creation, Diffusion, Utilization* 3: 327–37.

—— (1988). The Experimenting Society. In C. Campbell, *Methodology and Epistomology in the Social Sciences: Selected Essays*. Chicago: University of Chicago Press.

Canada (1962). *The Royal Commission on Government Operations* (Glassco Report). Ottawa: Queen's Printer.

—— (1991). *Speech from the Throne to Open the Third Session, Thirty-fourth Parliament of Canada*, May 13.

Canadian Centre for Management Development (1998). *A Strong Foundation*. Ottawa: CCMD.

Carter, N., P. Day, and R. Klein (1992). *How Organizations Measure Success*. London: Routledge.

Carter, N., and P. Greer (1993). Evaluating Agencies: Next Steps and Performance Indicators. *Public Administration* 71: 407–16.

Cate, F. A., and D. A. Fields (1994). The Right to Privacy and the Public's Right to Know: The "Central Purpose" of the Freedom of Information Act. *Administrative Law Review* 46: 41–74.

Cave, M., M. Kogan, and R. Smith (1990). *Output and Performance Measurement in Government: The State of the Art*. London: Jessica Kingsley.

Chapman, R. A. (1993). Reasons of State and the Public Interest: A British Variant of the Problem of Dirty Hands. In R. A. Chapman, ed., *Ethics in Public Service*. Edinburgh: University of Edinburgh Press.

—— (2000). *Public Service Ethics for a New Millennium*. Aldershot, UK: Dartmouth.

Chisholm, D. (1989). *Coordination Without Hierarchy*. Berkeley: University of California Press.

Christensen, T. (1994). Utviklingen av direktoratene—aktorer, tenking og organisasjons-former. In T. Christensen and M. Egeberg, eds., *Forvaltningskunskap*. 2d ed. Oslo: TANO.

Chubb, B. (1992). *The Government and Politics of Ireland*. 3d ed. London: Longman.

Chubb, J. E., and T. Moe (1990). *Politics, Markets and America's Schools*. Washington, DC: Brookings Institution.

Clark, I. D. (1991). Special Operating Agencies. *Optimum* 22 (2): 13–18.

Clark, P. B., and J. Q. Wilson (1961). Incentive Systems: A Theory of Organizations. *Administrative Science Quarterly* 6: 129–66.

Clarke, M., and J. Stewart (1992). *Empowerment: A Theme for the 1990s*. Luton, UK: Local Government Management Board.

Clinton, W. J. (1994). Remarks at the Group of Seven Jobs Conference in Detroit. *Weekly Compilation of Presidential Documents* 30 (11): 508–11.

Coase, R. H. (1960). The Problem of Social Cost. *Journal of Law and Economics* 3: 1–44.

Cohen, J., and J. Rogers (1994). Solidarity, Democracy, Association. *Politische Vierteil-jahrschrift,* Sonderheft 25: 136–59.

Cohn, D. (1997). Creating Crisis and Avoiding Blame: The Politics of Public Service Reform and New Public Management in Great Britain and the United States. *Admin-istration and Society,* 29: 584–616.

Commission on Social Justice (1994). *Social Justice: Strategies for National Renewal*. London: Vintage.

Common, R. K. (1998). Convergence and Transfer: A Review of Globalisation of the New Public Management. *International Journal of Public Sector Management* 6: 440–50.

Common, R., N. Flynn, and E. Mellon (1992). *Managing Public Services: Competition and Decentralization*. Oxford, UK: Butterworth Heinemann.

Connolly, M., P. McKeown, and G. Milligan-Byrne (1994). Making the Public Sector User Friendly? A Critical Analysis of the Citizen's Charter. *Parliamentary Affairs* 47: 23–37.

Cook, F. L., and E. J. Barrett (1992). *Support for the American Welfare State*. New York: Columbia University Press.

Cooper, P. (1995). Accountability and Administrative Reform: Toward Convergence and Beyond. In B. G. Peters and D. Savoie, eds., *Governance in a Changing Environ-ment*. Montreal: McGill/Queens University Press.

Cox, R. H. (1992). After Corporatism: A Comparison of the Role of Medical Profession-als and Social Workers in the Dutch Welfare State. *Comparative Political Studies* 24: 532–52.

Cronin, T. E. (1989). *Direct Democracy: The Politics of Initiative, Referendum and Recall*. Cambridge: Harvard University Press.

Crook, R. C. (1989). Patrimonialism, Administrative Effectiveness and Economic Devel-opment in Cote d'Ivoire. *African Affairs* 88: 205–28.

Crozier, M. (1964). *The Bureaucratic Phenomenon*. Chicago: University of Chicago Press.

Daley, D. (1988). Profile of the Uninvolved Worker: An Examination of Employee Attitudes Toward Management Practices. *International Journal of Public Administration* 11: 63–90.

Davies, A., and J. Willman (1992). *What Next? Agencies, Departments and the Civil Service*. London: Institute for Public Policy Research.

Day, P., and R. Klein (1987). *Accountabilities*. London: Tavistock.

Deleon, P. (1994). Reinventing the Policy Sciences: Three Steps Back to the Future. *Policy Sciences* 27: 77–95.

Deming, W. E. (1988). *Out of the Crisis: Quality, Productivity and Competitive Positions*. Cambridge: Cambridge University Press.

de Montricher, N. (1994). *La deconcentration*. Paris: Decouverte.

Department of Finance (1987). *FMIP and Program Budgeting: A Study of Implementation in Selected Agencies*. Canberra: AGPs.

Department of Health (October 1994). *A Framework for Local Community Care Charters in England*. London: Department of Health.

Derlien, H.-U. (1991). Horizontal and Vertical Coordination of German EC–Policy. *Hallinnon Tutkimus* 27: 3–10.

—— (1993). German Unification and Bureaucratic Transformation. *International Political Science Review* 14: 319–34.

—— (1994). Germany. In C. Hood and B. G. Peters, eds., *The Rewards of High Public Office*. London: Sage.

—— (1995). Germany. In J. Olsen and B. G. Peters, eds., *Learning from Experience: Lessons of Administrative Reform*. Pittsburgh: University of Pittsburgh Press.

—— (1999). On the Selective Interpretation of Max Weber's Theory of Bureaucracy. In P. Ahonen and K. Palonen, eds., *Disembalming Max Weber*. Jyvaskyla, Finland: Sophi.

Derlien, H.-U., and G. Szablowski (1993). *Regime Transitions, Elites and Bureaucrats in Eastern Europe*. Oxford, UK: Blackwell.

de Vries, M. S. (2000). The Bureaucratization of Participation. *International Review of Administrative Sciences* 66: 324–48.

Dexter, L. A. (1990). Intra-Agency Politics: Conflict and Contravention in Administrative Entities. *Journal of Theoretical Politics* 2: 151–72.

Dicken, P. (1992). *Global Shift: The Internationalization of Economic Activity*. London: Chapman.

DiIulio, J. J. (1994). *Deregulating the Public Service: Can Government Be Improved?* Washington, DC: Brookings Institution.

DiMaggio, P. J., and W. W. Powell (1991). Introduction. In DiMaggio and Powell, *The New Institutionalism in Organizational Analysis*. Chicago: University of Chicago Press.

Doern, G. B. (1993). The UK Citizens' Charter: Origins and Implementation in Three Agencies. *Policy and Politics* 21: 17–29.

Doig, J. (1983). "When I See a Murderous Fellow Sharpening a Knife Cleverly": The Wilsonian Dichotomy and the Public Administration Tradition. *Public Administration Review* 43: 292–304.

Donkin, R. (1995). Tales of the Office Nomad. *Financial Times* 29 (May).

Dopson, S. (1993). Are Agencies an Act of Faith? *Public Money and Management* 13 (2): 17–24.

Dowding, K. (1991). *Rational Choice and Political Power*. Aldershot, UK: Edward Elgar.

Downs, A. (1960). Why the Government Budget Is Too Small in a Democracy. *World Politics* 12: 541–63.

—— (1967). *Inside Bureaucracy*. Boston: Little, Brown.

—— (1972). Up and Down with Ecology—The "Issue-Attention Cycle." *Public Interest* 28: 38–50.

Downs, G. W., and P. D. Larkey (1986). *The Search for Government Efficiency: From Hubris to Helplessness*. Philadelphia: Temple University Press.

Draper, F. D., and B. T. Pitsvada (1981). ZBB—Looking Back After Ten Years. *Public Administration Review* 41: 76–83.

Dreyfus, F. (2000). *L'invention de la bureaucratie*. Paris: La Decouverte.

Dror, Y. (1986). *Policymaking Under Adversity*. New Brunswick, NJ: Transaction.

—— (1992). Future View: Fuzzy Gambles with History. *Futurist* 26 (4): 60–64.

Dryzek, J. S. (1990). *Discursive Democracy: Politics, Policy and Political Science*. Cambridge: Cambridge University Press.

du Gay, P. (2000). *In Praise of Bureaucracy*. London: Sage.

Duncan, A., and D. Hobson (1995). *Saturn's Children*. London: Sinclair-Stevenson.

Dunleavy, P. (1985). Bureaucrats, Budgets and the Growth of the State. *British Journal of Political Science* 15: 299–328.

—— (1991). *Democracy, Bureaucracy and Public Choice*. Brighton, UK: Harvester Wheatsheaf.

Dunn, W. N. (1988). Methods of the Second Type: Coping with the Wilderness of Conventional Policy Analysis. *Policy Studies Review* 7: 720–37.

Dunsire, A. (1995). Administrative Theory in the 1980s: A Viewpoint. *Public Administration* 73: 17–40.

Dunsire, A., and C. Hood (1989). *Cutback Management in Public Bureaucracies: Popular Theories and Observed Outcomes in Whitehall*. Cambridge: Cambridge University Press.

Dupuy, F., and J.-C. Thoenig (1985). *L'administration en miettes*. Paris: Fayard.

Durant, R. F., and L. A. Wilson (1993). Public Management, TQM, and Quality Improvement: Toward a Contingency Strategy. *American Review of Public Administration* 23: 215–45.

Economist (1995). E-lectioneering, June 17, 56–57.

Egeberg, M. (1995). Bureaucrats as Public Policy-makers and Their Self-Interests. *Journal of Theoretical Politics* 7: 157–67.

Ehrenhalt, A. (1993). The Value of Blue-Ribbon Advice. *Governing* 7 (August): 47–56.

Eisenberg, E. F., and P. W. Ingraham (1993). Analyzing the Pay for Performance Literature: Are There Common Lessons? *Public Productivity and Management Review* 17: 117–28.

Elcock, H. (1994). Editorial: Democracy and Management in Britain and the United States of America. *Public Policy and Administration* 9 (3): 1–5.

Elder, S. (1992). Running a Town the Seventeenth-Century Way. *Governing* 5: 29–30.

Ellul, J. (1980). *The Technological System*. New York: Continuum.

Elmore, R. F. (1983). *Forward and Backward Mapping: Reversible Logic in the Analysis of Public Policy*. Seattle: Graduate School of Public Affairs, University of Washington.

Epstein, R. A. (1990). No New Property. *Brock Law Review* 56: 747–86.

Ericksson, B. (1983). Sweden's Budget System in a Changing World. *Public Budgeting and Finance* 3: 64–80.

Etheredge, L. S. (1985). *Can Government Learn? American Foreign Policy and Central American Revolutions*. New York: Pergamon Press.

Etzioni, A. (1993). *The Spirit of Community*. New York: Crown Publishers.

Evans, P. (1995). *Embedded Autonomy: States and Industrial Tranformation*. Princeton: Princeton University Press.

FDA News (1995). "Competing for Quality" Gets Overdue Review (May): 1–2.

Feely, M. M., and E. L. Rubin (1998). *Judicial Policy-Making and the Modern State: How the Courts Reformed America's Prisons*. Cambridge: Cambridge University Press.

Feigenbaum, H. B., J. Henig, and C. Hamnett (1999). *Shrinking the State: The Political Underpinnings of Privatization*. Cambridge: Cambridge University Press.

Feller, I. et al. (1995). Decentralization and Deregulation of the Federal Hiring Process. Paper presented at Trinity Symposium on Public Management Research, San Antonio, TX, July.

Fiorina, M. P. (1989). *Congress: Keystone of the Washington Establishment*. 2d ed. New Haven: Yale University Press.

—— (1992). Coalition Governments, Divided Governments and Electoral Theory. *Governance* 4: 236–49.

Fischer, F. (1990). *Technocracy and the Politics of Expertise*. Newbury Park, CA: Sage.

Follett, M. P. (1940). *Dynamic Administration: The Collected Papers of Mary Parker Follett*. Ed. H. C. Metcalf and L. Urwick. New York: Harper.

Foreman, C. (1988). *Signals from the Hill: Congressional Oversight and the Challenge of Social Regulation*. New Haven: Yale University Press.

Forsberg, E., and J. Calltorp (1993). Ekonomiska incitament forandrar sjukvarden. *Läkartidningen* 90: 2611–14.

Fortin, Y., and H. Van Hassel (2000). *Contracting in the New Public Management*. Brussels: IOS Press.

Foster, C. D. (1992). *Privatization, Public Ownership and the Regulation of Natural Monopoly*. Oxford, UK: Blackwell.

Fournier, J. (1987). *Le travail gouvernementale*. Paris: Dalloz.

Frederickson, G. (1980). *New Public Administration*. Tuscaloosa: University of Alabama Press.

Frederickson, H. G. (1997). *The Spirit of Public Administration*. San Francisco: Jossey-Bass.

Frenkel, M. (1994). The Communal Basis of Swiss Liberty. *Publius* 23: 61–70.

Friedman, M. (1962). *Capitalism and Freedom*. Chicago: University of Chicago Press.

Frohlich, N., J. A. Oppenheimer, and O. R. Young (1971). *Political Leadership and Collective Goods*. Princeton: Princton Univeristy Press.

Fry, G. (1995). *Policy and Management in the British Civil Service*. London: Prentice-Hall.

Garvey, G. (1993). *Facing the Bureaucracy: Living and Dying in a Public Agency*. San Francisco: Jossey-Bass.

Geddes, B. (1994). *Politician's Dilemma: Building State Capacity in Latin America*. Berkeley: University of California Press.

Geddes, M., and S. Martin (2000). The Policy and the Politics of Best Value: Currents, Crosscurrents and Undercurrents in the New Regime. *Policy and Politics* 28: 379–95.

General Services Administration (1993). *Agenda for Action*. Washington, DC: GSA, April.

Germann, R. (1981). *Ausserparliamentarische Kommissionen: Die Milizverwaltung des Bundes*. Bern: Haupt.

Gibert, P., and J.-C. Thoenig (1992). La gestion publique entre l'apprentissage et l'amnesie. Communication presented at International Conference of the *PMP* journal. Paris.

Gidron, B., R. M. Kramer, and L. M. Salamon (1992). *Government and the Third Sector*. San Francisco: Jossey-Bass.

Gilbert, G. R. (1993). Employee Empowerment: Law and Practical Approaches. *Public Manager* 22 (3): 45–48.

Gillin, J. L., and J. P. Gillin (1948). *Cultural Sociology*. New York: Macmillan.

Gilmour, R. S., and A. A. Halley (1994). *Who Makes Public Policy? The Struggle Between Congress and the Executive*. Chatham, NJ: Chatham House.

Glynn, J., A. Gray, and B. Jenkins (1992). Auditing the Three Es: The Challenge of Effectiveness. *Public Policy and Administration* 7: 56–72.

Goetz, K. H. (1993). Rebuilding Public Administration in the New *Länder*: Transfer and Differentiation. *West European Politics* 16: 447–69.

Golembiewski, R. (1995). *Managing Diversity in Organizations*. Tuscaloosa: University of Alabama Press.

Goodin, R. E. (1982). Rational Politicians and Rational Bureaucrats in Washington and Whitehall. *Public Administration* 60: 23–41.

Goodman, J. B., and G. W. Loveman (1991). Does Privatization Serve the Public Interest? *Harvard Business Review* 69 (6): 26–38.

Goodnow, F. J. (1900). *Politics and Administration: A Study in Government*. New York: Macmillan.

Goodsell, C. T. (1976). Cross-Cultural Comparison of Behavior of Postal Clerks Toward Clients. *Administrative Science Quarterly* 21: 140–60.

—— (1981a). *The Public Encounter: Where State and Citizens Meet*. Bloomington: Indiana University Press.

—— (1981b). Looking Once Again at Human Service Bureaucracy. *Journal of Politics* 43: 763–78.

—— (1995). *The Case for Bureaucracy*. 3d ed. Chatham, NJ: Chatham House.

Gormley, W. T. (1989). *Taming the Bureaucracy: Muscles, Prayers and Other Strategies*. Princeton: Princeton University Press.

—— (1993). Counter-Bureaucracies in Theory and Practice. Paper presented at Annual Meeting of the American Political Science Association, September, Washington, DC.

Gormley, W. T., and D. Weimer (1999). *Organizational Report Cards*. Cambridge: Harvard University Press.

Gosling, P. (2000). An Inspector Calls. *Public Finance* (24 March): 5–9.

Gray, A., and B. Jenkins (1995). From Public Administration to Public Management: Reassessing a Revolution. *Public Administration* 73: 75–100.

Gray, A., B. Jenkins, and B. Segsworth (1993). *Budgeting, Auditing and Evaluation: Functions and Integration in Seven Countries*. New Brunswick, NJ: Transaction.

Gray, A. G., and W. I. Jenkins (1991). The Management of Change in Whitehall: The Experience of FMI. *Public Administration* 69: 41–59.

Gray, B. (1985). Conditions Facilitating Interorganizational Coordination. *Human Relations* 38: 911–36.

Greenwood, R., C. R. Hinings, and S. Ranson (1975a). Contingency Theory and the Structure of Local Authorities, Part 1: Differentiation and Integration. *Public Administration* 53: 1–23.

—— (1975b). Contingency Theory and the Structure of Local Authorities, Part II: Contingencies and Structure. *Public Administration* 53: 169–90.

Greer, P. (1994). *Transforming Central Government: The Next Steps Initiative*. Buckingham, UK: Open University Press.

Gregory, R. (1998). A New Zealand Tragedy: Problems of Political Responsibility. *Governance* 11: 231–40.

Grice, A. (1995). The Man with an Eye on No. 10: Blair Salutes Enterprise Culture. *Sunday Times,* April 23.

Grindle, M. S., and J. W. Thomas (1991). *Public Choices and Policy Change: The Political Economy of Reform in Developing Countries*. Baltimore: Johns Hopkins University Press.

Gruber, J. (1987). *Controlling Bureaucracies: Dilemmas in Democratic Governance*. Berkeley: University of California Press.

Guardian (2000). Is Ofsted Right to Attack Local Education Authorities? July 1.

Gulick, L. (1933). Politics, Administration and the "New Deal." *Annals of the American Academy of Political and Social Science* 169 (September): 45–78.

Gurwitt, R. (1992). A Government That Runs on Citizen Power. *Governing* 6 (3): 48–54.

Gustafsson, B. (1979). *Post-Industrial Society*. London: Croom Helm.

Guyomarch, A. (1999). "Public Service," "Public Management" and the "Modernization" of French Public Administration. *Public Administration* 77: 171–93.

HMSO (1988). *Improving Management in Government: The Next Steps*. London: HMSO.

—— (1991). *Competing for Quality*. London: HMSO, CM 1730.

—— (1993). *Career Planning and Succession Planning*. London: HMSO, November.

—— (1994a). *The Civil Service: Continuity and Change*. London: HMSO, CM 2627.

—— (1994b). *Better Accounting for the Taxpayer's Money: Resource Accounting and Budgeting in Government*. London: HMSO, CM 2626.

—— (1995). *Setting New Standards: A Strategy for Government Procurement*. London: HMSO.

Habermas, J. (1984). *The Theory of Communicative Action I: Lifeworld and System*. Boston: Beacon.

Halachmi, A., and G. Bouckaert (1996). *Organisational Performance and Measurement in the Public Sector*. London: Quorum Books.

Halligan, J. A. (2001). Australia and New Zealand. In J. Hesse, C. Hood, and B. G. Peters, eds., *Paradoxes of Public Sector Reforms*. Berlin: Nomos.

Hancock, M. D., J. Logue, and B. Schiller (1991). *Managing Modern Capitalism: Industrial Renewal and Workplace Democracy in the United States and Western Europe*. New York: Greenwood Press.

Handler, J. (1986). Dependent People, the State and the Modern/Postmodern Search for the Dialogic Community. *UCLA Law Review* 35: 999–1113.

Hanf, K., and F. W. Scharpf (1978). *Interorganizational Policy Making: Limits to Coordination and Central Control*. Beverly Hills, CA: Sage.

Hanushek, E. A. (1987). Formula Budgeting: The Economics and Analytics of Fiscal Policy Under Rules. *Journal of Public Policy Analysis and Management* 6: 3–19.

Haque, S. (1999). Relationship Between Citizenship and Public Administration: A Reconfiguration. *International Review of Administrative Sciences* 65: 309–25.

Harmon, M. M. (1995). *Responsibility as Paradox: A Critique of Rational Discourse on Government*. Thousand Oaks, CA: Sage.

Harrigan, P. (1994). Consumer Voices in Australian Drugs Approval. *Lancet* 344 (August 13): 464.

Harrison, S., N. Small, and M. Baker (1994). The Wrong Kind of Chaos? The Early Days of an NHS Trust. *Public Money and Management* 14 (1): 39–46.

Harter, P. (1982). Negotiating Regulations: A Cure for the Malaise. *Georgetown Law Journal* 71: 17–31.

Hatry, H. (2000). *Performance Management: Getting Results*. Washington, DC: Urban Institute Press.

Haves. J. R. (1993). Should Bureaucrats Make Decisions? *Forbes* 152: 247.

Hayek, F. A. von (1968). *The Constitution of Liberty*. London: Macmillan.

Hayes, M. (1992). *Incrementalism and Public Policy*. New York: Longman.

Heclo, H., and A. Wildavsky (1974). *The Private Government of Public Money*. Berkeley: University of California Press.

Helgason, S. (1997). International Benchmarking: Experiences of the OECD Countries. Paper presented at International Benchmarking Conference, April, Copenhagen.

Henkel, M. (1991). The New Evaluative State. *Public Administration* 69: 122–36.

Hennessy, P. (1989). *Whitehall*. New York: Free Press.

Hentic, I., and G. Bernier (1999). Rationalization, Decentralization and Participation in the Public Sector Management of Developing Countries. *International Review of Administrative Sciences* 65: 197–209.

Hesse, J. J. (1993). From Transformation to Modernization: Administrative Change in Central and Eastern Europe. *Public Administration* 71: 219–57.

Hesse, J. J., C. Hood, and B. G. Peters (2000). *The Paradoxes of Administrative Reform*. Berlin: Nomos.

Hirst, P. Q. (1994). *Associative Democracy: New Forms of Economic and Social Governance*. Cambridge, UK: Polity.

Hirst, P. Q., and G. Thompson (1999). *Globalization in Question*. Malden, MA: Blackwell.

Hogwood, B. W. (1993). Restructuring Central Government: The "Next Steps" Initiative. In K. A. Eliassen and J. Kooiman, eds., *Managing Public Organizations*. 2d ed. London: Sage.

——— (1995). The "Growth" of Quangos: Evidence and Explanations. *Parliamentary Affairs* 48: 207–25.

Hogwood, B. W., D. Judge, and M. McVicar (2000). Agencies and Accountability. In R. A. W. Rhodes, ed., *Transforming British Goverment*, vol. 1, *Changing Institutions*. Basingstoke, UK: Macmillan.

Hogwood, B. W., and B. G. Peters (1983). *Policy Dynamics*. Brighton, UK: Harvester.

Hood, C. (1990). De-Sir Humphreying the Westminster Model of Bureaucracy. *Governance* 3: 205–14.

——— (1991). A Public Management for All Seasons? *Public Administration* 69: 3–19.

—— (1995). "Deprivileging" the UK Civil Service in the 1980s: Dream or Reality? In J. Pierre, ed., *Bureaucracy in the Modern State*. Cheltenham, UK: Edward Elgar.

—— (1996). Of Shocks and Long-Tenure. In J. P. Olsen and B. G. Peters, eds., *Lessons from Experience: Learning About Administrative Reform*. Oslo: Scandinavian University Press.

Hood C., and B. G. Peters (1994). *The Rewards of High Public Office*. London: Sage.

—— (2000). Towards Paradox Free Reform? Paper presented at Conference of Public Administration in the New Millennium, City University of Hong Kong, January.

Hood, C., and G. F. Schuppert (1989). *Delivering Public Services in Western Europe*. London: Sage.

Hood, C., C. Scott, O. James, G. Jones, and T. Travers (1999). *Regulating Inside Government*. Oxford: Oxford University Press.

Hood, C., H. Wollmann, and B. G. Peters (1996). Sixteen Ways to Consumerize the Public Sector. *Public Money and Management* 16 (4): 43–50.

Horner, C. (1994). Deregulating the Federal Service: Is the Time Right? In J. J. DiIulio, ed., *Deregulating the Public Service*. Washington, DC: Brookings Institution.

Howard, P. K. (1994). *The Death of Common Sense*. New York: Random House.

Hula, R. C. (1990). *Market-based Public Policy*. New York: St. Martin's.

—— (1991). Alternative Management Strategies in Public Housing. In W. T. Gormley, ed., *Privatization and Its Alternatives*. Madison: University of Wisconsin Press.

Hult, K. M. (1987). *Agency Merger and Bureaucratic Redesign*. Pittsburgh: University of Pittsburgh Press.

Hupe, P. (1993). The Politics of Implementation: Individual, Organisational and Political Co-Production in Social Services Delivery. In M. Hill. ed., *New Agendas in the Study of the Policy Process*. London: Harvester/Wheatsheaf.

Inglehart, R. (1990). *Culture Shift in Advanced Industrial Societies*. Princeton: Princeton University Press.

Inglehart, R., and Abramson, P. R. (1994). Economic Security and Value Change. *American Political Science Review* 88: 336–54.

Ingraham, P. W. (1987). Building Bridges or Burning Them? The President, the Appointees and the Bureaucracy. *Public Administration Review* 47: 425–35.

—— (1993). Of Pigs and Pokes and Policy Diffusion: Another Look at Pay for Performance. *Public Administration Review* 53: 348–56.

—— (1995a). *The Foundation of Merit: Public Service in American Democracy*. Baltimore: Johns Hopkins University Press.

—— (1995b). Quality Management in Public Organizations: Prospects and Dilemmas. In B. G. Peters and D. J. Savoie, eds., *Governance in a Changing Environment*. Montreal: McGill/Queens University Press.

Ingram, H., and A. Schneider (1991). Target Populations and Policy Design. *Administration and Society* 23: 333–56.

International Monetary Fund (1998). *Transparency in Government Operations*. Washington, DC: IMF.

International Political Science Review (1993). Public Administration and Political Change (special issue) 14 (4).

Jain, R. B. (1998). Citizen Participation in Development Administration: Experiences in India. *International Review of Administrative Science* 65: 381–94.

Jann, W. (1994). *Moderner Staat und effizient Verwaltung*. Bonn: Friedrich Ebert Stiftung.

Jenkins, S. (1995). Milk and Water Communities. *Times* (London), March 25.

Jennings, E. T., and D. Krane (1994). Coordination and Welfare Reform: The Quest for the Philosopher's Stone. *Public Administration Review* 54: 341–48.

Jerome-Forget, M., J. White, and J. M. Wiener (1995). *Health Care Reform Through Internal Markets*. Montreal: Institute for Research on Public Policy.

Johnson, N. (1998). The Judicial Dimension of British Politics. *West European Politics* 21: 148–66.

Johnson, R. N., and G. D. Libecap (1994). *The Federal Civil Service System and the Problem of Bureaucracy*. New York: Cambridge University Press.

Jonsson, S., S. Rubenowitz, and J. Westerstähl (1995). *Decentraliserad Kommun: Exemplet Göteborg*. Goteborg: SNS.

Jordan, A. G. (1990). Political Community Realism versus "New Institutionalism" Ambiguity. *Political Studies* 38: 470–84.

—— (1994). *The British Administrative System: Principles Versus Practice*. London: Routledge.

Kato, J. (1994). *The Problem of Bureaucratic Rationality: Tax Politics in Japan*. Princeton: Princeton University Press.

Katz, D., B. A. Gutek, R. L. Kahn, and E. Barton (1975). *Bureaucratic Encounters*. Ann Arbor: Institute for Social Research, University of Michigan.

Katz, E., and B. Danet (1973). *Bureaucracy and the Public*. New York: Basic Books.

Katz, J. L., and S. J. Nixon (1994). Food Stamp Experiments Spark Welfare Debate. *Congressional Quarterly Weekly Report* 52: 2261–63.

Kaufman, H. (1956). Emerging Doctrines of Public Administration. *American Political Science Review* 50: 1059–73.

—— (1976). *Are Government Organizations Immortal?* Washington, DC: Brookings Institution.

—— (1977). *Red Tape: Its Origins, Uses and Abuses*. Washington, DC: Brookings Institution.

—— (1978). Reflections on Administrative Reorganization. In J. A. Pechman, ed., *Setting National Priorities: The 1978 Budget*. Washington, DC: Brookings Institution.

—— (1991). *Time, Chance, and Organizations*. 2d ed. Chatham, NJ: Chatham House.

Kavanagh, D., and P. Morris (1994). *Consensus Politics: From Atlee to Major*. Oxford, UK: Blackwell.

Kazin, M. (1995). *The Populist Persuasion: An American History*. New York: Basic Books.

Kearns, K. (1996). *Accountability in Public and Non-Profit Management*. San Francisco: Jossey-Bass.

Keating, M., and M. Holmes (1990). Australia's Budgetary and Financial Management Reforms. *Governance* 3: 168–85.

Kelman, S. (1985). The Grace Commission: How Much Waste in Government? *Public Interest* 78 (winter): 62–82.

—— (1992). Adversary and Cooperationist Institutions for Conflict Resolution in Public Policymaking. *Journal of Public Policy Analysis and Management* 11: 178–206.

—— (1994). Deregulating Federal Procurement: Nothing to Fear but Discretion Itself?

In J. J. DiIulio, ed., *Deregulating the Public Service: Can Government Be Improved?* Washington, DC: Brookings Institution.

Kemp, P. (1994). The Civil Service White Paper: A Job Half Finished. *Public Administration* 72: 591–98.

Kenis, P., and V. Schneider (1991). Policy Networks and Policy Analysis: Scrutinizing a New Analytical Toolbox. In B. Marin and R. Mayntz, eds., *Policy Networks: Empirical Evidence and Theoretical Considerations.* Boulder, CO: Westview, 1991.

Kernaghan, K. (1991). Career Public Service 2000: Road to Renewal or Impractical Vision? *Canadian Public Administration* 34: 551–72.

—— (1992). Empowerment and Public Administration: Revolutionary Advance or Passing Fancy? *Canadian Public Administration* 35: 194–214.

—— (1994). The Emerging Public Service Culture: Values, Ethics and Reforms. *Canadian Public Administration* 37: 614–30.

Kerwin, C. M. (1994). *Rulemaking: How Government Agencies Write Law and Make Policy.* 2d ed. Washington, DC: CQ Press.

Kettl, D. F. (1988). *Government by Proxy: (Mis?) Managing Federal Programs.* Washington, DC: CQ Press.

—— (1992). *Deficit Politics: Public Budgeting in Its Institutional and Historical Context.* New York: Macmillan.

—— (1993). *Sharing Power: Public Governance and Private Markets.* Washington, DC: Brookings Institution.

—— (2000). *The Global Public Management Revolution.* Washington, DC: Brookings Institution.

Kettl, D. F., and J. J. DiIulio Jr. (1995). *Inside the Reinvention Machine: Appraising Governmental Reform.* Washington, DC: Brookings Institution.

Kickert, W. J. M. (1994). Administrative Reform in British, Dutch and Danish Civil Service. Paper presented at ECPR Workshop on Administrative Reform, Madrid, Spain, April.

—— (1995). Public Governance in the Netherlands: An Alternative to Anglo-American Managerialism. *Public Administration* 75: 737–53.

Kiel, L. D. (1989). Nonequilibrium Theory and Its Implications for Public Administration. *Public Administration Review* 49: 544–51.

Kiggundu, M. N. (1998). Civil Service Reforms: Limping into the Twenty-first Century. In M. Minogue, C. Polidano, and D. Hulme, *Beyond the New Public Management.* Cheltenham, UK: Edward Elgar.

Kimm, V. J. (1995). GPRA: Early Implementation Lessons. *Public Manager* 24 (spring): 11–14.

King, D. S. (1987). *The New Right: Politics, Markets, and Citizenship.* London: Macmillan.

—— (1995). *Actively Seeking Work? The Politics of Unemployment and Welfare Policy in the United States and Great Britain.* Chicago: University of Chicago Press.

Klages, H. et al. (1995). Quality Improvement in German Local Government. In C. Pollitt and G. Bouckaert, eds., *Quality Improvement in European Public Services.* London: Sage.

Klein, A., and R. Schmalz-Bruns (1997). *Politische Beteiligung und Buergenengagement.* Bonn: Bundes fuer Politische Bildung.

Kliksberg, B. (2000). Six Unconventional Theses About Participation. *International Review of Administrative Sciences* 66: 161–74.

Knapp, A. (1994). *Le gaullisme après de Gaulle*. Paris: Le Seuil.

Kobach, K. W. (1993). *The Referendum: Direct Democracy in Switzerland*. Aldershot, UK: Dartmouth.

Koehn, P. H. (1990). *Public Policy and Administration in Africa: Lessons from Nigeria*. Boulder, CO: Westview Press.

Konig, K. (1993). Administrative Transformation in Eastern Germany. *Public Administration* 71: 135–49.

Kooiman, J. (1993). Governance and Governability: Using Complexity, Dynamics and Diversity. In J. Kooiman, ed., *Modern Governance*. London: Sage.

Korsgaard, M. A., D. M. Schweiger, and H. J. Sapienza (1995). Building Commitment, Attachment and Trust in Strategic Decision-making Teams. *Academy of Management Journal* 38: 60–84.

Koven, S. G. (1992a). Co-production of Law Enforcement Services: Benefits and Implications. *Urban Affairs Quarterly* 27: 457–69.

—— (1992b). Base Closings and the Politics- Administration Dichotomy. *Public Administration Review* 52: 526–31.

Kraan, D. J. (1996). *Budgetary Decisions: A Public Choice Approach*. Cambridge: Cambridge University Press.

Krarup, A.-S. (2000). Administrative Reform in Danish Central Government. Paper prepared for Administrative Reform Seminar, University of Aarhus.

Krause, G. (2000). *A Two-Way Street: The Institutional Dynamics of the Modern Administrative State*. Pittsburgh: University of Pittsburgh Press.

Krauss, E., and M. Muramatsu (1995). Japan's Administrative Reform: The Paradox of Success. In J. P. Olsen and B. G. Peters, eds., *Learning from Experience: Lessons from Administrative Reform*. Pittsburgh: University of Pittsbugh Press.

Laegreid, P. (1994). Norway. In Hood and Peters, *The Rewards of High Public Office*.

Laegreid, P., and P. G. Roness (1997). Political Parties, Bureaucracies and Corporatism. In K. Strom and L. Svasand, eds., *Challenges to Political Parties*. Ann Arbor: University of Michigan Press.

Lamont, B. T., R. J. Williams, and J. J. Hoffman (1994). Performance During "M-form" Reorganization and Recovery Time. *Academy of Management Journal* 37: 153–66.

Lampe, D. (1995). Welfare Reform: Congress Debates, States Move. *National Civic Review* 84: 60–61.

Lan, Z., and D. H. Rosenbloom (1992). Public Administration in Transition? *Public Administration Review* 52: 535–37.

Landau, M. (1969). Redundancy, Rationality and the Problem of Duplication and Overlap. *Public Administration Review* 29: 346–58.

Lane, J.-E. (1993). *The Public Sector: Concepts, Models and Approaches*. London: Sage.

Langton, S. (1978). *Citizen Participation in America*. Lexington, MA: Lexington Books.

LaNoue, G. R. (1993). Social Science and Minority "Set Asides." *Public Interest* 110 (winter): 49–62.

Larsson, T. (1986). *Regeringen och dess kansli*. Stockholm: Studentlitteratur.

Laughlin, R., and J. Broadbent (1994). The Managerial Reform of Health and Education: Value for Money or a Devaluing Process? *Political Quarterly* 65: 152–67.

Laux, J. A., and M. A. Molot (1988). *State Capitalism: Public Enterprise in Canada.* Ithaca, NY: Cornell University Press.

LeGrand, J. (1989). Markets, Welfare and Equality. In S. Estrin and J. LeGrand, eds., *Market Socialism.* Oxford, UK: Clarendon Press.

—— (1991). *Equity and Choice.* London: HarperCollins.

—— (1991). The Theory of Government Failure. *British Journal of Political Science* 21: 423–42.

Leichter, H. (1992). *Health Policy Reform in America: Innovations from the States.* Armonk, NY: M. E. Sharpe.

LeLoup, L. T., and P. T. Taylor (1994). The Policy Constraints of Deficit Reduction. *Public Budgeting and Finance* 14: 3–25.

Lemco, J. (1995). Canada: The Year of the Volatile Vote. *Current History* 94 (590): 118–22.

Leonard, M. (1988). *The 1988 Education Act: A Tactical Guide for Schools.* Oxford, UK: Blackwell.

Levacic, R. (1994). Evaluating the Performance of Quasi-Markets in Education. In W. Bartlett et al., *Quasi-Markets in the Welfare State.* Bristol, UK: SAUS.

Levine, C. H., and P. L. Posner (1981). The Centralizing Effects of Austerity on the Intergovernmental System. *Political Science Quarterly* 96: 67–86.

Lewis, N. (1994). Citizenship and Choice: An Overview. *Public Money and Management* 14 (October–November): 9–16.

Lewis, N., and P. Birkinshaw (1993). *When Citizens Complain: Reforming Justice and Administration.* Buckingham, UK: Open University Press.

Light, P. C. (1993). *Monitoring Government: Inspectors General and the Search for Accountability.* Washington, DC: Brookings Institution.

—— (1994). Creating Government That Encourages Innovation. In P. W. Ingraham and B. S. Romzek, eds., *New Paradigms for Government.* San Francisco: Jossey-Bass.

—— (1995). *Thickening Government: Federal Hierarchy and the Diffusion of Accountability.* Washington, DC: Brookings Institution.

Likert, R. (1961). *New Patterns of Management.* New York: McGraw-Hill.

Likierman, A. (1998). Recent Development in Resource Accounting and Budgeting. *Public Money and Management* 18 (4): 62–64.

Lindblom, C. (1965). *The Intelligence of Democracy: Decision-Making Through Mutual Adjustment.* New York: Free Press.

Linden, R. M. (1994). *Seamless Government: A Practical Guide to Re-Engineering the Public Sector.* San Francisco: Jossey-Bass.

Linder, S. H., and B. G. Peters (1987). A Design Perspective on Policy Implementation: The Fallacy of Misplaced Precision. *Policy Studies Review* 6: 459–75.

—— (1989). Instruments of Government: Perceptions and Contexts. *Journal of Public Policy* 9: 35–58.

—— (1995). A Design Perspective on the Structure of Public Organizations. In David Weimer, ed., *The Structure of Public Institutions.* Dordrecht, Netherlands: Kluwer.

Lindquist, E. (1994). Citizens, Experts and Budgets: Evaluating Ottawa's Emerging Budget Process. In S. D. Phillips, ed., *How Ottawa Spends, 1994–95.* Ottawa: Carleton University Press.

Lipsky, M. (1980). *Street-level Bureaucracy.* New York: Russell Sage Foundation.

Llewellyn, S. (1994). Applying Efficiency Concepts to Management in the Social Services. *Public Money and Management* 14 (2): 51–56.

Loeffler, E. (1997). *The Modernization of the Public Sector in an International Comparative Perspective.* Speyer, Germany: Forschungsinstitut fuer Offentliche Verwaltung.

Lofty, J. S. (2000). Teachers Talk About Standards in Britain and America. *English Journal* 89: 97–105.

Loughlin, J., and S. Mazey (1995). The End of the French Unitary State? Ten Years of Regionalization in France (1982–1992). *Regional Politics and Policy* 4, 3 (special issues).

Lovell, R. (1992). The Citizens' Charter: The Cultural Challenge. *Public Administration* 70: 395–404.

Lowi, T. J. (1972). Four Systems of Politics, Policy and Choice. *Public Administration Review* 32: 298–310.

Luhmann, N. (1990). *Political Theory in the Welfare State.* New York: De Gruyter.

Lundell, B. (1994). Sverige: institutionella ramar for forvaltningspolitiken. In P. Laegreid and O. K. Pedersen, eds., *Forvaltningspolitiken i Norden.* Copenhagen: Jurist og Økonomforbundets Forlag.

Macey, J. R. (1992). Organizational Design and Political Control of Regulatory Agencies. *Journal of Law, Economics and Organization* 8: 93–110.

Machinery of Government Committee (1918). *Report.* Haldane Report. Cmm. 9320. London: HMSO.

Mackenzie, G. C. (1987). *The In and Outers.* Baltimore: Johns Hopkins University Press.

Maidment, R., and G. Thompson (1993). *Managing the United Kingdom: An Introduction to Its Political Economy and Public Policy.* London: Sage.

Majone, G. (1989). *Evidence, Argument and Persuasion in the Policy Process.* New Haven: Yale University Press.

Malpass, P. (1990). *Reshaping Housing Policy: Subsidies, Rents and Residualization.* London: Routledge.

Mansbridge, J. (1994). Public Spirit in Political Systems. In H. J. Aaron, T. E. Mann, and T. Taylor, eds., *Values and Public Policy.* Washington, DC: Brookings Institution.

Maor, M. (1999). The Paradox of Managerialism. *Public Administration Review* 59: 5–13.

March, J. G. (1991). Exploration and Exploitation in Organizational Learning. *Organizational Science* 2: 71–87.

March, J. G., and J. P. Olsen (1983). Organizing Political Life: What Administrative Reform Tells Us About Governing. *American Political Science Review* 77: 281–97.

—— (1984). The New Institutionalism: Organizational Factors in Political Life. *American Political Science Review* 78: 734–49.

—— (1989). *Rediscovering Institutions.* New York: Free Press.

—— (1995). *Democratic Governance.* New York: Free Press.

March, J. G., and H. A. Simon (1957). *Organizations.* New York: John Wiley.

Marini, F. (1971). *Toward a New Public Administration.* Scranton, PA: Chandler.

Marshall, G. (1989). *Ministerial Responsibility.* Oxford: Oxford University Press.

Martz, J. D. (1997). *The Politics of Clientelism: Democracy and the State in Colombia.* New Brunswick, NJ: Transaction Press.

Masa, F. (1990). *Gestion privé pour services publics.* Paris: Inter Editions.

Massey, A. (1993). *Managing the Public Sector.* Aldershot, UK: Edward Elgar.

Mastracco, A., and S. Comparato (1994). Project: Federal and State Coordination — A Survey of Administrative Law Schemes. *Administrative Law Review* 46: 385–573.

Mayne, J. (1994). Utilizing Evaluation in Organizations: The Balancing Act. In F. L. Leeuw, R. C. Rist, and R. C. Sonnischen, eds., *Can Governments Learn?* New Brunswick, NJ: Transaction Press.

Mayntz, R. (1993). Governing Failures and the Problem of Governability: Some Comments on a Theoretical Paradigm. In J. Kooiman, ed. *Modern Governance.* London: Sage.

Mayntz, R., and F. W. Scharpf (1975). *Policy-Making in the German Federal Bureaucracy.* Amsterdam: Elsevier.

McCubbins, M. D., R. G. Noll, and B. R. Weingast (1989). Structure and Process, Politics and Policy: Administrative Arrangements and the Political Control of Agencies. *Virginia Law Review* 75: 431–82.

McGarrity, T. (1991). *Reinventing Rationality: The Role of Regulatory Analysis in the Federal Bureaucracy.* Cambridge: Cambridge University Press.

McLean, I. (1987). *Public Choice: An Introduction.* Oxford, UK: Basil Blackwell.

Meier, H. (1969). Bureaucracy and Policy Formation in Sweden. *Scandinavian Political Studies* 4: 103–16.

Mellett, H., and N. Marriott (1995). Depreciation Accounting in the Public Sector: Lessons from the NHS. *Public Money and Management* 15 (July): 39–43.

Meny, Y., and D. Della Porta (1997). *Democracy and Corruption in Europe.* London: Pinter.

Meyer, F. (1985). *La politisation de l'administration publique.* Brussels: Institut Internationale d'administration publique.

Meynaud, J. (1969). *Technocracy.* New York: Free Press.

Michiletti, M. (1990). Toward Interest Inarticulation: A Major Consequence of Corporatism for Interest Organizations. *Scandinavian Political Studies* 13: 255–76.

Miller, G. J. (1992). *Managerial Dilemmas: The Political Economy of Hierarchy.* Cambridge: Cambridge University Press.

Miller, G. J., and T. M. Moe (1983). Bureaucrats, Legislators and the Size of Government. *American Political Science Review* 77: 297–322.

Miller, T. (1984). Conclusion: A Design Science Perspective. In T. Miller, ed., *Public Sector Performance: A Conceptual Turning Point.* Baltimore: Johns Hopkins University Press.

Millett, R. A. (1977). *"Examination of Widespread Citizen Participation" in Model Cities Programs.* San Francisco: R and E Research Associates.

Mills, N. (1994). *Debating Affirmative Action: Race, Gender, Ethnicity and the Politics of Inclusion.* New York: Delta.

Milward, H. B. (forthcoming). Symposium on the Hollow State: Capacity, Control and Performance in Interorganizational Settings. *Journal of Public Administration Research and Theory.*

Ministere de la Fonction Publique (1994). *L'Etat dans tous ses projets.* Paris: La Documentation Francaise.

Mintzburg, H. (1979). *The Structuring of Organizations.* Englewood Cliffs, NJ: Prentice-Hall.

Mishan, E. J. (1988). *Cost-benefit Analysis: An Informal Introduction.* 4th ed. London: Unwin-Hyman.

Modeen, T., and A. Rosas (1988). *Indirect Public Administration in Fourteen Countries*. Åbo, Finland: Åbo Academy Press.

Moe, R. (1993). Let's Rediscover Government, Not Reinvent It. *Government Executive* 25: 46–48.

—— (1994). The Reinventing Government Exercise: Misinterpreting the Problem, Misjudging the Consequences. *Public Administration Review* 54: 111–22.

Moe, T. (1984). The New Economics of Organizations. *American Journal of Political Science* 28: 739–77.

—— (1989). The Politics of Bureaucratic Structure. In J. E. Chubb and P. E. Peterson, *Can the Government Govern?* Washington, DC: Brookings Institution.

Mommsen, W. J. (1989). *The Political and Social Theory of Max Weber: Collected Essays*. Oxford, UK: Polity Press.

Morgan, G. (1986). *Images of Organizations*. London: Sage.

Mosher, F. (1979). *The GAO: The Quest for Accountability in American Government*. Boulder, CO: Westview.

Moynihan, D. P. (1969). *Maximum Feasible Misunderstanding: Community Action Programs in the War on Poverty*. New York: Free Press.

Mulgan, G. (1993). *Politics in an Antipolitical Age*. Oxford, UK: Polity.

Mulhall, S., and A. Swift (1992). *Liberals and Communitarians*. Oxford: Oxford University Press.

Muller, P. (1985). Un schema d'analyse des politiques sectorielles. *Revue Française de science politique* 35: 165–88.

Müller, W. C., and V. Wright (1994). Reshaping the State in Western Europe: The Limits to Retreat. *West European Politics* 17: 1–11.

National Performance Review (March 1993a). *Creating a Government That Works Better and Costs Less* (Gore Report). Washington, DC: Government Printing Office.

—— (September 1993b). *Reinventing Human Resource Management*. Washington, DC: Government Printing Office.

Nelson, R. (1968). *The Moon and the Ghetto*. New York: W. W. Norton.

Niskanen, W. (1971). *Bureaucracy and Representative Government*. Chicago: Aldine/Atherton.

—— (1994). *Bureaucracy and Public Economics*. Aldershot, UK: Edward Elgar.

Norman, P. (1994). Cultural Revolution in Whitehall. *Financial Times,* July 18.

Norris, P. (1998). *Critical Citizens*. Oxford: Oxford University Press.

Northcote, S., and C. Trevelyan (1853). *Report on the Organization of the Permanent Civil Service*. Reprinted as appendix B, vol. 1, Committee on the Civil Service *Report* (Fulton Report). London: HMSO, 1968.

Novick, D. (1965). *Program Budgeting, Program Analysis and the Federal Budget*. Cambridge: Harvard University Press.

Nunberg, B. (1995). *Managing the Civil Service—Reform Lessons from Advanced Industrial Democracies*. Washington, DC: World Bank Discussion Paper.

Oates, W. E. (1995). Green Taxes: Can We Protect the Environment and Improve the Tax System at the Same Time? *Southern Economic Journal* 61: 914–22.

Obolonsky, A. V. (1999). The Modern Russian Administration in the Time of Transition. *International Review of Administrative Sciences* 65: 569–77.

OECD (1987). *Administration as Service, Public as Client*. Paris: Organization for Economic Cooperation and Development.

—— (1990). *Flexible Personnel Management in the Public Service*. Paris: Organization for Economic Cooperation and Development.

—— (1993). *Internal Markets*. Market-Type Mechanisms Series, no. 6. Paris: Organization for Economic Cooperation and Development.

—— (1997). *In Search of Results: Performance Management Practices*. London: OECD.

—— (2000). *Trust in Government: Ethics Measures in OECD Countries*. Paris: OECD.

Office of Management and Budget (2000). *Government-Wide Performance Plan*. Washington, DC: OMB.

Olsen, J. P. (1986). *Organized Democracy*. Oslo: Universitetsforlaget.

—— (1991). Modernization Programs in Perspective: An Institutional Perspective on Organizational Change. *Governance* 4: 125–49.

Olsen, J. P., and B. G. Peters (1995). *Learning from Experience: Lessons from Administrative Reform*. Pittsburgh: University of Pittsburgh Press.

Olson, M. (1965). *The Logic of Collective Action*. Cambridge: Harvard University Press.

Opheim, C., L. Curry, and P. M. Shields (1994). Sunset as Oversight. *American Review of Public Administration* 24: 253–68.

Orlans, H., and J. O'Neill (1992). Affirmative Action and the Clash of Experiential Realities. *Annals* 523 (September): 10–19.

Osborne, D., and T. Gaebler (1992). *Reinventing Government*. Reading, MA: Addison-Wesley.

Ostrom, E. (1986). An Agenda for the Study of Institutions. *Public Choice* 48: 3–25.

Oughton, J. (1994). Market Testing: The Future of the Civil Service. *Public Policy and Administration* 9 (2): 11–20.

Overman, E. S., and A. G. Cahill (1994). Information, Market Government, and Health Policy: A Study of Health Data Organizations in the States. *Journal of Public Policy Analysis and Management* 13: 435–53.

Page, E. C. (2001). *Governing by the Numbers: Delegated Legislation and Everyday Politics*. Oxford, UK: Hart.

Painter, J. (1991). Compulsory Competitive Tendering in Local Government: The First Round. *Public Administration* 69: 191–210.

Painter, M. (1981). Central Agencies and the Coordinating Principle. *Australian Journal of Public Administration* 40: 265–80.

—— (1987). *Steering the Modern State: Changes in Central Coordination in Three Australian State Governments*. Sydney: Sydney University Press.

Pallot, J. (1991). Financial Management Reform. In J. Boston, J. Martin, J. Pallot, and P. Walsh, eds., *Reshaping the State: New Zealand's Bureaucratic Revolution*. Auckland: Oxford University Press.

Parrado-Diaz, S. (1999). Introducing Rationality in Personnel Administration in Spanish Central Administration. In D. Farnham and S. Horton, eds., *Human Resources Flexibilities in the Public Service*. London: Macmillan.

Parris, H. (1969). *Constitutional Bureaucracy*. London: George Allen and Unwin.

Pateman, C. (1970). *Participation and Democratic Theory*. Cambridge: Cambridge University Press.

Peacock, A. T. (1983). Public X-Inefficiency: Informational and Institutional Constraints. In H. Hanusch, ed., *Anatomy of Government Deficiencies*. Berlin: Springer.

Peacock, A. T., and H. Willgerodt (1989). *Germany's Social Market Economy: Origins and Evolution*. Basingstoke, UK: Macmillan.

Pear, R. (1995). A Welfare Revolution Hits Home, but Quietly. *New York Times,* August 13.

Pennock, J. R., and J. W. Chapman (1975). *Nomos XVI: Participation in Politics*. New York: Lieber-Atherton.

Perrow, C. (1984). *Normal Accidents: Living with High-risk Technologies*. New York: Basic Books.

Perry, J. (1993). Transforming Federal Civil Service. *Public Manager* 21 (Fall): 14–16.

—— (1994). Revitalizing Employee Ties with Public Organizations. In P. W. Ingraham and B. S. Romzek, *New Paradigms for Government*. San Francisco: Jossey-Bass.

Perry, J., and H. G. Rainey (1988). The Public-Private Distinction in Organization Theory: A Critique and a Research Strategy. *Academy of Management Review* 13: 138–66.

Peters, B. G. (1985). Administrative Change and the Grace Commission. In C. H. Levine, ed., *The Unfinished Agenda for Civil Service Reform*. Washington, DC: Brookings Institution.

—— (1988). *Comparing Public Bureaucracies: Problems of Theory and Method*. Tuscaloosa: University of Alabama Press.

—— (1992). Public Policy and Public Bureaucracy. In D. Ashford, ed., *History and Context in Comparative Public Policy*. Pittsburgh: University of Pittsburgh Press.

—— (1994). Alternative Modellen des Policy-Prozesses: Die Sicht "von unten" und die Sicht "von oben." *Politische Vierteiljahrschrift,* Sonderdruck 24: 289–303.

—— (1995a). The Politics of Bureaucratic Change in Transitional Governments. *International Social Science Journal* 47: 127–40.

—— (1995b). *The Politics of Bureaucracy*. 4th ed. New York: Longman.

—— (1995c). *American Public Policy: Promise and Performance*. Chatham, NJ: Chatham House.

—— (1998). What Works? The Antiphons of Administrative Reform. In B. G. Peters and D. J. Savoie, eds., *Taking Stock: Two Decades of Administrative Reform*. Montreal: McGill/Queens University Press.

—— (1999). Managing Horizontal Government: The Politics of Coordination. *Public Administration* 76: 298–312.

—— (2001). *The Politics of Bureaucracy*. 5th ed. London: Routledge.

Peters, B. G., and B. W. Hogwood (1985). In Search of the Issue-Attention Cycle. *Journal of Politics* 47: 238–53.

—— (1988). Births, Deaths and Marriages: Organizational Change in the U.S. Federal Bureaucracy. *American Journal of Public Administration* 18: 119–33.

Peters, B. G., and J. Pierre (2000). Citizens Versus the New Public Managers: The Problem of Mutual Empowerment. *Administration and Society* 32: 9–28.

—— (2001). *Politicians and Bureaucrats: The Impact of Reform*. London: Routledge.

Peters, B. G., and D. J. Savoie (1994a). Civil Service Reform: Misdiagnosing the Patient. *Public Administration Review* 54: 418–25.

—— (1994b). Reinventing Osborne and Gaebler: Lessons from the Gore Commission. *Canadian Public Administration* 37: 302–22.

Peters, B. G., and V. Wright (1996). The Public Bureaucracy. In R. E. Goodin and H.-D. Klingemann, eds., *The New Handbook of Political Science*. Oxford: Oxford University Press.

Peters, T. J., and R. H. Waterman (1982). *In Search of Excellence: Lessons from America's Best-Run Companies*. New York: Harper and Row.

Petersen, J. E. (1992). The Property Tax Revolt: Here We Go Again. *Governing* 5 (4): 4.

Petersson, O., and D. Söderlind (1992). *Förvaltningspolitik*. 2d ed. Stockholm: Almänna Förlag.

Petersson, O., A. Westholm, and G. Blomberg (1989). *Medborgarnas Makt*. Stockholm: Carlsson.

Pharr, S. J., and R. D. Putnam (2000). *Disaffected Democracy*. Princeton: Princeton University Press.

Pierce, N. R. (1992). Oregon's Rx for Mistrusted Government. *National Journal* 29 (February): 529.

Pierre, J. (1991). *Självstyrelse och omvarldsberoende*. Lund, Sweden: Studentlitteratur.

—— (1995a). The Marketization of the State. In D. J. Savoie and B. G. Peters, eds., *Governance in a Changing Environment*. Montreal: McGill/Queens University Press.

—— (1995b). Administrative Reform in Sweden: The Decline of Executive Capacity? Paper presented at conference on Modernization of Administration in Europe, Paris, June.

—— (1997). *Partnerships in Urban Governance*. London: Macmillan.

—— (1998). Depolitisee, repolitise ou simplement politique? *Revue française d'administration publique* 86: 301–10.

Pierre, J., and B. G. Peters (2000). *Governance, the State and Public Policy*. London: Macmillan.

Pitt, D. C., and B. C. Smith (1984). *The Computer Revolution in Public Administration*. Brighton, UK: Wheatsheaf.

Piven, F., and R. A. Cloward (1993). *Regulating the Poor: The Function of Public Welfare*. 2d ed. New York: Vintage.

Plamondon, A. L. (1994). A Comparison of Official Secrets and Access to Information in Great Britain and the United States. *Communications and the Law* 16: 51–68.

Pliatzky, L. (1989). *The Treasury Under Mrs. Thatcher*. Oxford, UK: Basil Blackwell.

Plowden, W. (1994). *Ministers and Mandarins*. London: Institute for Public Policy Research.

Pollitt, C. (1984). *Manipulating the Machine: Changing the Pattern of Ministerial Departments, 1960–83*. Boston: George Allen and Unwin.

—— (1986). Beyond the Managerial Model: The Case for Broadening Performance Assessment in Government and the Public Services. *Financial Accountability and Management* 12: 115–20.

—— (1990). *Managerialism and the Public Service*. Oxford, UK: Basil Blackwell.

—— (1995). Management Techniques for the Public Sector: Pulpit or Practice? In B. G. Peters and D. J. Savoie, eds., *Governance in a Changing Environment*. Montreal: McGill/Queens University Press.

Pollitt, C., and G. Bouckaert (2000). *Public Management Reform: A Comparative Analysis*. Oxford: Oxford University Press.

Posner, P. L. (1998). *The Politics of Unfunded Mandates: Whither Federalism?* Washington, DC: Georgetown University Press.

Power, M. (1994). *The Audit Explosion.* London: Demos.

Pritzker, D., and D. Dalton (1990). *Negotiated Rulemaking Sourcebook.* Washington, DC: Administrative Conference of the United States.

Pross, A. P. (1992). *Group Politics and Public Policy.* 2d ed. Toronto: Oxford University Press.

Prottas, J. M. (1979). *People Processing: The Street-Level Bureaucrat in Public Service Bureaucracy.* Lexington, MA: D. C. Heath.

Public Money and Management (1994). Reorganizing Local Government 14 (1) (theme issue).

—— (1995). Fraud and Corruption in the Public Sector 15 (1) (theme issue).

Quah, J. S. T. (1999). Corruption in Asian Countries: Can It Be Minimized? *Public Administration Review* 59: 483–94.

Racine, D. P. (1995). The Welfare State, Citizens and Immersed Civil Servants. *Administration and Society* 26: 434–63.

Rainey, H. G. (1997). *Understanding and Managing Public Organizations.* 2d ed. San Francisco: Jossey-Bass.

Ramamurti, R. (1986). Public Entrepreneurs: Who They Are and How They Operate. *California Management Review* 28: 142–58.

Ranade, W. (1995). The Theory and Practice of Managed Competition in the National Health Service. *Public Administration* 73: 241–62.

Ranson, S., and J. Stewart (1994). *Management in the Public Domain.* Basingstoke, UK: Macmillan.

Rawls, J. (1972). *A Theory of Justice.* Cambridge: Harvard University Press.

Reich, C. (1973). The New Property. *Yale Law Journal* 73: 733.

Reich, R. B. (1983). *The Next American Frontier.* New York: Times Books.

Reichard, C. (1994). *Umdenken im Rathaus: Neue Steuerungsmodelle in der deutsche Kommunalverwaltung.* Berlin: Edition Sigma.

Rhodes, G. (1981). *Inspectorates in British Government.* London: Allen and Unwin.

Rhodes, R. A. W. (1992). Local Government Finance. In D. Marsh and R. A. W. Rhodes, eds., *Implementing Thatcherite Policies: Audit of an Era.* Buckingham, UK: Open University Press.

—— (1994). The Hollowing Out of the State. *Political Quarterly* 65: 138–51.

Rhodes, R. A. W., and D. Marsh (1992). New Directions in the Study of Policy Networks. *European Journal of Political Research* 21: 181–205.

Rhodes, T. (1995). U.S. Looks Longingly at Major's Citizens' Charter. *Times* (London), April 17.

Richards, S. (1992). Changing Patterns of Legitimation in Public Management. *Public Policy and Administration* 7: 15–28.

Richardson, J. J. (1984). Doing Less by Doing More: British Government 1979–1993. *West European Politics* 17: 178–97.

Riddell, P. (1995). When Ministers Must Decide. *Times* (London), May 29.

Riggs, Fred W. (1964). *Administration in Developing Countries.* Boston: Houghton-Mifflin.

Rist, R. C. (1990). *Program Evaluation and the Management of Government: Patterns and Prospects Across Eight Countries.* New Brunswick, NJ: Transaction.

Roberts. A. (2000). Less Government, More Secrecy: Reinvention and Weakening of Freedom of Information. *Public Administration Review* 60: 308–20.

Roberts, J. (1995). Food and Drug Administration Under Assault. *British Medical Journal* 310 (January 14): 82.

Robinson, M., and G. White (1998). Civil Society and Social Provision: The Role of Civic Organizations. In M. Minogue, C. Polidano, and D. Hulme, eds., *Beyond the New Public Management*. Cheltenham, UK: Edward Elgar.

Robinson, R., and J. LeGrand (1994). *Evaluating the NHS Reforms*. London: Kings' Fund Institute.

Rochefort, D. A., and R. W. Cobb (1993). Problem Definition, Agenda Access and Policy Change. *Policy Studies Journal* 21: 56–71.

Roethlisberger, F. J., and W. J. Dickson (1941). *Management and the Worker*. Cambridge: Harvard University Press.

Rogers, D. L., and C. L. Mulford (1982). The Historical Development. In D. L. Rogers and D. A. Whetten, eds., *Interorganizational Coordination*. Ames: Iowa State University Press.

Romzek, B. S. (1990). Employee Investment and Commitment: The Ties That Bind. *Public Administration Review* 50: 374–82.

Romzek, B. S., and M. J. Dubnick (1994). Issues of Accountability in Flexible Personnel Systems. In P. W. Ingraham and B. S. Romzek, eds., *New Paradigms for Government*. San Francisco: Jossey-Bass.

Roniger, L., and A. Ghuneps-Ayata (1994). *Democracy, Clientelism and Civil Society*. Boulder, CO: Lynne Reinner.

Rose, R. (1974). *The Problem of Party Government*. London: Macmillan.

—— (1984). *Understanding Big Government: The Programme Approach*. Beverly Hills, CA: Sage.

—— (1987). *Ministers and Ministries: A Functional Analysis*. Oxford, UK: Clarendon Press.

—— (1987). Giving Direction to Permanent Officials: Signals from Electorates, the Market and from Self-expertise. In J.-E. Lane, ed., *Bureaucracy and Public Choice*. London: Sage.

Rose, R., and B. G. Peters (1978). *Can Government Go Bankrupt?* New York: Basic Books.

Rose, R. et al. (1985). *Public Employment in Western Nations*. Cambridge: Cambridge University Press.

Rossi, P. H., and H. E. Freeman (1989). *Evaluation: A Systematic Approach*. 4th ed. Newbury Park, CA: Sage.

Rouban, L. (1991). Le client, l'usager et le fonctionnaire: quelle politique pour l'administration publique. *Revue française d'administration publique* 59: 435–44.

—— (1998). La politisation des fonctionnaires en France: obstacle ou necessite? *Revue française d'administration publique* 86 (avril–juin): 167–82.

Rubin, I. (1997). *Politics of Public Budgeting*. New York: Chatham House.

Sabatier, P. A. (1988). An Advocacy Coalition Model of Policy Change and the Role of Policy-Oriented Learning Therein. *Policy Sciences* 21: 129–68.

Sagie, A., and M. Koslowsky (2000). *Participation and Empowerment in Organizations*. Thousand Oaks, CA: Sage.

Salamon, L. M. (1979). The Time Dimension of Policy Evaluation: The Case of the New Deal Land Relief Programs. *Public Policy* 27: 129–84.

—— (1980). The Goals of Reorganization. In P. Szanton, ed., *Federal Reorganization: What Have We Learned?* Chatham, NJ: Chatham House.

Sampson, A. (1995). *Company Men: The Rise and Fall of Corporate Life.* London: HarperCollins.

Savoie, D. J. (1990). *The Politics of Public Spending in Canada.* Toronto: University of Toronto Press.

—— (1994a). *Reagan, Thatcher, Mulroney: In Search of a New Bureaucracy.* Pittsburgh: University of Pittsburgh Press.

—— (1994b). Truth About Government. *Ottawa Citizen,* October 13.

—— (1995a). What Is Wrong with the New Public Management? *Canadian Public Administration* 38: 112–21.

—— (1995b). *Central Agencies: Looking Backward.* Ottawa: Canadian Centre for Management Development.

—— (1995c). Globalization and Governance. In B. G. Peters and D. J. Savoie, eds., *Governance in a Changing Environment.* Montreal: McGill/Queens University Press.

—— (1999). *Governing at the Centre.* Toronto: University of Toronto Press.

Sawer, M. (1982). Political Manifestation of Australian Libertarianism. In Sawer, ed., *Australia and the New Right.* Sydney: George Allen and Unwin.

Schaffer, B. B. (1973). *The Administrative Factor: Papers in Organization, Politics, and Development.* London: Cass.

Scharpf, F. (1991). Die Handlungsfähigkeit des Staates am Ende des zwanzigsten Jahrhunderts. *Politische Vierteiljahrschrift* 4: 621–34.

Scharpf, F. W. (1989). Decision Rules, Decision Styles and Policy Choices. *Journal of Theoretical Politics* 1: 149–76.

Schick, A. (1978). The Road from ZBB. *Public Administration Review* 38: 177–81.

—— (1988). Micro-budgetary Adaptations to Fiscal Stress in Industrialized Countries. *Public Administration Review* 48: 523–33.

—— (1990). *The Capacity to Budget.* Washington, DC: Urban Institute Press.

Schmitter, P. C. (1974). Still the Century of Corporatism? *Review of Politics* 36: 85–131.

—— (1989). Corporatism Is Dead: Long Live Corporatism. *Government and Opposition* 24: 54–73.

Schoenbrod, D. (1993). *Power Without Responsibility: How Congress Abuses the People Through Delegation.* New Haven: Yale University Press.

Schön, D., and M. Rein (1994). *Frame Reflection: Resolving Intractable Policy Issues.* New York: Basic Books.

Schorr, P. (1987). Public Service as a Calling: An Exploration of a Concept. *International Journal of Public Administration* 10: 465–94.

Schultze, C. L. (1977). *The Public Use of Private Interest.* Washington, DC: Brookings Institution.

Scott, G., P. Bushnell, and N. Sallee (1990). Reform of the Core Public Sector: The New Zealand Experience. *Governance* 3: 138–67.

Scott-Clark, C. (1995). Parents Decry School "Choice" As a Failure. *Sunday Times,* June 4.

Sears, D. O., and J. Citrin (1985). *Tax Revolt: Something for Nothing in California.* 2d ed. Cambridge: Harvard University Press.

Seidman, H., and R. Gilmour (1986). *Politics, Power and Position: From the Positive to the Regulatory State.* New York: Oxford University Press.

Seldon, A. (1990). The Cabinet Office and Coordination 1979–87. *Public Administration* 68: 103–21.

Self, P. (1993). *Government by the Market?* Boulder, CO: Westview.

Selznick, P. (1957). *Leadership in Administration: A Sociological Interpretation.* Evanston, IL: Row, Peterson.

Sharp, E. B. (1994). *The Dilemma of Drug Policy in the United States.* New York: Harper-Collins.

Shepsle, K. (1989). Studying Institutions: Some Lessons from the Rational Choice Approach. *Journal of Theoretical Politics* 1: 131–48.

—— (1992). Bureaucratic Drift: Coalitional Drift and Time Consistency: A Comment on Macey. *Journal of Law, Economics and Organization* 8: 111–18.

Silberman, B. (1993). *Cages of Reason: The Rise of the Rational State in France, Japan, the United States and Great Britain.* Chicago: University of Chicago Press.

Simon, H. (1947). *Administrative Behavior.* New York: Free Press.

Simon, H. A. (1973). The Structure of Ill-Structured Problems. *Artificial Intelligence* 4: 181–201.

Sjölund, M. (1989). *Statens Lönepolitik, 1977–88.* Stockholm: Almänna Forlaget.

—— (1994a). Sweden. In C. Hood and B. G. Peters, *The Rewards of High Public Office.* London: Sage.

—— (1994b). Transition in Government Pay Policies. *International Journal of Public Administration* 17: 1907–35.

Skelcher, C. (1998). *The Appointed State: Quasi-governmental Organizations and Democracy.* Buckingham, UK: Open University Press.

Skogstad, G. (1993). Policy Under Siege: Supply Management in Agricultural Marketing. *Canadian Public Administration* 36: 1–23.

Skowronek, S. (1982). *Building a New American State: The Expansion of National Administrative Capacity, 1877–1920.* Cambridge: Cambridge University Press.

Smart, H. (1991). *Criticism and Public Rationality: Professional Rigidity and the Search for Caring Government.* London: Routledge.

Smith, M. J., D. Marsh, and D. Richards (1993). Central Government Departments and the Policy Process. *Public Administration* 71: 567–94.

Smith, S. P. (1977). *Equal Pay in the Public Sector: Fact or Fantasy?* Princeton: Department of Economics, Princeton Univesity Press.

Solovay, N., and C. K. Reed (1999). *Alternative Dispute Resolution.* New York: M. Bender.

Sorenson, E. (1997). Democracy and Empowerment. *Public Administration* 75: 553–67.

Spragens, T. A. (1990). *Reason and Democracy.* Durham, NC: Duke University Press.

Spulbar, N. (1989). *Managing the American Economy: From Roosevelt to Reagan.* Bloomington: Indiana University Press.

Squires, P. (1990). *Anti-Social Policy: Welfare, Ideology and the Disciplined State.* London: Harvester Wheatsheaf.

Ståhlberg, K. (1987). The Politicization of Public Administration: Notes on the Concepts,

Causes and Consequences of Politicization. *International Review of Administrative Science* 53: 363–82.

State Service Commission (1994). *New Zealand's Reformed State Sector*. Wellington: State Services Commission.

Statens Information (1998). *Forholdtet mellem minister og embedsmaend*. Copenhagen: Schultz.

Stein, E. W. (1995). Organizational Memory. *International Journal of Information Management* 15: 17–32.

Stein, J. (1995). Building a Better Bureaucrat. *Regulation* 3: 24–32.

Steinmo, S., K. Thelen, and F. Longstreth (1992). *Structuring Politics: Historical Institutionalism in Comparative Analysis*. Cambridge: Cambridge University Press.

Stillman, R. J. (1991). *Preface to Public Administration: A Search for Themes and Direction*. New York: St. Martin's.

Stockman, D. (1986). *The Triumph of Politics: How the Reagan Revolution Failed*. New York: Harper and Row.

Stromberg, L. (1990). Det svenska frikommunsforsoket. In K. Ståhlberg, ed., *Frikommunsforsoket i Norden*. Åbo, Finland: Åbo Akademi.

Summa, H. (1995). Old and New Techniques for Productivity Promotion: From the Cheese Slicing to a Quest for Quality. In A. Halachmi and G. Bouckaert, eds., *Public Productivity Through Quality and Performance Management*. Amsterdam: IOS Press.

Sutherland, S. L. (1991). The Al-Mashat Affair: Administrative Responsibility in Parliamentary Institutions. *Canadian Public Administration* 34: 573–603.

Swiss, J. (1993). Adapting Total Quality Management (TQM) to Government. *Public Administration Review* 52: 356–62.

Szanton, P. (1981). *Federal Reorganization: What Have We Learned?* Chatham, NJ: Chatham House.

Taggart, P. (1995). New Populist Parties in Western Europe. *West European Politics* 18: 34–51.

Talbot, C., C. Pollitt, K. Bathgate, J. Caulfield, A. Reilly, and A. Smullen (2000). The Idea of Agency: Researching the Agentification of the (Public Service) World. Paper presented at Annual Meeting of the American Political Science Review, Washington, DC, September.

Tarschys, D. (1981). Rational Decremental Budgeting. *Policy Sciences* 14: 49–58.

—— (1986). From Expansion to Restraint. *Public Budgeting and Finance* 6: 25–37.

Taylor-Gooby, P. (1985). *Public Opinion, Ideology and State Welfare*. London: Routledge and Kegan Paul.

Tellier, P. M. (1990). Public Service 2000: The Renewal of the Public Service. *Canadian Public Administration* 33: 123–32.

—— (1991). A New Canadian Public Service. *Business Quarterly* 55 (4): 93–98.

Terry, L. D. (1995). *Leadership of Public Bureaucracies: The Administrator as Conservator*. Thousand Oaks, CA: Sage.

Thain, C., and M. Wright (1992a). Planning and Controlling Public Expenditure in the UK, Part 1: The Treasury's Public Expenditure Survey. *Public Administration* 70: 3–24.

—— (1992b). Planning and Controlling Public Expenditure in the UK, Part 2: The Effects and Effectiveness of the Survey. *Public Administration* 70: 193–224.

Theakston, K. (1992). *The Labour Party and Whitehall*. London: Routledge.

Therkildsen, O. (2000). Public Sector Reform in a Poor, Aid-Dependent Country, Tanzania. *Public Administration and Development* 20: 61–71.

Thomas, J. C. (1993). Public Involvement and Government Effectiveness. *Administration and Society* 24: 444–69.

Thompson, G., J. Frances, R. Levacic, and J. Mitchell (1991). *Markets, Hierarchies and Networks*. London: Sage.

Thompson, V. A. (1975). *Without Sympathy or Enthusiasm: The Problem of Administrative Compassion*. Tuscaloosa: University of Alabama Press.

Tiebout, C. M. (1956). A Pure Theory of Local Public Expenditure. *Journal of Political Economy* 64: 416–24.

Tiihonen, S. (2000). *From Uniform Administration to Governance and Management of Diversity*. Helsinki: Ministry of Finance.

Timmins, N. (2000). Failing Hospitals to Face "Special Measures." *Financial Times*, July 1.

Timsit, G. (1988). *Les autorites administratives independentes*. Paris: Presses Universitaires de France.

Tomkys, R. (1991). The Financial Management Initiative in the FCO. *Public Administration* 69: 257–63.

Torstendahl, R. (1991). *Bureaucratization in Northwest Europe, 1880–1985: Dominance and Government*. London: Routledge.

Tritter, J. (1994). The Citizens' Charter: Opportunities for Users' Perspectives. *Political Quarterly* 86: 397–414.

Tsebelis, G. (1994). The Power of the European Parliament as a Conditional Agenda Setter. *American Political Science Review* 88: 128–55.

Tullock, G. (1965). *The Politics of Bureaucracy*. Washington, DC: Public Affairs Press.

United Nations Development Programme (1988). *Selected Studies on Major Administrative Reforms*. New York: UNDP.

U.S. General Accounting Office (1995a). *Federal Quality Management: Strategies for Involving Employees*. Washington, DC: USGAO, April 18, GAO/GGD-95-79.

——— (1995b). *Federal Hiring: Reconciling Managerial Flexibility with Veterans' Preference*. Washington, DC: USGAO, June 16, GAO/GGD-95-102.

Van Nispen, F. (1994). *Het dossier Heroverweging*. Delft, Netherlands: Eburon.

Vander Weele, M. (1994). *Reclaiming Our Schools: The Battle over Chicago School Reform*. Chicago: Loyola University Press.

Victor, P. (1995). Freedom of Information: It Will Cost You. *Independent on Sunday*, June 18.

Vinzant, J. C., and L. Crothers (1998). *Street-Level Leadership: Discretion and Legitimacy in Frontline Public Service*. Washington, DC: Georgetown University Press.

Waldo, D. (1968). Scope of the Theory of Public Administration. *Annals of the American Academy of Political and Social Sciences* 8: 1–26.

Walsh, K. (1991). Quality and Public Services. *Public Administration Review* 69: 503–14.

——— (1995). *Public Services and Market Mechanisms: Competition, Contracting and the New Public Management*. Basingstoke, UK: Macmillan.

Walsh, K., and J. Stewart (1992). Change in the Management of Public Services. *Public Administration* 70: 499–518.

Walsh, P. (1991). The State Sector Act of 1988. In J. Boston, J. Martin, J. Pallot, and P. Walsh, eds., *Reshaping the State: New Zealand's Bureaucratic Revolution*. Auckland: Oxford.

Walters, J. (1992a). How Not to Reform Civil Service. *Governing* 6 (2): 30–34.

—— (1992b). Reinventing Government: Managing the Politics of Change. *Governing* 6 (3): 27–37.

—— (1992c). The Cult of Total Quality. *Governing* 5 (8): 38–42.

Warner, N. (1984). Raynerism in Practice: Anatomy of a Rayner Scrutiny. *Public Administration* 62: 7–22.

Weber, M. (1958). Bureaucracy. In H. H. Gerth and C. W. Mills, eds., *From Max Weber: Essays in Sociology*. New York: Oxford University Press.

Wehrle-Einhorn, R. J. (1994). Reinventing the Government Contract for Services. *National Contract Management Journal* 25 (2): 63–72.

Weir, M. (1992). *Politics and Jobs: The Boundaries of Employment Policy in the United States*. Washington, DC: Brookings Institution.

Werth, W. (1973). *Mitbestimmung: Deutsche Reformpolitik auf falschen Weg*. Munich: Politisches Archiv.

West, W. (1985). *Administrative Rulemaking: Politics and Process*. New York: Greenwood.

Wex, S. (1990). Leadership and Change in the 1990s. *Optimum* 21: 25–30.

White, O. F., and J. F. Wolf (1995). Deming's Total Quality Management Movement and the Baskin Robbins Problem: Part 1: Is It Time to Go Back to Vanilla? *Administration and Society* 27: 203–25.

White, S. K. (1988). *The Recent Work of Jürgen Habermas: Reason, Justice and Modernity*. Cambridge: Cambridge University Press.

Wildavsky, A. (1969). Rescuing Policy Analysis from PPBS. *Public Administration Review* 29: 189–202.

—— (1978). A Budget for All Seasons? Why the Traditional Budget Lasts. *Public Administration Review* 38: 501–9.

—— (1979). Doing Better and Feeling Worse. In A. Wildavsky, *Speaking Truth to Power*. Boston: Little, Brown.

—— (1992). *The New Politics of the Budgetary Process*. 2d ed. New York: Harper Collins.

Willetts, D. (1994). *Civic Conservatism*. London: Social Market Foundation.

Williamson, O. E. (1975). *Markets and Hierarchies*. New York: Free Press.

—— (1985). *The Economic Institutions of Capitalism: Firms, Markets, Relational Contracting*. New York: Free Press.

Wilson, D. (1995). The Quango Debate. *Parliamentary Affairs* (special issue) 48 (2): 3–13.

Wilson, G. (1994c). The Westminster Model in Comparative Perspective. In I. Budge and D. McKay, eds., *Developing Democracy*. London: Sage.

Wilson, J. Q. (1989). *Bureaucracy*. New York: Free Press.

—— (1994a). Can the Bureaucracy Be Deregulated? Lessons from Government Agencies. In J. J. DiIulio, ed., *Deregulating the Public Sector*. Washington, DC: Brookings Institution.

—— (1994b). Reinventing Public Administration. *PS: Political Science and Politics* 27: 667–73.

Wilson, S. V. (1988). What Legacy? The Nielsen Task Force Program Review. In K. A. Graham, ed., *How Ottawa Spends, 1988/89: The Conservatives Heading into the Stretch*. Ottawa: Carleton University Press.

Wilson, W. (1887). The Study of Administration. *Political Science Quarterly* 2: 197–222.

Wolfe, C. (1988). *Markets or Governments?* Cambridge, MA: MIT Press.

Wolfe, R. (2000). Gore Promises to Scale Back Size of Federal Government. *Financial Times,* October 25.

Wright, V. (1994). Reshaping the State: Implications for Public Administration. *West European Politics* 17: 102–34.

Wright, V., and B. G. Peters (1996). Public Administration: Change and Redefinition. In R. E. Goodin, ed., *New Handbook of Political Science*. Oxford: Oxford University Press.

Zifcak, S. (1994). *New Managerialism: Administrative Reform in Whitehall and Canberra*. Buckingham, UK: Open University Press.

Zussman, D., and J. Jabes (1989). *The Vertical Solitude: Managing in the Public Sector*. Halifax, N.S.: Institute for Research on Public Policy.

Index